FAITH ON
THE HOME FRONT

Stephen Parker

FAITH ON THE HOME FRONT

Aspects of Church Life and
Popular Religion in Birmingham
1939–1945

PETER LANG

Oxford · Bern · Berlin · Bruxelles · Frankfurt am Main · New York · Wien

Bibliographic information published by Die Deutsche Bibliothek
Die Deutsche Bibliothek lists this publication in the Deutsche Nationalbiblio-
grafie; detailed bibliographic data is available on the Internet at
‹http://dnb.ddb.de›.

British Library and Library of Congress Cataloguing-in-Publication Data:
A catalogue record for this book is available from The British Library, Great
Britain, and from The Library of Congress, USA

ISBN 3-03910-252-4
US-ISBN 0-8204-7181-X

© Peter Lang AG, European Academic Publishers, Bern 2005
Hochfeldstrasse 32, Postfach 746, CH-3000 Bern 9, Switzerland
info@peterlang.com, www.peterlang.com, www.peterlang.net

Printed in Germany

To Fiona, Katy and Samuel,
who kept me smiling through,

And

To Gladys Parker and George Pilkington,
two who earned victory

Contents

Preface and Acknowledgements

Even though I grew up twenty years after the war had ended, in 1960s and 1970s Birmingham, the events of the Second World War impinged upon my early life. I grew up amidst many a wartime yarn of the experiences of sheltering from the falling bombs in a partially submerged metal box – the Anderson shelter – which was rendered more safe and comfortable by the proud efforts of my bricklayer grandfather. Tales about barrage balloons becoming snagged in local trees, causing alarm and mirth amongst neighbours, filled my imagination. As a child, I played inside a shed that was a salvaged Anderson, later excitedly digging in vain in our garden to find the remnants of another. Often, I sat nervously and respectfully whilst visiting an uncle of mine who had fought in the war. Blown up by a landmine during the invasion of Sicily in July 1943, his devastating injuries had left him permanently paralysed across half of his body and barely able to speak. Though I could not appreciate the horrors that had given rise to his condition or fully understand the familial ramifications of them, I was deeply affected by the experience of being around him. His frustrations at not being able to communicate clearly coupled with his recurrent illnesses brought home to me the personal cost of war. The significance of this personal suffering was further enhanced by the tale of how my uncle's near-fatal injuries were intuitively predicted by my grandmother in a dream; a prophecy which continues to puzzle me to this day. Thus, the war's aftermath left its impressions upon me – and by implication upon others – long after its conclusion.

Not only did the family context within which I grew up attest to the tangible results of war, so did the social circumstances of my childhood. Though I was oblivious to it, I grew up benefiting from the government-provided services of the post-war welfare state. As a result, I was on the receiving end of healthcare and educational opportunities massively superior to those my parents had experienced. Later I discovered that it was the Second World War that had accelerated the rate of social change from which I profited. Furthermore, I was nurtured within a cultural environment that loyally perpetuated, by various means, the mythological character of wartime Britishness as stoical, even in the face of defeat. Along with others, I accepted and enjoyed the various portrayals of this wartime character in the proliferation of war films and in television comedies such as *Dad's Army*. This characterisation of Britishness was, I unquestioningly believed, one which mirrored reality.

It was during a visit to Germany in the late 1990s that I began to query the widespread personal, social and religious influence of the war on a different level. Whilst on the visit, I was dumbfounded by the horror of the bombing of Dresden, amazed by the city's reconstructed beauty, and impressed by the Churches' part in the post-war work of reconciliation. Whilst in Berlin, and especially when visiting the Kaiser Wilhelm Memorial Church, I began to realise that the events of wartime had necessitated recourse to theological ritual and remorseful imagery to deal with the German national cataclysm. This building's nondescript concrete exterior belied its penitential purple interior seemingly embodying the nation's 'mea culpa' before God. Religion had been called upon to make sense of the war's aftermath. I began to ask, what role did it play at the time?

My experience in Germany engendered, in turn, other questions concerning the role of religion in British wartime society and the impact of the war upon faith, which forms the subject matter here. Amongst the questions explored are these: how were wartime trials and conditions responded to and coped with by both clergy and Church workers across denominations? In what sense did Birmingham's clergy, and the nation's Christians, believe this to be a just and justifiable war? How did the faithful, and their leaders, write, speak, and act in response to wartime events? How did they care in this time of crisis? Additionally, what was the character of wartime popular religion? Were changes wrought in the popular religious life of the nation by the war? Indeed, how did popular religion interact with people's self-understanding: did the war have any impact on this? How, and by what means, were the people encouraged to conceptualise the war, and what theological themes, motifs and moral motives were deployed in support of the conflict? How did the clergy and others instruct people to rationalise events? What kind of world was it hoped the war would give rise to?

Conceived as an opportunity to explore the interaction between religion and warfare historically, this study eventually focused upon the local experience of the Churches and citizens of Birmingham against the national socio-political and ecclesiastical backdrop. This is not a historical study of pacifism, nor is the focus the ethics of warfare or the thorny realities of living the Christian ideal; this is a consideration of the broader aspects of the religious experience of the citizens of Birmingham during the Second World War and the theological and pastoral response of the city's Churches. Asa Briggs characterised the vitality of Birmingham's nineteenth-century 'civic gospel' as being the 'leaven' in the city's life.[1] Whether the Churches lived up to a similar assessment in their involvement in Birmingham's wartime life is the issue here.

Based upon my PhD, this book represents the culmination of a lengthy process. I wish to record my thanks to the many, whose contribution has been essential to project's completion, especially former colleagues at the Universities of Birmingham, Westhill, and Chester. I am deeply grateful to Dr Michael Snape for the initial inspiration, his continual guidance and encouragement throughout, and for his true friendship to this sometime 'apprentice historian'. Along with all historians of religion, I always relied upon the goodwill of archivists; in this, my main debt is to the long-suffering staff of Birmingham's Central Library. My editor, David Edmonds, and Sue Leigh and Graham Speake of Peter Lang AG, have been a patient and steady presence in the final stages of the work; this is much appreciated. Most importantly, without the willingness of many oral history interviewees to divulge their life memories to me, this work would lack the colour, depth of insight and humanity their recollections provided; therefore sincere thanks go to them for their openness and hospitality.

1   A. Briggs, 1952, p.4.

Abbreviations

EWB   The papers of E.W. Barnes, wartime Anglican Bishop of Birmingham, kept at the University of Birmingham Special Collections.

IWM   Imperial War Museum, London.

M-O   Mass-Observation [hereafter M-O]. All Mass-Observation material is reproduced by permission of Curtis Brown Ltd, London, © the Trustees of the Mass-Observation Archive at the University of Sussex.

MOI   Ministry of Information.

PRO   Public Record Office, Kew, London.

Introduction: The Scholarly Context

Popular Religion and the Secularisation Debate

Concluding his examination of recent works on popular religion, David Hempton suggests that even 'more local studies of non-metropolitan urban' contexts are now needed.[1] Writing in the 1980s, Hempton reflected a growing interest in the popular religious dynamic that operates beyond the Church and institutional religious confines. This book contributes to the growing evidence of the importance of the popular religious dimension in British religious historiography, not least in the context of war.

Birmingham merits being a focus for such a study because of its place in the British war effort. The city was a major centre of arms production; consequently, every night of the blitz it endured heavy bombardment. The prevailing conditions of the blitz, and the disruptions to civilian life which resulted, demanded unique responses from the populace and, likewise, from the city's Churches. How popular religion was affected by war and how the Churches responded is the major focus of interest here.

Churchgoing statistics as the index of the population's religious commitment and sensibility have, of late, come to be regarded with suspicion. Reliance upon such figures to prove the theory of creeping secularisation within British society has given way to evidence for the continuing and vital influence of the Churches and of Christian symbol, ritual, and practice well beyond the previously accepted bounds, and well into the twentieth century. Gradually, historical research has unearthed evidence of the persistent relevance of Christianity within the people's communal life, and as a referent in the construction of individual character. Popular religion may be defined as:

1   Hempton, 1986, p.201.

a generally shared understanding of religious meaning including both folk beliefs as well as formally and officially sanctioned practices and ideas, operating within a loosely bound interpretative community [...] a system which gives meaning to the world.[2]

Arguably, the historical study of the phenomenon of popular religion now has its own integrity equal to that of other perspectives on the history of religion in Britain. Landmark contributions to the historiography of English and British[3] popular religion in the nineteenth and twentieth centuries are the works of Jeffrey Cox, Sarah Williams and Callum Brown.[4]

Jeffrey Cox's book, *The English Churches in a Secular Society: Lambeth, 1830–1930*, challenges the accepted understanding of secularisation as having its advent in urbanisation, industrialisation and scientific advance.[5] Far from being peripheral to late nineteenth-century life, the Churches were, in fact, central to its social functioning. Cox asserts that:

public worship was only one of a great number of church-related activities which enrolled thousands [...] By the 1880s both Anglicans and Non-conformists, drawing upon different ideological traditions but responding to similar urban problems, were deeply involved in the provision of charity and social services.[6]

However, despite the Churches' critical involvement in local life, which in part was driven by its 'civilising mission',[7] its leisure, educational and relief activities resulted in neither increasing, nor safeguarding, churchgoing figures.[8] What did result from the various ways in which the Churches succeeded in binding people to it was an increased exposure to religious symbols and language amongst the

2   Williams, 1999, pp.11 and 13.
3   As much of this work is about the local conditions prevalent in an English city, much that will be asserted can only be properly descriptive of the character of English popular religion.
4   In particular Cox, 1982; Williams, 1999; Brown, 2001.
5   Cox, 1982, pp.266f.
6   Cox, 1982, pp.23 and 58.
7   Cox, 1982, p.83.
8   Cox, 1982, p.83.

16

populace. The outcome for Cox was, in the words of Bishop E.S. Talbot of Rochester in 1903, a 'diffusive Christianity' amongst the general population. This 'diffusive Christianity', though clearly reliant upon and influenced by orthodoxy, characteristically maintained its own integrity and detachment from official norms. Thus of such 'diffusive Christianity' in Lambeth, Cox asserts: 'the people of Lambeth thought of themselves as Christians but insisted on defining their own religious beliefs rather than taking them from clergymen.'[9] 'Diffusive Christianity' proves a useful working concept descriptive of the dynamic and persistent popular religious life functioning elsewhere in this period and beyond.

For Cox, it was the erosion of the network of Church involvement in the communal life of English society, from the 1880s onwards, that defined the onset and cause of secularisation. Similarly, it was the decline in the Churches' pervasive participation, rather than the people's non-attendance at worship, that led to the Churches being viewed as remote and irrelevant.[10] What will be demonstrated in this work, contrary to Cox's conclusions, is the continuing resilience of the identified 'diffusive Christianity' some years on from his focus period, without the intricate props of Church social involvement that he identifies. Neither popular religion nor the Churches were peripheral to the people's lives during the Second World War. Nevertheless, Cox's contribution is foundational to this study in querying the assumed marginalisation of Christianity from popular life and culture heretofore.

Sarah Williams's work, *Religious Belief and Popular Culture in Southwark c.1880–1939* (1999) augments Cox's contribution. Where Cox's focus is predominantly the institutional aspects of the Churches' role in society, Williams's work approaches the subject of religion, and its place in Victorian and Edwardian life, from the people's recollected perspective. Drawing upon oral testimony, as Cox suggests should be the way forward,[11] Williams argues that it is the people themselves – rather than contemporary clerical commentators – that should

---

9   Cox, 1982, p.92.
10   Cox, 1982, p.273.
11   Cox, 1982, p.90.

characterise popular religious life.[12] From her oral history accounts, she finds evidence of 'the multidimensional character of religious experience', that is to say, that there may be a mixture of motives for engaging in a particular ritual (e.g. baptism) and that both orthodox understandings and quasi-magical beliefs may be operating at the same time.[13] What Williams succeeds in demonstrating is that popular belief and practice functioned outside the confines of the ecclesiastical and its orthodoxies, creating its own social meaning and purpose.

Sarah Williams's work also demonstrates that even though formal religious observance, evidenced by declining Church attendance, waned across the early and middle years of the twentieth century, Christian rites of passage, symbols, hymnody and stories remained deeply embedded in the social and cultural psyche of the British people. Christianity's idiom and influence, she argues, were:

> incorporated as part of a distinct popular identity and heritage [...] within a wider repertoire of religious belief [and within] a broader definition of religiosity [than that subscribed to by religious commentators]. The church was seen and its presence felt beyond the parameters of the institutional [...] within popular culture.[14]

Perhaps because Sarah Williams anticipated that the populace of Southwark would have been dispersed by the blitz, its community life disrupted and its patterns of life distorted, she concludes her study at the beginning of the Second World War. In so doing, however, Williams inadvertently creates a sense of false discontinuity between peacetime and wartime popular religion. What will be seen in this book, however, is that, in reality, the contours of wartime popular religion were similar to those of peacetime; 'diffusive Christianity' as such remained intact. Yet, despite this underlying consistency between wartime and peacetime popular religion, war gave rise to particular and unique characteristics in response to events; what may be termed an air-raid shelter spirituality emerged from experiences. Moreover, what will become clearer as this study goes on is that the character of

12   Williams, 1999, p.9.
13   Williams, 1999, p.10.
14   Williams, 1999, p.162.

18

wartime popular religion was shaped as much by wartime propaganda and popular culture as by the traditional sources of its popular heterodoxy.

Callum Brown, in *The Death of Christian Britain*, seeks to further revise assumptions concerning the genesis of the secularisation of British society.[15] He argues that the real death knell of people's enthralment to Christian notions of personal identity and to the Christian world view did not occur in the nineteenth century, as previously assumed, but in the 1960s.[16] Up until then, Christianity so 'infused public culture and was adopted by individuals, whether churchgoers or not, in forming their own identities' that it becomes reductionist and deceptive to rely simply upon statistics of churchgoing as the primary measure of the process of secularisation.[17] Brown's distinctive contribution lies in his utilisation of the notion 'discursive Christianity', which he classifies as:

> the people's subscription to protocols of personal identity [...] derived from Christian expectations, or discourses[: these are] rituals or customs of behaviour, economic activity, dress, speech and so on [...] manifest in [e.g.] going to church on a Sunday, or saying grace before meals [but also] discerned in the 'voices' of the people [and circulated in] the dominant media of the time [...] autobiography and oral record show a personal adoption of religious discourses [i.e.] 'subjectification' [...] where people have been reflexive to the environment of circulating discourses.[18]

He argues that it is when people no longer tangibly define themselves according to such Christian discourses, that is to say when there is 'decay in discursive religiosity', that the decline in Christianity's sway over British religious life begins.[19] For Brown, it is the post-1960s generation who when questioned display no such 'religious or quasi-religious discourse, motif or activity whatever' and, for him, this is conclusive proof that the secularisation of British society begins at this

---

15   Brown, 2001.
16   Brown, 2001, p.1.
17   Brown, 2001, p.8.
18   Brown, 2001, pp.12–13.
19   Brown, 2001, p.14.

point.[20] As well as finding evidence of so-called 'discursive Christianity' in a wide range of media (tracts, films, literature, and so on) up until then, Brown also demonstrates that the various discourses contained in these media shaped gender identity across the period. Personal narratives (such as those recounted in oral histories) were similarly reflexive of the particular religious protocols that formed such gender identities.

Brown's work challenges narrow understandings of the British people's personal and cultural attachment to Christianity. He demonstrates that Christian discourses continue to be circulated explicitly in the way that people live their lives, and implicitly in the way they define who they are, well on into the twentieth century. By listening to the people's voices and by examining some of 'the voices that speak to' people, he provides conclusive evidence of the persistent liveliness of Christian influence.[21]

In recent years, a number of other scholars have contributed to the historiography of British popular religion. Richard Sykes, for example, writing about another Midlands locale,[22] Dudley and the Gornals, provides significant evidence of the character of popular religion in this geographical area. However, his is a brief, and rather more negative, assessment of the impact of the Second World War upon popular religious belief and behaviour than that presented here. Similarly, Dorothy Entwistle, writing of rural Lancashire, discovers a religious vitality beyond the boundaries of institutional Christianity.[23] Alongside the work of Sykes and Entwistle, this locally focused study of wartime Birmingham adds to a now substantial volume of works attesting to the persistency of Christianity's influence over British life and the dynamics of such popular belief and practice.

20   Brown, 2001, p.183.
21   Brown, 2001, p.115.
22   Sykes, 1999.
23   Entwistle, 2001.

The Literature of the Impact of War on the Churches

The military historiography of the First and Second World Wars continues to proliferate. By contrast, the available literature concerned with the religious aspects of these two conflicts is decidedly limited, particularly that pertaining to the Second World War.[24] Presented below is a synopsis of some of the noteworthy contributions to the religious historiography of the two world wars.

By his two major works, one wholly concerned with the role of the established Church, the other with the nonconformist Churches in England across both conflicts, Alan Wilkinson has confirmed the significant part played by the mainline Protestant Christian denominations during the two world wars.[25] From an examination of their involvement, predominantly from a hierarchical and clerical level, it is clear that the Churches' response to the war, though diverse, was in the main supportive of each conflict. During the First World War, in particular, there existed a degree of belligerence amongst clerics bolstered by particular theological interpretations of events. Second-World-War clerics were much more tentative and subtle than this, and in the case of figures such as the renowned Bishop of Chichester, George Bell, critical of the way in which the war was being fought.

Wilkinson presents an extensive survey of the Churches' responses to the two world wars in his two books on the subject. By contrast, this study examines the religious aspects of the Second World War through the lens of the local experience of Birmingham's clergy, Church workers and general population. Whereas Wilkinson's work is little concerned with the popular religious experience of war, this study seeks to explore the distance between clerical teaching and popular faith.[26]

Adopting a similarly ecclesiastical focus, Arlie Hoover's book, *God, Britain and Hitler in World War Two*, examines in detail the

---

24   For First World War, for example: Mews, 1973; Marrin, 1974; Hoover, 1989. Ceadel, 1980; Hastings, 1991; Wolffe, 1994 deal with both conflicts.
25   Wilkinson, 1978; Wilkinson, 1986.
26   E.g. Wilkinson, 1978, p.179; Wilkinson, 1986, p.276.

published and private thinking of senior clerics across denominations concerning the Second World War.[27] Hoover is able to detect dominant themes in the life and theology of the wartime Churches. The responses of the Churches to pacifism, the changing theological landscape from liberalism to neo-orthodoxy and the extent to which the Second World War was understood to be a war for Christian civilisation are the key themes Hoover identifies. However, he does not deal with the day-to-day ministrations of the Churches, nor is he concerned with the extent to which clerics' ideas were diffused amongst the populace, two major considerations here.

Michael Snape's paper *British Catholicism and the British Army in the First World War* fills a demonstrable gap in the religious history of this denomination.[28] Through this piece Snape demonstrates the wider dynamic that shaped the Roman Catholic Church's response to the conflict, namely the need to exhibit Catholic loyalty (particularly in the context of Irish Nationalism and the neutrality of the wartime papacy), as well as uncovering the realities of the Catholic chaplains' and soldiers' trench experience. Snape's work is of particular relevance in providing evidence of the soldier's recourse to religion as a way of coping, which is in accord with the recorded experiences of many on the home front in the Second World War.[29] What Snape's work also reveals is that some chaplains tolerated the unorthodox application of religious devotion and the sacraments (by, for example, believing they provided protection in some way).[30] This contrasts well with the usual disparagement of such religious responses as 'second-rate religion' during the Second World War and at other times.

Adrian Hastings and Ian Machin, in their respective works, *A History of English Christianity* and *Churches and Social Issues in Twentieth Century Britain*, set the religious historiography of the Second World War in continuity with the rest of the century.[31] Hastings takes a global approach, setting the English Churches' history in the

27   Hoover, 1999.
28   Snape, 2002.
29   Snape, 2002, p.340.
30   Snape, 2002, pp.346–347.
31   Hastings, 1991; Machin, 1998.

context of socio-political events rather than in ecclesiastical isolation. His is a broad-brush but thoroughgoing and wise assessment of events. However, once more their impact upon the local citizen is little considered. Machin demonstrates how, even in the midst of hostility, the Churches' wider concerns differed little from their peacetime ones; ill-used leisure time, weak Sabbath observance, concerns about sexual promiscuity, the abuse of alcohol and the resort to gambling.[32] Despite the particular social problems, such as those highlighted by the evacuation of children, and challenges to the Churches to contribute to ideas for social reconstruction, Machin chooses to leave unexamined the wartime pastoral care and concerns of clerics, and the religious response people made during a time of fearful need.

Similarly, John Wolffe, in *God and Greater Britain*, has a broader canvas in mind in his study of the part religion played in bolstering national identity across the period 1843–1945.[33] Undoubtedly of relevance in underscoring aspects of wartime popular religion reported on here, his focus is more the First than the Second World War and his sources are less the voices of ordinary people and more the assessments of other scholars and commentators on the importance of events.

In *Pacifism in Britain 1914–1945*, Martin Ceadel analyses the form of Christian idealism exhibited by the pacifist movement of the interwar period, exploring its roots and the outworking of its ideology and surveying its chief protagonists.[34] Whilst an indispensable study of this particular aspect of Christian political life, Ceadel's is a focused study singularly concerned with a particular facet of interwar history. What he highlights, however, is that pacifism was one of the dominant political lobbies of the period, and that the Churches were by no means compliant when it came to support for the war; nor were Churchmen uniform in their outlook. However, the layer of socio-political life with which Ceadel deals overlaps little with the life of the ordinary majority of people, who during the Second World War were satisfied that this war was just from a moral and religious point of view.

32   Machin, 1998, pp.115–125.
33   Wolffe, 1994.
34   Ceadel, 1980.

Oral History as a Research Method

The works of John Wolffe (1994), Sarah Williams (1999) and Callum Brown (2001) have brought to the fore evidence of the continued and vital influence of Christian belief and practice upon the individual and collective self-identity of the British people and the reality that the 'religious behaviour of the great majority of men and women in the British Isles [...] only rarely conformed to the institutional structures devised for them.'[35] In particular, Williams and Brown each rely upon analyses of oral testimony to demonstrate the continued reality of Christianity's influence. It seemed, therefore, appropriate and necessary to follow their lead, in order to accurately ascertain the character of the people's religious experience in Birmingham during the Second World War, by both consulting the documentary evidence available and by creating further historiography from garnered oral historical accounts.

Twenty-six oral testimonies were collected for this research, for which the details of date of birth, birthplace and parental occupation appear in the Appendix.[36] Initially, oral testimonies were sought from amongst the churchgoing population of Birmingham by placing requests for interviewees in the local and national Church press. At this stage of the research, it was intended that the study focus upon the impact of the war upon churchgoers alone; seven of the twenty-six interviewees were collected during this phase. Of these seven, three were Methodists; one was self-described as independent evangelical; one as Welsh Non-conformist; one Anglican and one Jewish. Exhausting these initial sources of interview, fifteen questionnaires were then sent to retired Anglican, Roman Catholic and Methodist clerics from whom there were five written responses; three of these, two Anglican and one Roman Catholic, were followed up by interview. At this point, Sarah Williams's study of the popular religion

---

35 Hempton, 1988, p.182.
36 Following common practice, the names of individuals have been changed to protect their identity. Wherever possible, however, details of their dates of birth and social backgrounds are retained for the sake of the integrity of the research. The names of clerics, however, are kept intact.

of the London district of Southwark began to impact upon the direction and emphasis of my own work. In particular, the evidence that Williams found from Southwark, that religious belief and practice existed beyond the regular churchgoing population, caused me to seek a wider pool of interviewees. From then on the study invited responses from the general population of Birmingham, utilising personal contacts amongst local historians working in the city's radio and newspaper media. Potential interviewees were asked to come forward on the basis of their recollected general wartime memories; their memory of the particular role of the Churches, or their remembered impressions that personal religious belief helped to sustain them in wartime were mentioned as minor issues of interest. A further eleven interviewees emerged as a result, many of whom were from the Birmingham Air Raids Association, an existing support group for those whose civilian relatives were killed during the blitz. Of these eleven interviewees, ten were not currently churchgoers but, as it later emerged, all had at some point been so during the early years of their lives. The remaining four interviewees came from personal Church contacts; three of these were Anglican and one Roman Catholic. Thus, eleven men and fifteen women were interviewed drawn from a mix of denominational and non-denominational backgrounds. Prior to interview, ten of these people described themselves as non-churchgoers; eight as Anglicans; four as Methodists; one as Roman Catholic; one as independent Evangelical; one as Jewish and one as a member of a Welsh non-conformist Church. The majority of interviewees were adults during wartime, but eight were reflecting upon their memories of a wartime childhood. All but three of the interviewees lived in working class neighbourhoods of the city in wartime, and all but five were domiciled in central wards of the city during the war.

Despite their varied backgrounds what eventually emerged, and will be detailed later, was that, contemporary churchgoers or not, all exhibited a degree of facility with Christian language and concepts, and the majority displayed a deference towards things Christian: I was informed of the value and significance of Sunday school, the lasting impressions made by local Church leaders and the prevailing impact of hymnody and prayers upon interviewees' lives. Arguably, some of these positive remarks may have arisen because in the dynamic of the interview dialogue they were deemed to be 'the right thing to say', especially when statements originated from those interviewees who were churchgoers, or from those who were aware that their interlocutor was a clergyperson. Based upon the assumption that their religious memories would be received sympathetically and knowledgeably, and therefore an example of the effect of the interviewer's and interviewees' inter-subjectivity (that is to say that memory is social and that the past is reconstructed dialogically in interactions with others rather than in isolation, and that narrators often recount their story with reference to their perception of their audience) some interviewees were readily explicit in their illustrations of religious behaviour in wartime.[37] However, deference towards things Christian was general amongst interviewees and exhibited even by those who had no knowledge of the researcher's religious standing. Perhaps this deference towards Christianity lay in the assumption by interviewees that if one is asking questions about religious faith one is likely to be religious (and therefore sympathetic) oneself. Indeed, maybe the perceived congruence between interviewees' and interviewer's worldview positively enabled the vocalisation of aspects of remembered life not ordinarily spoken of. Notwithstanding the impact of the researcher's religious position, it is contended here that any deference towards Christianity displayed was, in reality, not out of pretence, nor solely for the benefit of the hearer, but actual evidence of the genuine character of wartime cultural life.

During the interview, interviewees answered a range of questions, about the character of their faith or religious devotion at the time, intended to provoke general discussion of the social and familial influences upon their spirituality. Questions about interviewees' family life and social background were based upon those suggested by Paul Thompson's work.[38] Other questions were added, intended to explore the interviewees' religious upbringing (if any) and the impact of war upon patterns of religious observance. It was found that these questions provided a framework for the interview. Tangents were permissible: indeed, these often brought to the fore the most telling information.

37   Summerfield, 1998, pp.20–23.
38   Thompson, 1988, p.296ff.

26

Naturally, some interviews elicited more useful information than others.

The value (and simultaneous pitfalls) of oral history to this study were twofold. Firstly, oral history provides unique perspectives upon the detail of wartime occurrences, often bringing to the fore facts and impressions that hitherto have not been adequately taken into account. For example, this was particularly true of the recorded testimonies of clergy gathered for this research. Herein lay a wealth of detailed anecdote, from which was gained insights into the patterns of ministry and pastoral practices adopted by wartime clerics. Memory for detail was, more often than not, reliable, providing coherence across separate accounts and between interviews and available documentary sources. However, memory is not simply a repository of facts stored pristinely in a human mind. Memory is a complex dynamic of the human psyche. As Freeman observes:

> The recapitulation of ages of existence, of landscapes and encounters, obliges me to situate what I am in the perspective of what I have been [...] Memory, gives me a certain remove and allows me to take into consideration all the ins and outs of the matter, its context in time and space, just as an aerial view sometimes reveals to an archaeologist the direction of a road or fortification [...] invisible to someone on the ground.[39]

Therefore, the oral historian needs to tread cautiously, as well as respectfully, when dealing with the somewhat symbolic world of the human memory. Oral recollections need to be treated with care and deftly interpreted, not haphazardly reported out of context to prove a point. The integrity of the whole text needs to be taken into account for the truest picture of the reality it represents to emerge. This has been the endeavour in the handling of material quoted in this study.

The second worth of personal narratives of wartime memories is that they tend to reveal the social constructs and discourses by which people patterned and conceptualised their existence during wartime. Viewed as a text to be interpreted, much in the same way as other texts, it becomes clear that 'the manner of [the story's] telling seems to

---

39   Freeman, 1993, p.29. Freeman herein quotes Gusdorf, 1980.

us as important as what is told.'[40] The dialogue between interviewer and interviewee and the reflection of the interviewee upon their past are viewed as one narrative account:

> a vital document of the construction of consciousness, emphasizing both the variety of experience in any social group, and also how each individual story draws upon common culture [thereby demonstrating] a defiance of the rigid categorization of private and public, just as of memory and reality.[41]

In a sense, the details of the account and their accuracy fade into insignificance as the broad impact of the narrative's social discursivity becomes clear. In order for its social mythology, or its reflexivity of the cultural discourse of the period to be teased out, the text of the account needs to be taken as a whole: details of dates, and so on, are, in fact, less important. Penny Summerfield's *Reconstructing Women's Wartime Lives* demonstrates the value of oral testimony in uncovering the patterns of social relationships and expectations placed upon women in wartime. Outlining as she does the degree to which the whole text of the interview interaction, from first contact with the interviewee onwards, are evocative of social understandings, she powerfully indicates that oral history is far more than a mere subjective index of personal remembrances:

> [People giving oral history accounts] are using language and so deploying cultural constructions [...] no one's personal testimony represents a truth which is independent of [social] discourse. Historians who base their work on accounts of 'lived experience', claiming that such accounts give access to social reality apart from the controlling forces of the social relations in which their subjects are implicated, falsely separate discourse and experience: experience cannot exist outside discourse, agency cannot exist independently of language [...] this means that accounts of lived experience [...] should not be considered outside the discursive constructions of the aspects of wartime life to which that testimony refers, be that mother–child relationship, family life, war work, post-war expectations or whatever.[42]

---

40   Samuels and Thompson, 1990, p.2.
41   Samuels and Thompson, 1990, p.2.
42   Summerfield, 1998, p.11.

Just as Penny Summerfield asserts that social constructions of work or familial relationships may be construed from oral history narratives, Callum Brown likewise indicates that texts of many kinds, not just oral testimony, may also be illustrative of the degree to which religion, its language, concepts and mythologies, are a referent, in the construction of social and personal identity.[43] Myths abounded in wartime. Some of these myths, such as the famous and often widely accepted 'Dunkirk Spirit' notion of a resilient people going it alone against the odds, still enchant the British self-consciousness.[44] Discerning those religious mythologies which interacted with, and which were perpetuated by cultural means, is one of things commented upon later.

A dislocation between the historical context studied (in this case the Second World War) and the cultural conditions of the present make interpretation of oral historical accounts problematic. Characteristically, in order to uncover the religious reality forming the backcloth of the social world of interviewees, it was sometimes necessary to overcome the initial discomfort of admitting religious belief or upbringing, and then the relief of finding, in the interviewer, someone sympathetic towards this world view.[45] This is evidence of the 'stunting of the concept of religion' and the notion of 'discursive bereavement' which Callum Brown identifies: that is to say, the degree to which the place and function of religion in British cultural life has altered across the generations.[46] This interesting reaction of interviewees represents a general challenge to the interviewer to accurately characterise the disparate socio-religious conditions existent during distinct periods and in different cultural settings.

Thus, this study joins recent works, such as that of Callum Brown, which represent an attempt to challenge the secularisation narrative, using oral testimony as a key source of evidence. This work

43   Brown, 2001, p.12.
44   For a fuller discussion of these 'mythologies' and their enchantment of the British people see Calder, 1991.
47   Occasionally, familiarity with the background of the interviewer meant that such initial discomforts were missing.
46   Brown, 2001, p.182 and p.184.

seeks to add to the accumulating evidence for a popular religious vitality well into the twentieth century. Far from being marginalised and irrelevant, evidence here demonstrates that Christianity was part of the warp and weft of cultural discourse and functional in shaping people's narratives of self-identity prior to and during the Second World War in Birmingham. Moreover, these prevailing socio-cultural conditions enabled the Church to play its part in wartime life comfortably, and the government propagandist to communicate meaningfully to people, using religious language and motifs. Similarly, this Christian language and its motifs was also readily, naturally, and often, drawn upon by individuals to frame wartime experiences and activities, acting to legitimate the moral purposes of the war, providing a spiritual security in adverse circumstances. Evidence that religious and quasi-religious motifs were utilised to bolster the collective mythology of wartime Britishness will become apparent.

The following chapter sets the context for a study of wartime Birmingham, by an examination of the prevalent socio-economic, political and ecclesiastical conditions of the city between the wars.

1: Birmingham before the War

> In the midst of the russet solitude, we came upon a notice board saying, 'This is the City of Birmingham.' There was nothing in sight but hedgerows, glittering fields and the mist of the autumn morning. For a moment, I entertained a wild hope that this really was the City of Birmingham, that the town had been pulled down and carted away [...] I had always thought of the place, vaguely, as perhaps the most typical product in civic life of nineteenth-century industrialism, as a city of big profits and narrow views, which sent missionaries out of one gate and brass idols and machine guns out of another.[1]

The scholarly debate about the origins of the Second World War continues. Clearly, the war resulted from a combination of factors that cannot be fully entered into here. However, with Brecht, it is possible to observe that this war had a 'thousand fathers'.[2] Hitler's ascendancy over Germany during the 1930s had a quality of inevitability about it, founded as it was upon a fatal combination of personal opportunism and charisma, and national and international politics. The complexities of these events aside, what were the political, social and cultural conditions of Britain during the 1920s and 1930s? In particular, what was it like to live in Britain's second city, Birmingham, during this twenty-year inter-war respite?

From his journey across England in 1933, J. B. Priestley, the popular radio broadcaster responsible for rousing the spirits of the population with his wartime political commentary *Postscripts*, presented in an idiosyncratic way his impressions of England. Reflecting upon the urban sprawls spawned by the nineteenth-century industrial expansion and their domination of the landscape, he described a feeling of anger and shame at the squalor and poverty that he met upon his way.[3] In contrast, he proudly and optimistically

---

1   Priestley, 1968, p.78.
2   Bertolt Brecht, 'Great Babel Gives Birth' (quoted in Graham, 1998).
3   Priestley, 1968, p.415.

concluded that culturally England had contributed much to the world: thereby, he averred, it had redeemed itself.

Priestley's priggish estimate of England was likewise demonstrated in his characterisation of Birmingham, a city that, at heart, he wished could be spirited away. After admiring the architecture of the city centre and praising the city's museums, he described setting off on a tram journey to the town's outskirts. To his dismay he found

> mile after mile […] a parade of mean dinginess […] so many miles of ugliness, squalor, and the wrong kind of vulgarity […] there was nothing […] to light up a man's mind for one single instant.[4]

It was only in the pleasant, well-planned garden suburb of Bournville that Priestley discovered an antidote to the city's overall wretchedness. Bournville, for him, was

> infinitely superior to and more sensible than most of the huge new workmen's and artisans' quarters that have recently been built on the edge of many large towns in the Midlands.[5]

Such were Priestley's overall impressions of the city in the 1930s. To what extent are his observations borne out by other evidence?

Birmingham's Population and Geography

Between 1921 and 1931 Birmingham's population rose from 919,444 to 1,002,603, an increase of some 9%.[6] This was due, at least in part, to the boundary changes of 1928, which expanded the city northwards, incorporating Perry Barr and then, a year later, embracing Castle Bromwich and Sheldon.[7] The city itself, according to the 1931 census,

4   Priestley, 1968, p.86.
5   Priestley, 1968, p.91.
6   Pedley, 1951, p.3.
7   Bournville Village Trust, 1941.

32

covered an area of some 51,147 acres. By 1938, then, the city's population had grown to an estimated 1,048,000.[8]

The health of the city's inhabitants, measured by infant mortality and death rates, improved significantly across the interwar years. Death rates fell from an average of 16.5 per thousand to 11.4 for the city as a whole, though they remained higher in the city's central wards.[9] Infant mortality rates, mirroring national trends, fell due to a decline in family size – as a result of the increasing use of contraceptive methods – and because of some improvements in public health.

A particular and pressing challenge for Birmingham and its politicians during the 1920s and 1930s was housing. The city's difficulty – that of a shortage of good quality homes – was shared by many towns after the First World War. Birmingham needed an estimated 12,000 additional houses due to an increase in population from an influx of workers during wartime and the demobilisation of the armed forces.[10] Birmingham needed even more homes to replace its dilapidated stock and because the city was continually expanding. In response, Birmingham Corporation rose impressively to the task, building some 50,000 municipal homes during the interwar period. However, even this ambitious building programme and the demolition of older homes, resulting in a gradual migration to the newly built outer estates, are regarded by some commentators as inconclusive, not being as vigorous and determined as the programmes undertaken by other towns and cities.[11]

Birmingham continued in its endeavour to improve the housing of its citizens right up the outbreak of the next war. Indeed some 8,000 houses were declared unfit for habitation and demolished between 1930 and 1939 alone.[12] Gordon Cherry wryly remarks upon the way in which the blitz continued the city's slum-clearance efforts, commen-

---

8   A. Briggs, 1952, p.302.
9   Hopkins, 1990, p.136.
10   Cherry, 1994, p.113.
11   Leeds and London councils carried out the most radical slum clearance programmes; Cherry, 1994, p.122.
12   Cherry, 1994, p.124.

ting that evacuation, migration and conscription helped its progress by rendering a further 4,400 back-to-back homes redundant.[13]

By the end of the 1930s Birmingham, economically and geographically, consisted of three concentric circles, termed as its inner, middle, and outer rings. The inner ring contained the old, nineteenth-century, heart of the city. It was a densely populated, bustling neighbourhood of 187,900 people, or 62 people per acre, living for the most part in back-to-back houses. The majority of these had shared sanitary and washing facilities[14] and nearly 60,000 of the homes had no toilet facilities of their own.[15] This poorer inner ring contained a diminishing population even though migration to the outer ring demanded a greater degree of income and mobility. Therefore, inevitably, the city centre population was made up of the poorest, a high proportion of these unattached, elderly, or widowed.[16] This remnant lived in a busy central location, but often their homes were deteriorating in quality. Despite rents here being relatively cheap, many front doors concealed levels of poverty and malnutrition greater than elsewhere.

Though these seven inner wards of Ladywood, St. Paul's, St. Mary's, Duddeston and Nechells, St. Bartholomew's, St. Martin's and Deritend and Market Hall were of decreasing importance as residential areas they were still an important focus for employment in the city. The evidence shows that 58.2% of those living in the inner ring were still employed there, and 34.4% of those living in the outer ring continued to find their employment in the centre of the town.[17] This meant that many now living beyond the city's central areas relied upon the transport network of buses and trams to take them to and from home to their place of employment and to the leisure and basic amenities still only to be found in the city's centre.[18]

---

13   Cherry, 1994, p.140.
14   Bournville Village Trust, 1941, p.45.
15   Hopkins, 1990, p.137.
16   Hopkins, 1990, p.47.
17   Hopkins, 1990, p.68.
18   A. Briggs, 1952, p.312.

Because of the migration to areas of better housing, where basic facilities remained as yet underdeveloped, many found that they were spending a greater proportion of their time and money journeying back to the centre of the city to work or to play.[19] This reliance upon public transport naturally hit the working classes worst of all, thereby acting as a form indirect taxation.[20]

The majority of employment and leisure opportunities were to be found in the centre; this truly was the city's heart. A summary glance through a business gazette of the period provides a taste of city-centre commercial diversity. Within its bounds were the famous Market Hall and the associated meat, fish and vegetable markets.[21] There was a choice of many hotels, The Grand Hotel on Colmore Row, the Midland on New Street or the Queen's on Stephenson Street amongst them. There were numerous places to eat, including Kunzel's at Five Ways, famous for its chocolates, or Barrow's on Corporation Street. And there were shops to cater for every income level, whether it was the clothier Marshall and Snelgrove or Lewis's department store. Birmingham's centre gave the appearance of being the vital heart of a prosperous city. J.B. Priestley described it thus:

> So long as you keep within a very narrow limit in the centre, Colmore Row, New Street, Corporation Street, Birmingham has quite a metropolitan air, and on the fine afternoon I first explored them, these streets had quite metropolitan crowds in them too, looking at the windows of big shops and hurrying in and out of cafes and picture theatres. The city has a passion for arcades, and I never remember seeing more. It also has a passion for bridging streets, usually by joining two tall buildings somewhere on the third or fourth storey.[22]

Birmingham's middle ring, with a population of some 288,600, consisted of a further seven wards which contained two sevenths of the city's housing. Houses here were predominantly of the 'tunnel back' type and built prior to 1914. Priestley captured the mood of the serried rows of these streets, describing them as: 'a monotonous repetition [...] each has approximately the same accommodation and the same

---

19   Bournville Village Trust, 1941, p.75.
20   A. Briggs, 1952, p.311.
21   Eyles, 1931.
22   Priestley, 1968, p.84.

external appearance [of which] gloom was the chief characteristic'.[23] These communities lacked the colour and character of the 'back-to-back' inner-ward areas. Though houses were more functional and structurally sound they were architecturally unimpressive.

Anomalous to this middle ring of the city was Edgbaston. Described as 'Birmingham's Belgravia', this was an area of larger residences set in tree-lined streets.[24] It was here that the wartime Roman Catholic archbishop, Thomas Williams, lived, together with many of the city's public dignitaries. The main arteries into the centre of the city, such as the Bristol and Hagley Roads, drove through these middle zones bringing goods and people to and from the heart. Additionally:

> Local shopping centres, churches and chapels, public houses and clubs tended to cluster around these roads, some of the shopping centres being sufficiently large to cater for all the daily wants of the people who lived round about.[25]

By the late 1930s, some 60% of the city's population lived in the city's expanding outer ring. Both council and private development provided these new districts, which were noted for their spaciousness, 'designed not to draw people together, but rather to divide them from each other'.[26] Ironically, some inhabitants missed the neighbourliness of the inner city, perhaps because the foci of community life, such as churches and other social amenities, were relatively underdeveloped. Migrants to these spacious new areas complained of other implications of their moves, the burden of higher rents and food prices and, especially, the weakening of family ties because of the greater distances involved in maintaining contacts.[27] The need for additional places of worship had been envisaged by some denominations, but

---

23 Bournville Village Trust, 1941, pp.36–38.
24 Stevenson, 1984, p.25.
25 A. Briggs, 1952, p.305.
26 R.V. Glass, *The Social Background of a Plan*, 1948. Quoted in A. Briggs, 1952, p.306.
27 Hopkins, 1990, p.140.

36

only the Roman Catholics managed to build sufficient churches to keep pace with their increasingly scattered flock.[28]

Soon community centres were built, funded initially by private entrepreneurs and religious bodies, then later by the council. Ten of these had been completed by 1938, tenants paying for them by a token 2d. per week from their rents. However, these community developments remained insufficient. In 1932, Shrewsbury, a smaller town in population terms than Kingstanding, one of Birmingham's new estates, had twenty community halls to Kingstanding's one.[29] Thus, Birmingham was an expanding metropolis, but its physical growth was not without problem.

Leisure in the Interwar Years

Leisure facilities as a whole in this growing city were numerous, an expanding leisure industry being a feature of the 1930s in particular. The people of Birmingham were catered for by a range of attractions meeting the countless tastes naturally evident in a population of this size. Large-scale spectator sports were served by three venues. Association football was played by two major clubs at Villa Park, in the north of the City, and at the St. Andrew's ground in the city's south-east. The Warwickshire County Cricket Club had its ground at Edgbaston. People could participate in sport themselves at one of the '186 football pitches, 117 cricket pitches, 80 hard tennis courts, 345 grass courts, 19 putting greens, 38 bowling greens, [and] 12 boating pools' within the city's boundaries.[30] As well as this, they could swim and bathe in one of the city's 24 public baths.[31] Greyhound racing, a newer form of entertainment, along with speedway or dirt-track, could be betted upon, legally and illegally, as could horse racing: bookies'

28   A. Briggs, 1952, p.307.
29   Hopkins, 1990, p.139.
30   Hopkins, 1990, p.141.
31   Pedley, 1951.

runners being a familiar sight, particularly in working-class areas of Birmingham.[32] The betting habit was so ingrained that by 1937 there was a rail delivery from Liverpool each week of 235,000 football coupons.[33] Dancing was a popular form of entertainment amongst the young and was often hosted by the Churches. Theatregoing, in its culturally distinct incarnations of variety and repertory, was well represented in Birmingham. The Theatre Royal, the Alexandra, the Hippodrome, the Empire, the Prince of Wales and the Birmingham Repertory Theatre were amongst the four theatres and three music halls all existing within a radius of half a mile of the city centre. Public houses were another and consistently favoured form of recreation. The city council, in its characteristically paternalistic fashion, tried to restrict the popularity of drink by limiting the number of licenses it gave, reducing them in number by 600 between 1911 and 1930. Despite this, a number of new large pubs were built between the wars. The council positively encouraged, however, the populace's apparent affinity with gardening. Consequently, by 1938 there were over 12,000 allotments in the city, covering some 1,300 acres of land.[34] As well as this, new outer-ring homes had generous-sized gardens that were especially appreciated by those migrants who had lived in cramped quarters without gardens prior to this. In tune with this fostering of the more sedate and self-improving forms of leisure, Birmingham's publicly provided lending libraries also expanded in the interwar years, doubling their issues between 1919 and 1940.

Of all the leisure pursuits of the 1920s and 1930s, however, two stand out as being meteoric in their growth and popularity: cinema and wireless. By 1939 there were some 109 cinemas in the city; indeed, 'Birmingham was in the forefront of cinema developments,'[35] not least because Oscar Deutsch, founder of the highly successful Odeon cinema chain, was a Birmingham-born scrap-metal merchant.[36] Collectively, in 1939 Birmingham's cinemas held around 115,000 people. By

32   Thank you to my cousin, Mr Charles Parker, for his recollections of this.
33   Hopkins, 1990, p.141.
34   A. Briggs, 1952, p.309.
35   Richards, 1983, p.35.
36   Richards, 1983, p.36.

then, Birmingham citizens visited the cinema on average at least once a week. Indeed, the city's cinemas were a matter of pride 'as vital social amenities'.[37] The cinema not only entertained but informed; and as testimony to this view in 1932 Neville Chamberlain opened the city's first news theatre, which promised to take the audience 'Round the World in 50 minutes'.[38]

Wireless licences trebled in number in 1930s Birmingham, from 99,221 to 286,995.[39] By the end of the 1930s, wireless had gained the status of necessity rather than luxury amongst the population at large. The increasing audiences and popularity accrued by cinema and wireless between the wars cemented its potency of influence during the Second World War.

The year 1938 marked the centenary of Birmingham's incorporation. By then, the magnitude of its population and geography meant that it had established itself as a significant player in national affairs. In July of that year a pageant was held, attended by the Duke and Duchess of Gloucester, to celebrate the city's incorporation. This centenary was marked by their laying of the foundation stone of the new civic centre, Baskerville House, a grandiose building which was emblematic of the city's flourishing state.

The Economic Conditions of Interwar Birmingham

For Britain as a whole, the 1920s and 1930s were a time of mixed economic fortunes. In Birmingham, however, the economic situation was more stable, and indeed buoyant, than the experience nationally. During this period Britain's staple industries of coal-mining, shipbuilding, textiles and iron and steel suffered decreased demand in increasingly competitive world markets. However, Birmingham's fortunes were coming to depend much more upon the newer industry

37   Richards, 1983, p.37.
38   Richards, 1983, p.36.
39   Hopkins, 1990, p.140.

of motor manufacturing, its spin-off businesses, plastics, electrical goods and rubber, and the city's more established multitude of light engineering concerns rather than any single traditional staple. According to Briggs, it was the adaptability of Birmingham's workforce to these new products and markets, as well as the introduction of mass production, that stood the local economy in good stead during a time of national (and international) economic stringency.[40]

Unemployment nationally rose sharply into the early 1930s, peaking at over 20% of the insured working population in 1931. Many regions fared much worse than this 'national average'. For example, in Jarrow 68% of the working population were out of work, leading to the oft-vocalised sentiment that: 'in the Midlands and the South, you just don't know what we in the North have been through.'[41] By contrast, Birmingham's highest unemployment rate during the same period was 14%, some 76,000 out of work. Naturally, beneath these cold statistics lay the realities of the hardship of unemployment for whoever was facing it. However, as the 1930s went on, Birmingham's economic fortunes improved, not least because of the effects of the government's decision to rearm from 1935 onwards, spawning a number of expanded industrial operations and 'shadow factories' to produce the anticipated hardware of warfare.[42] These were sited near existing plants such as Birmingham Small Arms, or B.S.A., at Small Heath (providing munitions), Rover at Acocks Green (making aero-engine parts), and Morris at Castle Bromwich (constructing aircraft frames). Because of Birmingham's relative good fortune and economic stability, the city's population rose by 1.7% due to a migration of workers from the more depressed areas of Britain, changing, it must be noted, the make-up of the city's ecclesiastical as well as its working population. Birmingham was a city founded upon industry, and a city that played its part in the Second World War because of this industrial base.

40   A. Briggs, 1952, p.287; Mackay, 1999, pp.19–20.
41   A. Briggs, 1952, p.290.
42   The details of this expansion and its effects upon the region are traced in Thoms, 1989.

The City's Preparations for War

The rearmament of the nation from the mid 1930s onwards followed events on the continent.[43] The Midlands', and Birmingham's, manufacturing specialisms meant that they became the geographical focus for increased armaments production by an adaptation of existing skills and facilities. Shadow factories, government-owned but privately managed concerns for the construction of aeroplanes and ordnance, were gradually established from 1936 near to existing plant.[44] Though these sites promised employment opportunities and therefore financial security for the people of Birmingham, they also meant that, in the likelihood of a war, Birmingham would become an important strategic target. It was ironic therefore, that when it came to planning air raid precautions the city planners displayed comparatively little prescience, perhaps believing that precautions taken in this regard might be understood as lack of trust in their local M.P., Prime Minister Neville Chamberlain's, judgement. Shadow factories had been built at the instigation of the government; air raid precautions were left up to the city; some believed that Birmingham was not in danger of attack from potential enemy bombers. Notwithstanding a government grant for civil defence given in July 1938, precautions were not completed by the outbreak of war and the council still urged frugality upon its A.R.P. Committee.[45] Despite this, by the summer of 1939 the city's civil defence comprised thirty-two first-aid posts and twelve mobile medical units, an early warning system, and extensive fire precautions. Shelter provision, however, remained unsatisfactory for a large majority of Birmingham's population even by the time war was declared. This may have been due to a degree of confusion about the best way to protect the civilian population from air raids, to arguments about the expense involved, or to laxity-cum-hostility towards civil defence. It

---

43   Discussion about rearmament actually began much earlier, in 1927. See: Thoms, 1989, p.2.
44   For a detailed account of the wartime industrial economy see: Thoms, 1989, esp. ch.1.
45   Sutcliffe and Smith, 1974, p.18.

was initially felt that a policy of 'dispersal', the evacuation of vulnerable people to so called 'safe' areas, would be the most successful course of action. For those in areas designated low risk in terms of bombardment, Anderson shelters were provided: 82,000 had been installed by October 1939, providing rudimentary shelter for 410,000 people, or around half the city's population. For Birmingham, with its mixed residential and manufacturing areas, these outdoor shelters were plainly not an adequate answer. Moreover, because of the nature of back-to-back housing in the high-risk areas, the city was forced to rely upon underground shelters, trenches, and, later, the Morrison indoor shelter, which was provided free to most families. This slow diffusion of precautions, which suggested a lack of urgency on the part of the council, put the city at grave risk; for 'if Birmingham had been heavily bombed on the outbreak of war, as most people expected it would be, the results would have been disastrous.'[46] Fortunately, the period of the so-called 'Phoney War' allowed for nearly all of the city's services to be brought up to a satisfactory standard, though the provision of adequate domestic and public/deep shelters remained a point of contention well into the conflict. In the event, however, Birmingham, along with other cities, proved unprepared for the kind of bombardment that actually occurred. Pre-war planners foresaw a greater number of high-explosive attacks and the use of poisonous gas but much greater damage was done by incendiary devices, some 90% of industrial damage in Birmingham being caused by fire. It was only after the big blitz of 1940 and 1941 that it was decided, by the then Home Secretary Herbert Morrison, to organise fire defences in a much more coherent way; this decision being made at the time of a civic row about the inadequacy of fire precautions in the city.

46   Sutcliffe and Smith, 1974, p.23.

An Interwar Political History of Birmingham

In the 1931 general election, Stanley Baldwin's Conservatives won 500 seats. This decisive victory, taken at face value, creates the impression that this was a period of political consensus. However, this was far from being the case. The interwar period was in many ways an era of political change, unrest and uncertainty. Moreover, it was a time of increasing social polarisation, of a widening gap between the social classes. Of these political conditions Adrian Hastings sardonically observes, 'only Hitler would break down the middle wall that lay between them.'[47] Unsurprisingly, amidst industrial strife and economic instability, the 1920s and 1930s were the heyday of the extremist political ideologies of communism and fascism. Likewise, these years saw the growth of the Labour movement, as well as sounding the virtual death knell of Liberalism.

It was Liberalism and Conservatism, the latter in its Unionist form, which dominated Birmingham's parliamentary politics in the late nineteenth and early twentieth centuries. Into the 1920s and 1930s Unionism still held sway, no doubt because of the prevailing loyalty to the legacy of Joseph Chamberlain, and in memory of the public service offered by local politicians of his ilk. The Labour Party, however, gradually replaced the Liberals in Birmingham as the second largest party, reflecting the national trend of the 1920s.

Overall, the electorate of Birmingham grew from 427,085 in 1918 to 662,967 in 1937, because of the widening of the franchise and the expansion of the boundaries of the city. In 1919 many women obtained the right to vote. It is difficult to show statistically how women's votes may have affected particular parliamentary seats, but in the judgement of one commentator the inclusion of the female electorate may have been one factor serving to increase the strength of the Labour Party in Birmingham.[48] The slow advent of socialism in the city during the interwar years meant a gradual shift in the political representation of the city in parliament. For example, in the election of 1924 Labour

47   Hastings, 1991, p.245.
48   Hastings, 1980, p.84.

won a Westminster seat in Birmingham, the first it had managed to obtain in the city. Fielding a candidate in every Birmingham ward for the first time, the party succeeded in nudging Neville Chamberlain down to a majority of just seventy-seven in his seat.[49] In the 1929 general election Labour won four of Birmingham's twelve parliamentary seats, taking an interwar high of 40% of the vote.[50] This time Neville Chamberlain opted to stand for the safer seat of Edgbaston. As things turned out, this was a timely decision, his former seat of Ladywood being won by the Labour candidate by eleven votes.[51] However, each Labour seat won in 1929 was returned to the Conservatives in the 1931 election. Perhaps because of relative economic prosperity locally or perhaps because amidst the fear invoked by growing fascism abroad, patriotism seemed to demand voting Conservative, this election was a resounding victory for the Conservative Party. However, this was to be a temporary hiccough in socialist fortunes.[52] Though the period of budding socialism seemed to be short-lived in Birmingham, in 1945 the Labour Party, winning ten of Birmingham's expanded number of thirteen seats, would conclusively overturn the Unionist–Conservative political hegemony.[53] Significantly to the city's life, the 1945 general election was the first in which no Chamberlain had stood for parliament in eighty years.[54]

Contrastingly, in the intervening pre-war election of 1935, Unionists won all of Birmingham's seats once again, despite Labour polling a higher share of the vote than previously (some 35% as opposed to 20% in the 1931 elections). The war most certainly transformed the parliamentary political landscape in Birmingham, altered by the changing make-up of voters (many migrants from other areas of the Britain), the decline of the Chamberlains' apparent enchantment of the people, and the progress of the Labour movement.[55]

49   A. Briggs, 1952, p.320.
50   A. Briggs, 1952, p.320.
51   Hastings, 1980, p.84.
52   A. Briggs, 1952, p.321.
53   Hastings, 1980, p.88.
54   Hastings, 1980, p.88.
55   Hastings, 1980, p.89.

Division	Member of Parliament
Aston	Capt. The Hon. A.O.J. Hope
Deritend	J. Smedley Crooke
Duddeston	Oliver E. Simmonds
Edgbaston	Rt. Hon. A. Neville Chamberlain
Erdington	J. F. Eales K.C.
Handsworth	Commander O.S. Locker-Lampson
Kings Norton	J. R. H. Cartland
Ladywood	G. W. Lloyd
Moseley	P. J. H. Hannon
Sparkbrook	Rt. Hon. L. C. M. J. Amery
West Birmingham	Rt. Hon. J. Austen Chamberlain
Yardley	E. W. Salt

Members of Parliament elected for Birmingham in 1935.[56]

However, Birmingham's twelve elected members of parliament in 1935, and therefore for the duration of the war, were all Conservatives.

The local elections of the 1920s were successful ones for the Labour Party. In 1921 they secured ten seats in the City Council, two of which were gains. In 1926, after the General Strike, Labour succeeded in winning twelve seats; eight of these were gains. Labour by this time held 30 out of the 120 seats on the council. Labour could not penetrate and rarely contested the Unionist strongholds of the city such as Edgbaston, Moseley, King's Heath and Sparkhill. In the early thirties, years of depression, the swing back towards the Unionists on the council reflected national political trends. In 1932 Labour polled well, winning some 10,000 more votes than the Unionists and secured 13 seats. By 1938, indicating the city's latest pre-war political trend, Unionists returned to a strong position with 83 councillors and 20 aldermen: Labour at this time had 20 councillors and 7 aldermen.

---

56   Black, 1957, p.659. Several changes occurred after 1935: Squadron Leader J.A.C. Wright was elected for Erdington in October 1936; Mr W.F. Higgs was elected for West Birmingham in March 1937; Major E. Kellett elected for Aston in May 1939; Mr P.F.B. Bennett returned unopposed for Edgbaston in Dec. 1940; Captain B.A.J. Peto was returned for King's Norton in May 1941; Lt. Comm. R.M. Prior was returned for Aston in June 1943.

Other parties hardly figured at this time; the Liberal Party held three seats, whilst independent candidates also held three.

Fascism had little appeal for Birmingham's moderate electorate. Despite Oswald Mosley's links with Birmingham, the British Union of Fascists did not manage to gain a popular mandate in the city. In 1934, at its peak in the Midlands, the Birmingham branch of the B.U.F. had a membership of only 2,000. This relatively small membership gained only a trivial electoral success. The reason for its lack of popularity in Birmingham seems to have been that there was little anti-Semitism upon which to play. The local B.U.F. reasoned that to stir up such political anti-Semitism in Birmingham would be futile; the conditions for the success of this political ideology simply did not exist. As Brewer observes: 'the manipulation of ethnic hostility and ethnic hatred was reserved for those areas where it was assumed to have the greatest effect on the host and the immigrant communities.'[57] It was elsewhere in the country, most notably in London's East End where the Jewish community was more conspicuous, that the energies of the B.U.F. were targeted. Because Birmingham's Jewish population was more dispersed amongst the populace and more assimilated into the city's life the community was a lesser focus for victimisation.[58]

Likewise, the Communist Party obtained relatively little support in Birmingham and few votes in local elections,[59] only having real influence in trades union affairs.[60] In fact, Communists canvassed on behalf of Birmingham Labour candidates in the 1935 general election, as a strategy to oppose fascism and assure that voting was not diffused across the socialist parties.[61] Though the Communists had little electoral support, their voices were as likely to be heard as others in the Bull Ring market area, a longstanding and popular place of public oratory.[62] It appears that neither fascism nor communism found a sub-

57 Brewer, 1984, p.119.
58 Brewer, 1984, p.113.
59 Sutcliffe and Smith, 1974, p.108.
60 Hastings, 1980, p.84.
61 Hastings, 1980, p.87.
62 Rogers, 1956, pp.219–220.

46

stantial niche in the seemingly moderate political climate of interwar Birmingham.

In the 1945 general election the Labour Party polled some 53% of Birmingham's votes.[63] Though not susceptible to revolutionary forms of politics, Birmingham's political landscape had nevertheless changed dramatically across the interwar and wartime years. The electorate were now much more sympathetic to issues rather than loyal to the established personalities. A number of influences had served to create these new circumstances, including an increase in workers' power during the war years, and the people's will to make significant social improvements in the post-war world.[64]

The Pre-war Churches of Birmingham

Contemporary commentators were often scathing of Birmingham's popular piety. For instance, despite one in three of the population being in attendance at churches across Birmingham for the *Birmingham News Religious Census* of 1892, and over half of the children of school age in attendance at Sunday school, the editor of the *Birmingham News* felt able to assert that 'a large proportion of our population is alienated by habit, as well as by taste, from regular attendance upon the ordinances of religion.'[65] Only twenty or so years later, whilst reflecting upon the partial success of missionary efforts, another investigator concluded disdainfully that 'irreligion' remained the chief cause of the city's ills:

> Looking back over the whole field of our inquiry in the life of Birmingham, our feeling should be a mingling of satisfaction and disquiet. Against the decline in church attendance we have to put the decline of blatant unbelief and the increasing popularity of men's meetings, the character of which, if not always directly religious, are for the most part run on Christian lines. Gambling

---

63   Sutcliffe and Smith, 1974, p.82.
64   Hastings, 1980, p.89.
65   *Birmingham News*, 10 December 1892, quoted in Peacock, [undated], p.15.

increases its hold on Birmingham, but against this we may set the undoubted fact that, consuming as this vice is the cure is at hand if we will only use it [...] Against the distressing fact that there is to-day in Birmingham more intemperance among women than formerly may be set the statement that drunkenness among men is diminishing. Birmingham has noble social forces at work for her amelioration. But we believe that not by these, but by religious agency must the city be saved. 'Uncertainty of employment', says one observer, 'is one cause of improvidence and recklessness. But irreligion is the chief cause.'[66]

In contrast to this cynical assessment of the religion of the masses, Birmingham undoubtedly had a formidable Christian elite. One only has to consider such celebrated clerical characters as George Dawson, R.W. Dale and John Henry Newman; the socio-political influence of the 'Quaker' and Unitarian family dynasties, such as the Cadburys and the Chamberlains, and the vitality of particular congregations such as the Graham Street Chapel and the Church of the Messiah, to realise that the city had an impressive Christian pedigree of pervasive influence which, in reality, left an indelible mark upon the city's public inheritance.[67] Thus, at the hierarchical level, at least, one can be persuaded that Birmingham's Christianity suffused and moulded the life of the Victorian city. Moreover, as Kim Wasey has clearly demonstrated in her study of the working-class central wards of Birmingham of the late nineteenth and early twentieth centuries, such communities were not as immune to missionary endeavours as some media commentators believed them to be.[68]

Asa Briggs, one of the authors of the principal history of the city, comments upon the changing ecclesiastical and religious landscape of interwar Birmingham:

Although religion did not obtrude so obviously as it had done in the nineteenth century, when it acted as the great dynamic in city development, and although many of the tendencies of the times encouraged secularisation, the churches and chapels still acted as focal points of their districts, and the values they taught

66 The Sunday at Home's Special Commissioner, "Greater Birmingham: its religious life, moral and spiritual condition", *Sunday at Home*, January 1911.
67 See also A. Briggs, 1990 edition, p.195ff in which Briggs names the key figures in Birmingham Victorian Christianity.
68 Wasey, 2002.

influenced the daily conduct of thousands of citizens. At the same time powerful new religious leaders emerged who preached Christianity to a new generation.[69]

According to Briggs, then, Christianity was as critical to the life of interwar Birmingham as it had been in former generations, though its practical life was somewhat more insular, and its influence more parochial than city-wide. His assessment is that the Christian Churches had adapted themselves to the ever-changing needs of the locality, and though other leisure interests had emerged, the Churches still played a noteworthy and influential part in the lives of the populace.

Certainly, Birmingham was a city well served by places of worship. By 1938 Birmingham had some 584 churches, chapels or meeting houses.[70] Denominationally, the city had more Anglican and Roman Catholic Churches than those of other traditions, and its respective denominational leaders maintained a good relationship with the city's Corporation. Given the city's historic domination by non-conformity, and the lasting influence of the 'Pope of nonconformity', R.W. Dale, it might have been expected that this arm of Christianity would still have a certain pre-eminence.[71] Instead, nonconformity was locally, as well as nationally, experiencing a general numerical decline. Indeed, Birmingham's religious life seemed to mirror national trends, in that Church membership was in overall decline (except for Roman Catholicism where, mainly because of Irish immigration, the Catholic population of the Birmingham Archdiocese rose from 152,243 in 1931 to 179,894 in 1946),[72] and the numbers of clergy were diminishing.[73] There is no single survey of Birmingham churchgoing in the interwar period. However, Easter communicant figures for one central Birmingham parish, St. John's, Sparkhill, exemplify the pattern of gradual decline across wartime: total communicants on Easter Day 1933 were 722, but by 1947 this had dwindled to 307.[74] Similarly, in the parish of

69   A. Briggs, 1952, p.320.
70   According to *Cornish's Birmingham Year Book 1938–1939*, Birmingham: Cornish Brothers Ltd.
71   R.W. Dale is described as such in Feiling, 1946, p.2.
72   *The Catholic Directory of the Archdiocese of Birmingham*, 1931 and 1946.
73   Sutcliffe and Smith, 1974, p.256.
74   Register of Services, St. John's Sparkhill.

Aston, Easter communions shrank from 602 in 1933 to 274 in 1947.[75] However, other Anglican parishes, such as King's Norton, experienced stable and increasing Easter communicant figures during wartime, rising from 415 in 1939 to 468 in 1946.[76] Nonetheless, according to available national statistics of Church membership, over the longer term, Church-affiliation was becoming a lesser priority in a growing proportion of the population's lives. Figures for England show that, for the Church of England in 1911, 6.74% of the population were Easter communicants; by 1931, this had fallen slightly to 6.05%. Similarly, these figures support the same trends of the erosion of Church membership for Methodists (2.32% falling to 2.09%), and Con-gregationalists (0.85% falling to 0.76%) across the same period. It is only the Roman Catholic Church that experienced an increase in membership from 4.74% in 1911, rising to 5.65% of the population in 1931.[77] Similar deterioration, this time in Church attendance figures, was reported of the city of York in *English Life and Leisure,* a post-war survey of various aspects of people's lives.[78] From the researcher's census, taken on a number of Sundays throughout the year, in 1901 43.7% of the city's population attended an Anglican church; by 1948, this figure was 33.1% of the population.[79] Nonconformist churches were attended by 37.8% of the population of York in 1901; by 1948, this had fallen to 34.4%. Roman Catholic church attendance, by contrast, was 13.8% in 1901 and 30.1% by 1948.[80] Naturally, beneath this data lie variations in the construction of results within and across surveys, making comparison between them difficult. These variations need to be taken into account before basing any conclusions upon them. Notwithstanding the need for a cautious interpretation, the general impression created by these surveys is one of decline in membership and attendance across the Protestant denominations and, by contrast, steady increases in Roman Catholic Church membership

75   Register of Services, St. Peter and St. Paul, Aston.
76   Register of Services, St. Nicholas, Kings Norton.
77   Wolffe, 1994, p.69. Figures are based upon Currie, Gilbert and Horsley, 1977.
78   Rowntree and Lavers, 1951.
79   Rowntree and Lavers, 1951, p.343.
80   Rowntree and Lavers, 1951, p.343.

and attendance figures across the inter-war and wartime period. Every indication is that these trends were generally true of Birmingham too.

Later commentators propose that the Churches in Birmingham struggled to find a role in interwar Birmingham society, abandoning evangelisation for a gospel of social concern.[81] Perhaps, they suggest, this priority made the Church one voice amongst many in an increasingly idealistic political climate, thereby leading to a diminution of the Churches' uniqueness.[82] Surely, however, this is to trivialise the impact of a number of noteworthy movements in Birmingham during these years. For instance, such events as the interdenominational *Conference of Christian Politics, Economics and Citizenship* (COPEC), hosted by the city in April 1924, could not have gone unnoticed by the population at large. COPEC and its 1,400 delegates were presided over by William Temple and produced some 12 volumes of reports after a single week's consultation. Afterwards, a body of the same name was formed to deal with substantive issues raised by the conference upon which prominent Christians could continue to ponder and plead. In Birmingham itself, an ecumenical Christian Social Council was formed in the early 1930s, partly stemming from COPEC and partly from a shared mission to the city by the Churches in 1930.[83] Chaired by the redoubtable Rector of Birmingham, T. Guy Rogers, the stated aim of this ecumenical Council was 'to quicken the social conscience of Birmingham'.[84] Despite its lofty objective of protesting 'against the un-Christian conditions under which so many of our fellow Christians live in the slums of Birmingham',[85] the Council often seemed more concerned about Sunday opening of cinemas and campaigning for a restriction on public-house licences.[86] However, the Council's coordinated programme of help for refugees in the latter part of the 1930s apparently led to 'a real inter-racial, inter-religious and inter-political fellowship'.[87] The strength of the relationship between Jews

81   Sutcliffe and Smith, 1974, p.264.
82   Sutcliffe and Smith, 1974, p.264.
83   Rogers, 1956, p.215.
84   Rogers, 1956, p.215.
85   Rogers, 1956, p.215.
86   Richards, 1983, pp.37–43.
87   Rogers, 1956, p.222.

and Christians was proven in a unique united worship service held in the late 1930s at St. Martin's, attended by both the Bishop and Archbishop of Birmingham and other representatives from both faiths, praying 'for a common deliverance from a common tyranny'.[88] Such evidence shows that Birmingham was a city for which religion continued to have a vital social function.

Leading the two largest Christian denominations of the city in 1938 were the Anglican bishop Ernest Barnes (1874–1953) and the Roman Catholic archbishop Thomas Williams (1877–1946). Each of them had been brought up in Birmingham (Barnes was born in Altrincham and Williams in Handsworth), and now they found themselves leading their respective denominations in their home city. Barnes and Williams had been sometime acquaintances at Cambridge but, it appears, there the parallels between them end.

Barnes, a scientist, mathematician and theologian, was also a published, and somewhat controversial, author. He has been variously described as paradoxical and contentious, preferring people of intellect but at the same time 'loved for his humanity, independence, and healthy disrespect for established authority and precedent'.[89] Barnes was a pacifist and a dedicated scourge of anything irrational in religion, especially in relation to Eucharistic doctrine.[90] Because of this, a number of Birmingham clergy were subject to Barnes's episcopal discipline. He forbade sacramental reservation and devotion, and some notable Anglo-Catholic clerics rebelled against his wishes. Such acrimony between Barnes and a sizeable group of his clergy led to a breakdown of the pastoral relationship between the bishop and his flock, and this overshadowed the early years of Barnes's episcopate. Given to stridency, Barnes often made inappropriate and tactless statements in sermons and addresses. For instance, he was very much in favour of eugenics, and on several occasions he suggested compulsory sterilisation for some members of the population.[91] Puritanical and Victorian in outlook, his aloofness from his clergy distanced him from

---

88   Rogers, 1956, p.223.
89   Rogers, 1956, p.265.
90   Barnes, 1979, p.162ff.
91   Vidler, 1974.

them during wartime, when a more informal leadership style might have been more effective.

Williams's talents appear to have been more unassuming. He was reputed to have been a man of iron will and relentless energy, a good listener and fair in his judgement. Assiduous in his pastoral care, in 1937 he became President of the Catholic Social Guild, which allowed him to pursue his concerns with regard to social and political issues; concerns reflected by many of his pastoral letters of the period. However, in the years leading up to the war Williams's health declined, sometimes hampering him in his duties and necessitating the appointment of an assistant bishop, Bernard Griffin, in 1939 (Griffin was later to become Archbishop of Westminster). But Williams's ill health did not seem to stifle his pastoral zeal, as the volume and temper of his correspondence illustrates.[92]

Leslie Tizard ministered at Carrs Lane Congregational Church in wartime. This historic church, at which the influential Victorian, R.W. Dale, had been minister, remained a prominent pastorate to hold. Following on from the pacifist co-founder of the Fellowship of Reconciliation, Leyton Richards, minister at Carrs Lane from 1924 until 1938, Tizard came to Birmingham from a ministry in Colchester: he remained at Carrs Lane from October 1941 until 1957.[93] It appears that Tizard was not overawed by comparisons with his predecessors, despite his invitation to minister being opposed by some of the pacifist members of his new congregation.[94] The author of seven books, Tizard was particularly interested in pastoral psychology and the practical application of the Christian faith. In wartime, he wrote *Facing Life with Confidence,* a book of advice to those dealing with life's changes, which curiously, however, did not deal with the vicissitudes experienced by many during the war.[95] His chief contribution to wartime city life was his organisation and input to the Carrs Lane seminars on

92   With thanks to The Revd. Dr. John Sharp of St. Chad's Cathedral Archive for letting me have sight of his *Dictionary of National Biography* article on Thomas Williams prior to its publication.
93   Guntrip, 1959, p.16.
94   Guntrip, 1959, p.16; Driver, 1948, p.89.
95   Tizard, 1941.

social reconstruction, which will be explored in detail below. Tizard's wartime ministry was characterised by its preaching, of which it was said that it 'never shies away from the difficulties of faith to the modern mind'.[96]

Were the Churches Prepared for War?

The signs of an impending international crisis were many, and few could fail to see them. The city's clergy interpreted events and the causes of them in subtly different ways, though they often agreed that the origins of war lay in the nation's spiritual and moral bankruptcy. Typical of the remarks of clerics are those of Father Rosenthal, Anglican vicar of St. Agatha's, Sparkbrook, an Anglo-Catholic parish near the centre of the city, who, along with others, had been subject to his Bishop's wrath concerning Eucharistic devotion. Writing in perhaps the most public organ of clerical thinking of the period, the parish magazine, he ruminated upon the events of the Munich crisis of September 1938. His reflections are typical of the temper of the time, and demonstrate how international events caused many clerics to urge greater devotion from the people.

> I turn to write this letter from listening to the Prime Minister speaking at Heston Aerodrome on his return from his historic visit to Germany […] It would be puerile and unworthy if we were to be occupied with local and parochial affairs while the world is in the throes of a crisis of a most serious and dangerous kind […] I urge you then to pray with faith and conviction about the world situation in your private prayers, to use the opportunities provided by the Masses and the Holy Hour [to pray] that God's will may be done.[97]

96 Guntrip, 1959, p.28.
97 *The Fiery Cross*, parish magazine of St. Agatha's, Sparkbrook, Vol. XIII, No. 10, October 1938.

54

Along with other clerics, Rosenthal identified the causes of the war as being rooted, not in economic instability or political tension, but in the creeping spiritual malaise infecting European society:

> the troubles of the world are the result of forgetfulness of God, and in that forgetfulness can we claim that England has had no share? [...] The process goes on without violence, continuously, steadily, as a kind of impersonal motion of secular change. It marks the passing of our English civilization away from the Faith in which it is founded, and out of which it has been fashioned. The great sin of our country is forgetfulness of God [...] Our present troubles, grave and serious as they are, will prove to be a blessing in disguise if only they make us realize that apart from God we can do nothing, that 'unless the Lord build the city their labour is but vain that build it. Except the Lord keep the city the watchman worketh [sic] but in vain'.[98]

Undoubtedly, these were gloomy and fearful days for all. Clergy reflections of the time mirrored Rosenthal's pessimism. In fact, such pessimism ran within and across denominations. For example, Father Francis Drinkwater, the Roman Catholic parish priest of The Holy Family, Small Heath, and an armed-forces chaplain during the First World War, also pondered the possible causes of the war and the course events might take in his Christmas sermon of 1938. His words contrasted the orderly spirituality and peacefulness of the season with the reality and chaos of war, attributing the onset of conflict not to international events alone but to political decisions being made closer to home and to the acquisitive nature of society:

> Outside there is still darkness, but here at Mass there is still light. Outside is universal madness rushing helplessly on to self-destruction; here in the stable of Bethlehem there is still sanity, and belief in love and peace. As soon as you look at the Infant Jesus you know [what] He is asking you to do, it is not to go scattering bombs and terror and death [...] You all know the reason why mankind is preparing to destroy itself – it is simply because men refuse to share with each other the good gifts of God; and even this very Christmas, [...] our own rulers [...] are going to perpetuate [evil by way] of that wicked means test which brings so many people in this country close to starvation.[99]

---

98 *The Fiery Cross*, the parish magazine of St. Agatha's, Sparkbrook, Vol. XIII, No. 10, October 1938.

99 The Papers of Fr. Francis Drinkwater, St. Chad's Cathedral Archive.

Parish life at the Anglican low-church parish of St. Luke's, Bristol Street, however, appeared to go on as usual right up to the outbreak of war, with a garden fete, a jumble sale and a failed heating boiler to focus attention upon rather than a European cataclysm. Wars and rumours of wars got little mention in the Reverend Thomas Tunstall's columns. In fact, when war broke out, it seemed to take him somewhat by surprise, but, yet again, the cause of war was easily identifiable. In October 1939 Tunstall wrote:

> My Dear Friends, when I was writing my letter last month I little thought that this month's letter would be written under war conditions. At that time we were hoping and praying that such a tragedy might be averted, but in the end, it came upon us. It was a shock to some. How could God allow it when millions of prayers were being offered for peace? And herein is the greatest tragedy that the world has not realised that man's selfishness and pride can seriously hamper and even temporarily defeat the carrying out of God's plans for the human race. But it cannot be so forever. God will win the final victory.[100]

Hence, a mood of sombre inevitability greeted the declaration of war amongst Birmingham's churchmen. Canon Guy Rogers, the Rector of Birmingham, another who had been an armed-forces chaplain in the First World War, preached as war was declared on Sunday 3 September 1939; as with many of his wartime sermons, the following day his words were reported in *The Birmingham Post*. In his address, Rogers lamented the laxity and complicity of the Church and politicians alike which failed to deal with the 'The philosophy of life which creates and sustains the Nazi regime'.[101] He lent his support and that of the Church to the war, arguing, however, that in contrast with the previous conflict the Church should not be a recruitment agency for the army. Rather in this war: 'the function of the Church and the state must be kept apart [...] it is to the spiritual care of the nation that the Church through its officers and through its members [...] must devote itself.'[102] Moreover, in this war, the Church needs to be the conscience of the nation for, as he pointed out, 'there are ideals to be held up

100   *The Parish Magazine of St. Luke's, Bristol Street*, October 1939.
101   *The Birmingham Post*, Monday 4 September 1939.
102   *The Birmingham Post*, Monday 4 September 1939.

before the nation which are to become sadly soiled in the course of conflict.'[103]

Other Birmingham clerics urged their people to look no further than their own souls for the true source of the war. The war was both representative of spiritual and moral inertia and, thereby, a spiritual opportunity. Because of this, sometimes the war was characterised as a retreat, an opportunity for spiritual recollection and renewal, as in the detailed spiritual advice given by the Reverend Dudley Clark, Vicar of St. Alban's, Bordesley, to his parishioners in his parish magazine of October 1939:

The important thing for us, as a parish and congregation, is to ask ourselves what message has the war for us? What are we to learn in this time of trouble? [...] First, there is the need for penitence [...] 'Sin lieth at the door.' It is not Christianity that has brought about this war; it is that which is the exact opposite to Christianity, namely sin and selfishness. And if we are tempted to look abroad and fasten the chief of the guilt elsewhere, we hear the voice of Our Lord saying to each nation and to every individual in each nation, 'Let him that is without sin first cast a stone.' [...] England in the twentieth century cannot afford to throw many stones. And the war is a call to us to look at sin and selfishness – our own sins and selfishness – in their true light [...] our first duty is to deepen our penitence. We are to learn from this war to hate our sins [...] surely another lesson for us to learn is the duty and power of prayer [...] we must see whether we cannot re-learn the lesson that prayer and sacraments must once more be the centre of our lives under all circumstances. We must re-learn the elementary fact that in joy and in sorrow in the ways of light as well as in the paths of darkness, we are dependent moment by moment on the guidance and upholding strength of God. 'His never failing providence ordereth all things.' Let us buy this opportunity which is given to us of becoming once again men and women of regular habits of prayer. Never let us wilfully neglect the duty of public worship [...] and besides penitence and prayer there is another lesson for us to learn at this time and that is the lesson of self-discipline. The war demands that we should put self and the pleasures and interests of self right in the background. It is a direct and urgent call to spend and be spent for others. And there is need for a good deal of self-discipline in speech at a time like this. It is so easy to spread rumours and to say many things that are against the law of love. A permanent spirit of self-discipline is the lesson that we need to learn [...] Under modern conditions of warfare the civil population is exposed to great dangers [...] Common sense would urge us to make provision for the safety of our souls at a

103 *The Birmingham Post*, Monday 4 September 1939.

time like this. We would try to keep in a state of grace, but if we fall into sin, small or great, let us make confessions and get forgiveness. Then our acts of Communion should be regular and frequent.[104]

However, for the average Birmingham citizen the declaration of war did not engender such piously purposeful thoughts; instead, it evoked a degree of spiritual uncertainty and fearfulness. As one Birmingham Mass-Observation diarist wrote:

> I feel like one on the brink of many unknown forces and counter forces [...] at breakfast the radio told us that at eleven fifteen we would know. At eleven o'clock, there was a general pacing about the house. Perhaps we were trying to brace ourselves to accept the news, although we knew in advance what it would be. At eleven fifteen we knew, one woman began to cry. Not much was said [...] Now may God Bless You [the Prime Minister went on] I thought for a moment he was going to bring God in on our side. But he continued, 'May God defend the right' without specifically stating the right.[105]

Thus, from the outset many of the city's religious leaders primed the populace with a spiritual slant upon events. In the coming months, clerics would not shy from stirring the people's spiritual sensibilities, nor shirk the chance of turning the experience of difficulty into a religious opportunity. Generally, clerics held back from belligerence, but on many occasions they would seek to point out that the war offered a chance to change, prophesying various possible religious and social outcomes. How people responded to the experience of war, what part religious belief and practice played in it, and how their religious experience was shaped by it, is the subject to which we now turn.

104 *The Parish Magazine St Alban's, Bordesley*, October 1939.
105 M-O Diarist DR 5228 3 September 1939.

2: Popular Religion and the Experience of War

It all depends on you, and you depend on God.[1]

In the assessment of the Birmingham historians Anthony Sutcliffe and Roger Smith, the Second World War had a negligible impact upon the continuing decline of the city's Churches during the twentieth century.[2] Discounting spontaneous shows of religiosity such as attendance at national days of prayer as 'superficial', they conclude that wartime 'boredom and fear did not make people turn to religion.'[3] Granted that narratives of Church decline (supported by churchgoing statistics as the gauge of religious sentiment) and an appreciation of the extent to which wartime Church life was disrupted might lead to such pessimistic conclusions, what this chapter seeks to reveal is that the everyday religious reality of people's wartime life was very different from these assumptions. In the context of the relative neglect of the study of wartime religion – perhaps because of the assumed secularity of the period or reflective of the view that the study of religion and the experience of war are, at face value, mutually exclusive – what will be revealed here is the potency of wartime popular religion. The war may not have led to a decisive rise in Church attendance but the popular religious milieu of the years 1939–1945 was much more vital and vibrant than has previously been imagined. Just as the works of Sarah Williams and Callum Brown have shown that Christianity remained a pervasive socio-cultural influence across the early to middle years of the twentieth century, this chapter provides oral and textual evidence that this also the case for wartime.[4]

As I have stated elsewhere, wartime popular religion resulted from a dynamic process that is best characterised by the term

1   The words of a wartime government poster referred to in *The Parish Magazine of St. Nicholas, Lower Tower Street, Birmingham*, July 1940.
2   Sutcliffe and Smith, 1974, p.256.
3   Sutcliffe and Smith, 1974, p.256 and p.38.
4   Williams 1999, Brown 2001.

'promiscuous eclecticism'.[5] That is to say, popular religion was determined by a deliberate (though often unconscious) personal and social selection of beliefs and practices dependent upon the degree to which the belief or practice lubricated social relations (to progress rites of passage such as birth and marriage, for example), and the extent to which it structured and made sense of reality (by supporting gender roles or providing particular rationales for coping in light of wartime circumstances, for example). Akin to Williams, who argues that the content of the popular religion of the early twentieth century was drawn from myriad sources which were selected not by the imperative to orthodoxy but on a decidedly ad hoc basis determined by cultural expediency, I argue here that wartime popular religion was likewise heterodox, formed in a somewhat arbitrary 'pick-and-mix' fashion founded mainly upon its personal and socio-cultural utility.[6] Better adjectives than 'secular' to describe wartime religion are 'variegated' (used to define patterns and degrees of belief) and 'selective' (in terms of particular expressions of commitment). Religion, in the main the Christian religion, remained critical to the cultural life of the people in the mid-twentieth century and oral testimony underscores that it was a rich source of meaning and purpose in wartime. In reality, there was a popular theology and self-understanding of the Second World War that determined how events were interpreted, and this was exhibited in the piety of the population at large. This spirituality operated to aid people in coping and to strengthen their resolve in their daily war effort. Wartime Britain, in many ways, was tangibly and self-consciously religious, and generally assumed itself Christian. Indeed, the Second World War, it was often asserted, was a battle for the very soul of Christian civilisation.[7]

In order to characterise wartime popular religion, oral history testimonies were gathered at first from those with a stated Christian adherence – either in the form of churchgoing or denominational allegiance – and later from those with no apparent religious conviction at all. As the study progressed, what became clear was that, despite

5   Snape and Parker, 2001, p.410.
6   Williams, 1999, p.12.
7   Churchill, 1947, p.234; Robbins, 1985; Robbins, 1995, p.937

people's disclaimers of religious adherence at the interview stage and earlier, evidence often emerged from the interview of an identifiable religious influence upon them, whether in upbringing, in dealing with wartime events, or in the setting of the wartime experience in a broader context. As it became evident that the majority of interviewees had grown up within more-or-less palpably religious environments suffused with Christian ritual, story and language, it was necessary to conclude that their recollected experience reflected the general nature of wartime British society. This chapter explores how people's religious conceptualisations were formed and how they made a difference to people's experience of war. Moreover, it investigates how religious faith and ideas were shaped and utilised by various means during the conflict. Such an analysis of the character of wartime popular religion shows how it helped many to get through the privations and vicissitudes with which war greeted the civilian, confirming the reality of an air-raid shelter spirituality by which events were circumscribed. Far from being a spasmodic attempt to control panicky emotional states, a kind of 'magic thinking' as Joanna Bourke would have it, the religiosity in evidence is indicative of the character of wartime religious culture.[8]

As well utilising oral testimony, evidence for the vitality of British wartime popular religion is drawn from a variety of sources: diaries and published memoirs, the wartime media of radio and cinema and the various religious and quasi-religious publications demonstrating some of the popular beliefs of the time. In addition, more mainstream evidence is provided for the continuing part played by hymnody and prayer, particularly during air raids.

Here, then, is an elucidation of the underlying religious consciousness of British wartime society; an exploration of both the religious experience of the individual, predominantly drawn from the citizens of Birmingham, and a study of the extent to which this war, for many in wider British society, was seen in spiritual and cosmological terms. Many in the nation instinctively believed that the events unfolding before their eyes were historically pivotal, and religious concepts and practices acted to strengthen this conviction.

8   Bourke, 2005, p.251.

Childhood Nurture and Popular Religion

Many individuals spoke in oral history interviews of the ways in which their faith had been formed in their childhood by religious nurture and by early socialisation, by the routines of family prayers, churchgoing and schooling. In several cases it was Church and Sunday school membership that emerged as a significant and early formative factor in their lives: this, coupled with the religious routine and commitments of the home, and the explicit religious instruction of schooling, had a lasting impact upon them, the detailed memories of which sustained them through the trials of wartime suffering. As Dorothy Entwistle has shown of the part played by the Churches in the life of working-class Lancashire, Churches 'were successful in creating viable communities, satisfying religious and social needs, mobilizing local effort and helping people cope with the challenges of a mature industrial society […] "where there was hope […] music […] ritual […] flowers, and colour, and comradeship".'[9]

An example of the conditions operative in Birmingham communal life, and of early socialisation's influence upon personal faith, is from Enfys Jones's childhood spent in a mining community in South Wales (she later migrated to Birmingham to train as a school teacher). The significant role of the Church to which she testifies is not untypical of others collected for this research, demonstrating the centrality of the Churches in cultural perpetuation and community cohesion. Akin to Entwistle's findings for Lancashire, not only did Birmingham's Churches function to inculcate in people the idiom and practices of Christianity, they also served as a focus for social interaction as well as leisure pursuits, and a place where cultural identity was constructed and preserved. Often the Church provided, alongside working life, a pattern, structure and scaffold to the community's social existence. The Church, the school, and the home, each fed values and cultural patterns into the other dimensions of childhood existence, reinforcing the beliefs and practices of the other

---

9   Entwistle, 2001, p.22 and p.35.

facets of life. Childhood nurture occurred within a set of coherent cultural discourses and moral expectations, propounded by these disparate elements of life. In childhood nurture, religion was a dominant instructor mediated by more than one social forum. Thus were many children nurtured and socialised. Of the Church Enfys Jones remembered:

> [It] was a place, well you developed all your culture there really because there was something on nearly every night […] you had, on a Sunday […] the morning service, you came home, you had your lunch, you went back for Sunday school, you came back and had your tea, you went back for Band of Hope and then you had the evening service, and then during the week there was a prayer meeting and there was also a discussion group during the week. Also, we had social events […] we had [magic lantern] shows […] it was surprising how much you learnt from them really […] then of course we had musical evenings as well, and we always had an oratorio or a music kind of event during the year […] there was always something to do. Your father or mother would take you down into the Church and leave you there and someone would bring you home […] we learnt the Lord's Prayer.

Similarly, of school it was said:

> Now school was very good that way, we had religious assembly in the mornings and once a week either the local vicar or one of the ministers of one of the Churches came in […] we learnt the little prayers: 'Now I lay me down to sleep' […] they live with you all your life.

Of family life it was recalled:

> We had a Bible and one of us would read and Dad would choose the passage of scripture and then we'd all say a prayer together, every night that would happen because we couldn't do it in the day because he worked shifts in the pits […] but we always kept that ritual of the family prayers […] My [religion] was part of me [as a child] I don't know what I'd have done without it really because that's how we learnt everything really […] you learnt your principles and values in life, it all came from that really. What your father told you, you believed, you see. He told you from the Bible and you would think 'Dada' said that and you can find it in the Bible and it's true and it's worth living by. [10]

10   Interview with Mrs Enfys Jones, September 1999.

By the time the Second World War came, notwithstanding falling Church attendances and diminishing contact with Sunday schools amongst the general population, such a diet of religious socialisation as that served up in Enfys Jones's early life would have been typical of a significant minority, especially amongst the working classes of the city of Birmingham. Church activities and involvement, for many working-class communities, provided the superstructure of social existence. According to Angus Calder, the numerical decline in regular religious attendance during the early years of the twentieth century[11] is suggestive of 'the godlessness of the urban masses'.[12] Despite this overall decline in numerical affiliation oral history evidence suggests, on the contrary, that a diet of familial religious activity persisted; that school religion added to the religious vocabulary of the child; that Christianity continued to function as a scaffold of cultural and social life, acting as a significant cohesive force in local and national society. As Jean Cuthbert, born and brought up in Small Heath, Birmingham described it: 'religion was an everyday thing. I wasn't crowded with it [...] It was just there.'[13] Similarly, Dorothy Leather, of Nechells, depicted the substantive religious character of Birmingham's popular culture: 'unless people went to Church regular you found a lot of people never mentioned religion; they took it for granted [...] they just acted out their lives.'[14] Christianity was a commonplace of the cultural and family milieu in 1930s and wartime Britain. Christopher Charles, born in 1929, in Balsall Heath, Birmingham, attested to this. It was so much an assumed part of his existence that recourse to the Church's ministrations seemed natural to him after the death of his father:

We was brought up to be aware of God; that religion is important without necessarily taking part. I knew umpteen prayers and carols learnt at school. And then in October 1939 my father, who was living in the United States, died; so my mother was a widow just a few weeks after war started. At that time, I suddenly took it on myself [bearing in mind I was only 10] to go down to Church for Matins, the 11am service; to St. Thomas's, Lincoln St [...] after a

11   For remarks upon these figures, see Snape and Parker, 2001, pp.397–398.
12   Calder, 1969, p.478.
13   Interview with Jean Cuthbert, March 2002.
14   Interview with Dorothy Leather, February 2000.

64

while they noticed that I was attending regularly on a Sunday morning [...] I think it was a choir master who approached me 'would I be interested in joining the choir' which I did 'cos I enjoyed singing hymns [...] I went of my own free will to seek solace and comfort.[15]

Likewise, Martin Ryland, who was brought up on the semi-rural edges of the Birmingham conurbation, further bore out the degree to which churchgoing was a widespread, even if burdensome, practice in 1930s Birmingham. His telling of an exciting wartime childhood was narrated against the backdrop of a cultural milieu where various degrees of religious affiliation were universal. The common practice of Church attendance was influenced by the extent to which local social networks were Church focused, and familial and educational reinforcement of children's religiosity was widespread:

[Attending Church was a routine practice], you understood that you went. We used to go to the evening service mostly but I also used to go to Bartley Green because I was very friendly with the vicar's son [...] I was taught to say my prayers and when I used to stay with my grandparents in Reigate, they were Baptists, we used to say grace before meals as well [...] and at school we used to say it in Latin [...] we were just brought up in the sort of religious background.[16]

Churches were, in many places, the focus of local leisure activities. Indeed, the social activities they organised served not only to draw young people into their influence, ensuring that the Churches were able to maintain a watchful moralistic eye, but also benefited the young with a forum to meet potential marital partners. Betty Law, whose lifelong contact with her parish church in Bearwood on the fringes of Birmingham began as a child, described the breadth of facilities available to the young:

Yes, oh yes, I had a crush on Len Law [...] I joined the [Church] tennis club so I could play with him. I joined the dramatic society because he was in it [...] eventually we married [...] He was a real Christian, the finest man I ever met.[17]

15   Interview with Christopher Charles, March 2001.
16   Interview with Martin Ryland, March 2002.
17   Interviews with Betty Law, January 2000, Arthur Brownsword, February 2000 and Penny Stephens, March 2000.

Many interviewees listed the plethora of additional social activities offered by the Churches. In addition to acts of worship and the uniformed organisations, Churches offered concerts, dances, rambles and camping. Because of the array of possibilities, and the social networks created by the Churches, their social utility became a bond with wider society. Thus, Dorothy Leather, a stalwart member of a Rocky Lane Methodist mission, was able to claim: 'your friends were your religion.'[18]

However, regular churchgoing was not a necessary prerequisite for the descriptor 'Christian'. More sporadic contact and evidence of a 'good' life were enough to merit this designation.[19] Jean Cuthbert of Small Heath, Birmingham, described her grandmother in such terms:

> [My grandmother] couldn't read or write, but she was a very kind person, she didn't go to Church, I don't think she liked to go because she couldn't read anyway [...] but she believed in God, and I remember if I was ill at any time I had to go to Church before I went anywhere else [to say] thank goodness that I'm well [...] You could tell from the way she talked [she was a Christian]. I think she led a Christian life in my way of thinking. I don't think you have to go and stay in Church for hours to have a Christian life [there were] little things; she just gave the impression she was. Her father, I believe, was a lay preacher [...] I think he died and her mother was a drunkard [...] she had a bad childhood and I think she went into service.[20]

Another woman, Betty Jones, stressed that the evidence of her parents' faith lay not in their Church attendance but in prayerful devotion and the remembered moral virtue of being a good mother and father:

> My mom never went to bed without her prayer book by her side and saying her prayers [...] my dad was very, very placid [...] our dad never raised his voice to any of us [...] dad always used to go to town and bring us things back [...] they were believers in Church [...] we were always dressed nicely [...] they didn't

18 Interview with Dorothy Leather, February 2000.
19 Williams, 1999, p.108.
20 Interviews with Jean Cuthbert, March 2002 and with Kitty Drummond, March 2002 contain other examples of the descriptor 'Christian'.

have time to go to Church […] whether you go to Church or not we're all God's children […] you haven't got to go into a Church to believe in God.[21]

Similarly, Penny Stephen recalled:

[My mother] hadn't got time to go to Church, she'd got six little children, my mother was always working [however], she was definitely a Christian, and my father, he was a very good man. Oh yes, they were good. My mother always used to say: 'I've had six children, and not one of them has brought me any trouble', which was something to be proud of.[22]

And Dorothy Leather recounted:

[When we sat down to eat and there wasn't enough food to go round] my mother would [sometimes] say, 'Oh, I'm not very keen on that' […] I think they'd got a religion, not by going to Church; but if they could help each other they would […] I'm not so much about psalm-singing myself.[23]

Moreover, Christopher Charles deemed meritorious the spontaneity of neighbourliness that occurred in wartime:

I think this is as Christian an ethic as you can have to offer assistance […] these neighbours used to come into [our shelter] and they had a daughter who was blind […] and she played the accordion and so we quite happily had a sing-song in the shelter.[24]

Sundays continued to be significant in the weekly pattern of British family life.[25] Even if the whole of the family did not attend Church, familial and quasi-religious rituals were observed, as one child of the time recollected:

You wore the best clothes on the Sunday, as I say, you couldn't listen to anything on the radio […] you didn't go playing out like you did in the week, you didn't make too much noise […] it was a day of rest […] we used to go to the cemetery most Sundays. I always remember going with my aunt up to

---

21   Interview with Betty Jones, March 2002.
22   Interview with Penny Stephens, March 2000.
23   Interview with Dorothy Leather, February 2000.
24   Interview with Christopher Charles, March 2001.
25   Williams, 1999, p.144f.

Yardley cemetery and then we used to have some of Granddad's relations call on the way [home]. You seemed to get a lot of people calling.[26]

Betty Jones recalled a similarly structured day: looking one's best and following social etiquette on Sunday had a moral imperative:

> Sundays, she used to put our hair in rags Saturday night, bathed in front of the fire [...] we wore our best dresses to go to Church all our hairs done in ringlets, bows in our hair [...] and off to Church we'd go, sometimes we'd go twice because we'd go to the service in the morning and Sunday school in the afternoon but my mom [didn't go to Church she] was doing dinner of a morning, clearing up, getting us ready for Sunday school. [The afternoon was my parents'] private time I think, and then we always had salmon on Sunday, always have a tin of salmon [...] and a cake [...] I couldn't sit in a chair like this, if you eat you eat at a table, that was the rule [...] that was manners, that was the way we was brought up.[27]

What is more, as Callum Brown has noted, and as Betty Jones described above, women often had to sacrifice the opportunity of Church attendance for the sake of their household duties, in particular preparing the family's Sunday lunch.[28] Peter Whitnall, one in a family of twelve children, proudly recounted:

> Mother never went to work; she was a wonderful woman, wonderful cook. She never had a pair of scales; she could do anything [...] she was on her hands and knees polishing the grate, sweat was pouring off. Wonderful worker she was [...] she used to go with Dad [to Church] when she got a chance, she didn't have a lot of time [...] we always had a good table.[29]

Peter Whitnall's childhood spanned the years of the First World War, but was characterised by the same priority given to Sunday school attendance common to those brought up a generation or so later. This interwar generation, from which oral history interviewees were drawn, were predominantly Sunday school scholars. Penny Stephens, in common with the majority others interviewed, recalled that: 'the

---

26 Interview with Jean Cuthbert, March 2002. This was supported by comments made during the interview with Joan and Norman Oswald, March 2002.
27 Interview with Betty Jones, March 2002.
28 Brown, 2001, pp.160–161.
29 Interview with Peter Whitnall, March 2000.

children were always sent to Sunday school [...] my mother used to come occasionally to different services, but not on a regular basis.'[30] For many interviewed, Sunday school teachers were significant figures in their young lives, thus they could easily recall their name and particular character or personality traits.[31]

Precedence was given to the religious nurture of children, even if the parents did not consider regular Church attendance of importance for themselves. This 'religion by deputy', as Sarah Williams terms it, of which Sunday school attendance was a part, represented a widespread desire to maintain an affiliation with the Churches, albeit often a tenuous one.[32] The Churches therefore remained of recognisable import in organizing and structuring familial and social life:

> My father was a Catholic, mother wasn't; but we children used to go down to St. Patrick's regularly on a Sunday [...] and then onto my grandmother's where we had our lunch and sometimes our tea [...] we moved to Smethwick [but] still kept up our religious instruction [...] My father's family were strict Catholic, so we did follow the Catholic religion [...] we used to be able to get the tram or the bus down to the Church [...] I think children were more independent in a way – well there wasn't the traffic. [Religion meant] a great deal [to me as a child] a lot of it stayed with me [...] it does set a standard to keep to. We learnt all about the commandments and how we should be with other people. That sort of thing stays with you. [33]

Home and family life, and in particular one or other of an interviewee's parents (or a grandparent), were often idealised in oral history accounts. Amidst large families and in conditions of poverty, the undoubted reality of parental (usually maternal) sacrifice was transformed into saintliness for the child. For instance, Laura Evans, a stalwart member of Wattville Chapel, Handsworth, remembered:

---

30   Interview with Penny Stephens, March 2000.
31   For example, interview with Dorothy Leather, February 2000. Williams, 1999, p.135.
32   Williams, 1999, p.142.
33   Interview with Kitty Drummond, March 2002.

I've seen my mother sit at the table and feed us all and go without herself. 'Aren't you going to have anything?' 'No, I'm not hungry.' Mother was a very quiet sort of woman but she was a lovely Christian.[34]

Likewise, though fathers were often emotionally and practically remote from household duties with regard to childcare, their moral and spiritual influence remained integral to this generation's upbringing:

Dad was saved from being a real drunkard [...] his conversion was wonderful [...] Dad taught us all the hymns. We'd got an organ and he couldn't read music but he would go to Church, hear a hymn, come home and play it, and teach it to us.[35]

Large families existed, in part, to counteract high rates of infant mortality. However, though childhood deaths were quite commonplace, it should not be thought that they failed to affect. Perhaps because of such regular bereavements popular Christianity devised consoling theologies such as that depicted by Laura Evans below. Indeed, maybe it was the proximity of death that strengthened people's recourse to particular aspects of Christian ministration (such as the churching of women) because such rituals were deemed likely to ward off potential suffering.[36] Recalling the impact of the death of a sibling upon her and the Church membership's response to it, Laura Evans, asserts the personal significance of such interpretations of death:

When I was thirteen the youngest, a little girl of three died [...] at that time I remember sitting on the step, on the step like, and a lady come past and said you mustn't cry because you little sister is one of the Lord's lambs. So, I thought if she could be a lamb for the Lord I could as well [...] I realised that I would never be able to enter into heaven and see my little sister that had died if I didn't belong to the Lord.[37]

If Christianity formed the religious backdrop to the lives of the majority of the nation in the pre-war period, this prevailing milieu spilled over into wartime conditions. Beryl Keith's recollections

34   Interview with Laura Evans, May 1999.
35   Interview with Laura Evans, May 1999.
36   Williams, 1999, p.90
37   Interview with Laura Evans, May 1999.

provide evidence of the continuity between popular religious life before the war and patterns of belief and practice during it. They also reveal the social barriers keeping some from formal Church affiliation:

> You'd find people [...] on the whole where I lived [...] didn't go to Church but they still believed in God and I think they were pleased to do that sort of thing [attend national days of prayer] and of course it was a very lively Church where I was and on Sundays, I'm going back now before the war, Sunday evenings (after the evening service), we used to have open-air services and we used to go round with an organ on wheels and we used to have a little service and you'd be amazed the people that would come round and join in [...] they weren't Churchgoers. One thing, being poor, people felt you had to dress up for Church and you see once you get in a Church there are things you contribute to and they felt they couldn't contribute [...] although we lived with them our lives were a little bit different [...] I mean nobody used bad language in the shop.[38]

Popular religion, strongly informed by Christian norms, provided the backdrop to the majority's childhood nurture, as demonstrated by oral testimony. Consequently, popular religiosity was influential in sustaining people amidst wartime difficulties.

The War and People's Faith and Self-understanding

War, for good or ill, changes individuals and societies that experience it: the multitude of ways in which the Second World War impacted upon the ordinary British citizen are well known,[39] even in the particular case of the City of Birmingham.[40] For social historians, the extent to which war acted as a catalyst for social change remains a matter of debate. A case in point is the question of the extent to which the traditional roles of women were altered by wartime (because of wartime labour demands) so that a return to the old social patterns and

38   Interview with Beryl Keith, March 2001.
39   The archetype of wartime home-front historiography is Calder, 1969.
40   The scholarly work of Sutcliffe and Smith, 1970 (especially ch.2) and the more popular works of Ballard, 1985 and Chinn, 1996 are good examples.

gender roles became impossible for the succeeding generations.[41] Similarly, John Costello has presented considerable evidence to show that wartime sexual mores were distinctly different than those of peacetime. Emotional traumas, resulting from such things as long periods of separation from loved ones, led, he observes, to a general loosening of the normal pattern of peacetime moral restraint.[42] Additionally, in the Midlands, changes to the patterns of industrial relations, and to the manufacturing processes, occurred because of the war, as David Thoms has revealed.[43]

Rarely, however, have questions of change resulting from war been posed about the individual's religious life and spiritual experience.[44] Perhaps this is because of the subjective nature of the concept of personal faith and the extent to which it is intricately bound up in and influenced by other dimensions of human identity and social nurture. Consequently, it being hard to differentiate someone's spirituality from other aspects of their individuality, their predisposition, emotional support, childhood nurture and so on, it is difficult to generalise. Granted that it is almost impossible to say which of the many influences (including wartime events) impacted most significantly upon a person's spiritual identity, below are some examples of acknowledged personal religious change resulting directly from the experience of wartime difficulty. The content of personal faith which is challenged or changed is represented by the stated values, theologies and spirituality of people's lives expressed in biographies and oral interviews and exhibited by the moral and religious priorities purportedly lived out in their lives at the time (for example, their habits of Church attendance, routines of prayer, and remembered understanding in relation to concepts of faith). Aspects of people's faith (and, interconnected with this, their self-understanding) were also evidenced indirectly by the way in which people told their stories to the

41 See, for example, Marwick, 1988; Summerfield, 1998.
42 Costello, 1985, pp.353f.
43 Thoms, 1989.
44 The effects the war had upon congregational life is to be explored in other chapters.

researcher. The structure and way their tale was told revealed as much as the content of their narrative testimony.[45]

In 1942, Mass-Observation, an organisation established in 1937 with the intent of studying people and their reactions to life in general, reported on the interim effects of the war upon faith. Its conclusions are noteworthy, reporting as they did upon opinions expressed during difficult times in the early part of the war. To summarise its findings: if faith existed prior to the conflict, 26% of the sample claimed that this was being strengthened. Only 3% of the sample claimed a loss of faith in the 1942 responses. However, those who claimed not to have a faith prior to the conflict were said to be 'even less favourably disposed towards religion' by the end, in the main because of questions of theodicy.[46] When questioning more closely, Mass-Observation researchers heard such typical statements as: war 'has made me think more than ever about spiritual things and very occasionally I have found that this can be expressed in the form of an organised service [however] Churchgoing has increasingly irritated me because it seems unreal and irrelevant.'[47] Arguably, then, the spiritual sensibilities of some were awakened by the conflict: but not enough for them to make permanent recourse to 'organised' religion. It cannot be claimed, on this evidence at least, that war was a catalyst for the permanent mass conversion of British civilians on the Home Front. However, the religious revival of the 1950s may conceivably have had its roots in wartime's popular awareness of God and of the assurances derived from wartime religion.[48] What is clear, from the Mass-Observation statistics at least, is that war was undoubtedly a determinative factor in shaping the spiritual and emotional lives of a significant number of people – especially, though not exclusively, it seems, if those individuals were predisposed to faith before the outbreak of war.

For children wartime events were especially formative. Moreover, the power of circumstances to influence the individual appears to have been in direct proportion to the amount of suffering he or she

45   Samuels and Thompson, 1990, p.2; Brown, 2001, p.70.
46   Mass-Observation FR1525.
47   Mass-Observation FR1566.
48   Green, 2000, p.164.

confronted; that is, the more suffering the more marked the change. For example, Jean Cuthbert remembered vividly the day war was declared precisely because of the upset that its declaration confronted her with:

> We were in Sunday school the day war was declared [...] we weren't that interested, I was only 12 [...] All of a sudden the man who was taking the service stopped and he said, 'I'm afraid I need you to go home now because they've declared war', and he started to cry. I'd never seen a man cry before.[49]

Kitty Drummond of Brookfields, Hockley, remembered this eventful day quite differently:

> I do remember being in Church on Sunday morning when the Priest told us that war had been declared, partly because it was my birthday the next day and I thought 'what a wonderful birthday present to have a war'; not that I knew what a war was like at 11.[50]

Wherever the fateful news of war's outbreak was heard, it evoked memories of the previous conflagration and the costs already borne. Beryl Keith, whose father was badly traumatised by his experiences as a soldier in the First World War, and whose resultant nightmares regularly disturbed her childhood sleep, remembers how her own indifference to events on 3 September contrasted with the emotions of those around her:

> That Sunday we didn't go to Church because we wanted to hear the broadcast; what we didn't know was that the vicar had got a radio in Church and all those that wanted listened to it there [...] I always remember my mother was leaning over the back of my chair as [Chamberlain] spoke [...] I looked at her and the tears were streaming down her cheeks [...] she said, 'oh, but you don't know.'[51]

Similarly, for those with particular memories of wartime tragedy the agenda of oral history interviews was dominated by the desire to recount these significant events. Although the structure of the interview remained unaltered, the interviewee usually hurried through

---

49   Interview with Jean Cuthbert, March 2002.
50   Interview with Kitty Drummond, March 2002.
51   Interview with Beryl Keith, March 2001.

the standard questions in order to tell the story that shaped their wartime experience most of all. The retelling of these stories was markedly rehearsed, though not without considerable emotion. For example, Kitty Drummond, born in 1928, recounted her father's death in April 1941, and the starkly insensitive way it was disclosed to her, demonstrative perhaps of the degree to which death became commonplace in wartime:

> The 9 April 1941 was my father's birthday [...] he was working nights as a taxi driver in the New Street Station, Birmingham, and there was a raid that night. Mom and I used to go to next door to our neighbour's Anderson shelter [...] I remember feeling terrified every time the siren went [...] we must have gone to bed I imagine cos when we got up my mother had already been to the garage where my father worked to see if they'd heard anything; because by that time he would have normally been home [...] She came back and she asked me later in the morning if I'd go to the phone box to find out [...] if there was any news [...] They said he'd been killed but they didn't know where he was and someone else, another taxi driver, was coming to join us [...] I don't remember how my mother reacted but I remember the sun was shining through the kitchen window and she'd got gold curtains which she'd washed, and the sun was shining through them [...]she probably sent me because she was afraid to go herself [...] she probably hoped they wouldn't tell a child such sad news but of course they had to [...] We went into town and I remember standing in Stephenson Place and seeing the wreck and everything and all the rubble and there was a taxi in a tank [sic] [...] he'd been waiting to pick someone up [...] we finally finished up in Station Street. I think it was the undertaker's [...] he'd been killed by blast mainly but I think he'd lost his leg [...] that was an awful day [...] the next thing I can remember was his funeral [...] He was very, very popular [...] and all the other taxi drivers followed the cortege [...] afterwards it was just my mother and myself.[52]

Kitty Drummond's life beyond these events continued to be dominated by the loss of a husband and father, whose personality was kept alive by her mother's memory of him and an ongoing parental expectation of educational success. Similarly, Penny Keel of Lozells, aged nine at the outbreak of war, tearfully recollected the lasting and influential impact of wartime deaths upon her life since:

---

52   Interview with Kitty Drummond, March 2002.

We had some very distressing experiences. I blame the war for the nervous wreck that I am. I could have done with brothers and sisters I think. And I wouldn't talk about what I saw to my parents, which was a pity I think. I think I really needed to talk to people. I took things very much to heart [...] its memories of friends being killed. Having to go to school and seeing their coffins come out the house [...] There was a wonderful manager at Lozells picture house, Mr Jennings [...] Do you know I loved that man. I was always in trouble, and he said, 'It doesn't matter' [...] he was killed by an incendiary bomb [the gory details of which were insensitively reported in my hearing] [...] My Mr. Jennings who'd been so nice to me.[53]

For this woman, and undoubtedly many others like her, who as children sheltered from the dangers of the blitz, minor details of the experience became personally seminal and long remembered. Penny Keel recalled:

You'd come home from school and start taking things down the air-raid shelter [...] the dog would go and hide behind a chair. We'd see this and say 'he's coming'. This would always happen before the sirens went. The dog picked up the drone of the plane. There was one night when Rexy went behind the chair. Mom said, 'take the cushions down.' I got into the garden and they dropped flares and they were like little falling stars amongst the flowers. I stopped and I thought, 'Oh, the flowers do look pretty' [...] they were all lit up, just like sparklers, not realising I was in full view [...] My mother and father hid behind a door in the kitchen and mom shouted, 'Run, Penny, run' and I ran into the shelter, which was dark and you had to go down steps, which you fell down. And I put a cushion over my head, saying, 'Please God, not my head, not my head.' [...] That is when I lost faith in my parents because they should have run out to me [...]. I would not have shouted to my child to go on alone.[54]

Norman Oswald of Sparkbrook, whose religious upbringing meant strict attendance at Church three times on Sundays, was nonchalant about many aspects of wartime life save the death of his father, who had fought in the First World War:

At the back of where I lived there was a wood factory [...] mom and me was in our Anderson shelter when this place caught fire. There was five houses in our road, and the five husbands all congregated outside, and a bomb came along and dropped in the middle of them – wiped the lot out. We was shook up in the

53   Interview with Penny Keel, March 2002.
54   Interview with Penny Keel, March 2002.

shelter of course [...] my father was [...] taken to the Co-op mortuary in Ashted Row [...] that was bombed [too] that was a nightmare that. I was fourteen.[55]

Another factor that strengthened a changed self-conception was the extent to which the individual felt that they had been plucked by an invisible hand from disaster. Dennis Harris, a child in wartime, recollects a confusing scene in which he and his family narrowly escaped death; for him it provided part of the accumulating evidence of providence at work in his life:

> I was aware that God's hand was upon me from a very early age [...] as I look back I can see things I didn't see at the time [...] I was in a lot of scrapes that I escaped from [for example] my Dad was a fatalist in the sense that he believed that if he was going to die he would die in his own house, he would never go into an air-raid shelter [...] so mom and I would traipse up the road at 7 o'clock every evening to a neighbour's shelter [...] On the occasion that I remember we were in the shelter at the usual time, mom was anxious to go to the loo, so she toddled off down the path, she saw this parachute thing disappear over the roof and guessed what it was [...] she ran down the garden path and she was in the shelter as it exploded. The door was slammed shut and blocked [...] we had to climb out of the escape hatch at the back of the Anderson shelter [...] where we were was covered in bricks from the houses and the wall of the park [...] I followed mom and it was dark, she went down the crater which the landmine had left losing her slipper in the hot water at the bottom of the crater [...] she ended up in one shelter and I ended up in another [...] we had to move because of a delayed action landmine and I found mom and dad in the neighbouring shelter, he'd come to find his wife and son. He'd had an experience himself [...] during the [same] raid he'd wanted to make himself a cup of tea [...] there was a bang and click while he was making it and he felt his feet were wet [...] he looked down and saw that the kettle of water had a hole in the top and bottom, some shrapnel had come through the roof and the kettle narrowly missing him.[56]

A member of Birmingham's Jewish community related a significant childhood memory, their first self-acknowledgement of their difference from others. Evacuated to Leicestershire early in wartime, he and his sisters were lodged with a non-Jewish household who served them pork as their welcome meal.[57]

55   Interview with Joan and Norman Oswald, March 2002.
56   Interview with Denis Harris, March 2001.
57   Interview with Martin Davies, October 1999.

Laura Evans linked the lessons of wartime suffering with difficulties encountered later in her life. Alongside others, she believed that the war acted to strengthen her faith:

> [The war] made us cling to the Lord more really, you see you depended on him for your safety didn't you […] You see trouble always makes you cling to the Lord more […] I suppose it strengthened my faith […] I had my husband ill for ten years [after the war] and I really depended on the Lord then. 'When thou pass through the waters I will be with thee.'[58]

For many, then, the war meant a revision of priorities, a change of values and an altering of self-conception, especially when the war had brought people face to face with danger, death, bereavement or dislocation: this war was replete with this type of experiences for many of the people of Birmingham. Indeed, the haphazardness of falling bombs and flying shrapnel enhanced rather than diminished the apparent significance of events and heightened their consequent power in shaping the future concerns and destinies of many. As the Birmingham-born theatre critic Kenneth Tynan recalled of a conversation with his sometime tutor C.S. Lewis:

> [Lewis] reminded me how I had once told him about the parachuted landmine which, dropping from a German bomber during an air raid in 1940, so narrowly missed our house in Birmingham that the next morning we recovered some of the parachute silk from our chimney. (The mine destroyed six houses across the road and blew out all our windows). But for that hair's breadth – matter of inches only – I would already (Lewis gently pointed out) have been dead for eight years. Every moment of life since then had been a bonus, a tremendous free-gift, a present that only the blackest ingratitude could refuse. As I listened to him, my problems began to dwindle to their proper proportions; I had entered the room suicidal, and I left it exhilarated.[59]

For others, another effect of the war upon their outlook was to halt and change their previous priorities, often causing them to live for the moment, especially because of the uncertainty of the future. As a Birmingham Mass-Observation diarist reported:

58   Interview with Laura Evans, May 1999.
59   Excerpt from the memoirs of Kenneth Tynan, *The Times*, 10 October 2001.

Saw an old friend of mine who is in the searchlight unit here and we spent the night at a local pub. He tells me he is doing okay, is getting plenty of leave and good food. His fiancé has joined the WAAF. He says that if war continues he will get married in two or three months time, he is about 23, and has become a part fatalist if there is such a thing. He lives for the present most of the time, and does not think about the future like he used to before the war broke out.[60]

Thus, the impact of the Second World War upon many individuals and their religious outlook seems clear. From this glimpse of war's defining power in the lives of a few it is possible to assert of the general population, that war left an indelible mark upon the character and post-war religious lives of the many: especially because it was difficult to avoid a confrontation with the suffering which is symptomatic of conflict.

Prayer, Worship and Personal Devotion

As one might expect in times of grave fear, as in those conditions encountered during the blitz, expediency elicited a certain type of prayer, an expletive cry for comfort and security in the face of extreme adversity. Graham Greene's novel *The End of the Affair*, set in wartime London during the blitz, explores poignantly such prayerful pleas, and the consequences of striking a deal with the Divine in the face of danger to oneself or a loved one.[61] Undoubtedly, Greene's portrayal of this kind of contract of desperation was, in reality, a recurrent event in this war, as in all wars. Winifred Harrison, a lifelong Methodist, Sunday school teacher and a firewatcher during the Second World War, described the conditions in which reliance on such intercessions became critical:

> Where we would have been sleeping, there was shrapnel on the bed, the windows had gone […] we might not have been alive after that […] you didn't

60 Diarist 5114, Thursday 5 October 1940.
61 Greene, 1974, pp.98–99.

know whether you were going to get up the next morning or not [...] prayer helped [...] just 'God help me'; 'look after me'; 'keep me safe'; 'keep so-and-so safe'; a thought going upwards as much as anything. If you got frightened, if you were on the bus or anything, you first thought, your first reaction was 'please, please, please Lord', you know. I remember asking my mother once: 'Mum, do you ever say your prayers?' She said: 'Lass, I don't say my prayers as such, but I'm praying all day.'[62]

However, whether or not this kind of communication with God constitutes genuine religiosity is a question that was thrown up time and again in wartime. For instance, in the previous war, G.A. Studdert-Kennedy, the most famous of First World War chaplains, deplored this kind of prayer as a misconstruing of the concept of prayer in Christian spirituality. Preferring that men should swear and blaspheme than pray in this fashion, he urged a reconceptualising. Prayer, he asserted, 'is not a means to protection, but a means to courage and nobility of conduct [a means of] spiritual support and strengthening of men to face death and danger with the single and sole aim of doing God's will in both [...] Much of prayerlessness is due to disappointment with the results of prayer which is not real prayer but a pseudo-sanctified selfishness.' His assessment of this kind of prayer was in line with that of his contemporaries in the *The Army and Religion* report, which in turn scorned the men's prayerful intention as 'childish', with a 'touch of superstition about it'. The report continued: 'Prayer as a natural impulsive cry for help and security has greatly increased. Prayer as a habit of the soul, as a living fellowship with a living God, regulated and developed, is much less apparent.'[63] Whether understandable in the circumstances or not, these prayer-like outbursts were similarly disparaged in the Second World War. Writing of the thousands of people to be found on their knees before the outbreak of war, W. Thompson Elliott, then Vicar of Leeds, argued for a corrective theology; a non-magical, rational notion of God, a God whose freedom to act is limited because of the imperative of human freewill:

Our crisis prayers should have depth enough to carry us into the realm of the spirit [...] people whose prayers were in this spirit [...] were prepared for any

62   Interview with Winifred Harrison, December 1999.
63   Cairns, 1919, p.166.

event. They were not of those whose faith required them to expect that God would intervene in some miraculous non-moral way to avert catastrophe; but they did believe, and still believe, that the Holy Spirit of God was working in the hearts of men [...] the achievement of a just peace can only come by the output of immense human endeavour and by a willingness to suffer and to sacrifice [and] a reassertion in our common life of the things of the spirit.[64]

Birmingham's clerics, moreover, were in favour of a theology of prayer which perceives it more as an instrument for the refinement of character, a spiritual motivator to moral action, than one which expects sudden divine intervention. Clerics urged, more properly, a deferential approach in prayer. The Vicar of Sparkbrook, Alban Tilt, wrote:

At such times as these [people] will turn to God with wild cries for mercy and help and preservation, but will find little help or peace [...] from doing so. Coming to God in prayer, forget yourself and your fears [...] Your comfort from prayer will come when you forget yourself and remember God.[65]

Also, the Vicar of Bordesley wrote:

Prayer is not merely asking God to help us out of a difficult position, but it means trying to find out what is the will of God and then, having discovered it, to set to work to do something.[66]

And, similarly, the Vicar of St. Jude's Birmingham, William Brooke argued:

One day of National Prayer is well enough, but unless it has a habit of prayer as a background, it can easily encourage false ideas and degenerate into a magic charm to be applied in times of special difficulty. Prayer is a habit that cannot be acquired suddenly; no individual or nation can expect to ignore God all the year and then pray [...] the King made it plain that prayer is not a quick and easy means of getting our own way, but rather of finding and accepting God's [...] Such is the truly Christian prayer: continual and dedicated.[67]

64   Thompson Elliott, 1939, pp.41–42 and 49.
65   *The Fiery Cross*, the parish magazine of St. Agatha's, Sparkbrook, Vol. XV, No.11, November 1940.
66   *The Parish Magazine of St Alban's, Bordesley*, September 1940.
67   *The Parish Newsletter St Jude's, Birmingham*, July 1944.

Notwithstanding clerical exhortations to the laity to refine their theology of prayer, many clergy often exhibited this disdained theology themselves. Indeed, the hand of God was seen to be at work in the miraculous events of the Dunkirk evacuation, an intervention that seemed to be in direct response to the National Day of Prayer of May 1940. In its June 1940 edition, the wartime propaganda organ of the Religions Division of the Ministry of Information, *The Spiritual Issues of the War,* though urging caution upon others who proposed a miraculous answer to prayer in recent events, itself seemed torn between reading proceedings in favour of divine intervention and the need for a balanced theology:

> There is evidence that the evacuation of the Allied armies from Flanders was experienced by many who took part in it as a miraculous intervention of Providence, and is associated in their minds with the national day of prayer which immediately preceded it. It is these unexpected and inexplicable happenings that awaken in men's minds a sense of the mystery of existence and the operation of forces beyond human calculation. We must be on our guard, however, against a too naïve interpretation of the connection between our prayers and the deliverance granted to us. Besides the mystery of answered prayers we have to set the mystery of unanswered prayers. Prayer is not one among other natural causes. If it were, science could determine its relative importance among those causes, and it would be the business of the High Command to provide for it along with its orders for munitions. On the other hand, it is a fact of religious experience, as many who took part in the recent evacuation have come to know, that when we have prayed and truly committed our lives and fortunes into God's hands, the events which happen to us are charged with new meaning. The succour which comes to us has a personal quality. The experience is suffused with an awareness of God. We know with a deep certainty that the deliverance comes from Him. Through prayer […] we enter into a new order or dimension of reality. The relation between the world of things with its chain of cause and effect, which it is the function of science to investigate and enable us to control, and the sphere of free, personal relations in which we experience the Fatherly love, protection and deliverance of God remains a mystery. The two are intimately connected. The laws of the world of time and space are the same for the religious man and the irreligious; the sun rises and the rain falls on the good and evil alike. But there is another plane of existence in which as persons we respond to the unconditional demand and

experience the succour of a personal God. To those who enter into it everything that happens appears in a fresh light.[68]

Others were less careful about linking national prayer and providence in a miraculous way. In a retrospective look at the events of war, Canon Tilt, Vicar of St. Agatha's, Sparkbrook, reminded his people of the circumstances at the height of the war and the efficacy of prayer in prompting Providence:

> Four years ago on a certain Sunday, the nation went to church. Cinemas, pubs and clubs were deserted. Churchyards were packed with cars instead. Vicars found themselves preaching to congregations which crowded the churches to the doors. Why? The nation was in a desperate corner. The nation wanted something, something that seemed well nigh impossible. All the people and things in which the nation had trusted for its defence had crumpled [...] allies, armaments, leaders. There was only one thing it could do. It went down on its knees and prayed for deliverance and breathing time. And what happened? A miracle took place. The miracle of Dunkirk – a calm sea and hazy sky on one hand; and on the other, the miracle of Germany not immediately attacking us – an historic miracle of deliverance; of reprieve snatched from disaster [...][69]

And, as one Church magazine insert dramatically described events in 1940:

> [On] Sunday millions of men, women and children in Great Britain joined in a nation-wide service of prayer [and as a result] the English Channel, that notoriously rough stretch of water which has brought disaster to so many holiday-makers in happier times, became as calm and smooth as a pond [...] while the smooth sea was aiding our ships, a fog was shielding our troops from the devastating attack by the enemy's air strength. As the German official News Agency stated: 'Conditions unfavourable for the employment of great numbers of aircraft.' [Thomas Tunstall, Vicar of St. Luke's, Bristol St., adds] Perhaps you who read this will wish to go to your Church today?[70]

Furthermore, the possibility of a link between the people's prayerfulness and divine action was never far from many people's minds.

68 *The Spiritual Issues of the War*, No. 34, 19 June 1940.
69 *The Fiery Cross*, the parish magazine of St. Agatha's, Sparkbrook, Vol. XIX, No. 9, September 1944.
70 *The Parish Magazine of St Luke's, Bristol St.*, July 1940.

Thus it was said to have been noticed by enemy P.O.W.s, who exclaimed, according to Birmingham's local press: 'How can my country hope to win when such faith exists in England?'[71]

However, more regular and ritualised forms of prayer were also to be found amongst the ordinary populace. As Mass-Observation reported in 1942, these prayers were also focused upon the wellbeing of the individual and their private concerns.[72] Clergy urged such prayer in the language of the moment. The Vicar of St. John's Sparkhill wrote in April 1940:

> Have you organised a personal ARP around your life? If not do so without delay. As a first line of defence, organise your spirit. Perhaps religion has been allowed to slip in to [sic] the background of your consciousness. Take it up again. The present crisis will give it a new meaning [...] If you can recapture the vision of simple faith and prayer of a little child and place yourselves in God's hands, bombs, fires, mutilation and sudden death will have little power to disturb your equanimity. Courage and fear are both conditions of the mind. [Take up] your spiritual defences if you would survive mental collapse when the great trial comes. A wise man prepares his spiritual ARP and leaves the rest to God and the King.[73]

Accordingly, in many homes, amidst the list of practical tasks undertaken to see a family through a lengthy air raid (for example, the preparation of food, light, warmth and so on) there was often the unspoken spiritual duty of prayer for divine protection. Interestingly, more often than not, this prayer was tempered with the realism clergy hoped for, not a prayer for victory, but the Gethsemane proviso: 'nevertheless not my will but yours be done.' One Methodist woman spoke of the place of prayer in her almost nightly experience of sheltering in the Morrison shelter in the family lounge during the blitz:

> We used to pray for my mother and father and sister [...] for their safety and our own [...] we always used to thank God for keeping us safe during a raid [...] We

71   The Birmingham Post, 5 March 1942.
72   From the Mass-Observation National Panel of 1500 respondents: Mass-Observation FR1525, 29 November 1942.
73   The Parish Magazine of St. John the Evangelist, Sparkhill, April 1940.

prayed when the all clear went [...] we used to say the Lord's prayer after our own little prayer.[74]

For another woman, Iris Smith, a Roman Catholic, and a parishioner of the Birmingham Oratory, praying whilst sheltering was done as a matter of course:

I used to pray a lot to St Theresa, the Little Flower [when sheltering] for Ray to come home, and [the safety of] members of the family in the forces, to keep us all safe [...] I'd usually got my Rosary [...] I'd have my Rosary beads, my book and maybe something to eat.[75]

Jean Cuthbert remembered the shelter behaviour as:

Reading, knitting, listening for bombers to come over [...] most tried to sleep [...] people used to talk [...] I think they used to tell everyone their life story [...] we all prayed.[76]

Christopher Charles affirmed the reality of the people's spiritual exertions:

I think everyone tended to pray outwardly or inwardly during the raids cos it was a rather fearsome time. Well it is surprising how strong people were I think it helped to make them strong, it put a little iron into people's souls and it took some time to get rid of that. They were genuinely stoical. They [...] resorted to prayer as a refuge; it was a great help to them.[77]

Betty Jones's mother encouraged her young family to sing the hymn 'All things bright and beautiful' to blot out the noise of the bombs falling. Evidently, her family prayed and though tragic circumstances negated belief in providence, there remained an overwhelming belief in the efficacy of prayer:

We prayed and prayed and prayed and he answered our prayer in a way. He took my nan and granddad we know, but he saved us. I mean we came out the shelter one day, we had to get back in the shelter because there was an incendiary bomb

74   Interview with Betty Law, January 2000.
75   Interview with Iris Smith, August 2000.
76   Interview with Jean Cuthbert, March 2002.
77   Interview with Christopher Charles, March 2001.

in mom and dad's house that hadn't exploded [...] it hadn't exploded weren't we lucky, it's just one of those things; it could have took our house down, no [...] God must have been on our side.[78]

Prayer brought some degree of reassurance to those who engaged in it and, contrary to Mass-Observation's survey findings, prayer was not always confined to topics of purely personal concern. People were often very aware of the suffering of others, and recognised that if they were not getting the brunt of the raids then someone else was. One Birmingham woman wrote with profundity and with awareness of the spiritual connectedness of herself and others:

> I feel as though a magic ring has been drawn round our shelter and that I could only suffer for others [...] As the planes come over and things seem to come closer I realise that some poor things are in agony, my heart is pierced with sharp arrows, it may be our turn next [...] I say a prayer for all my people and by the time I have gone all round I feel a degree of peace descend upon me and I can sleep.[79]

Continuing in this vein she went on:

> Every night at 9 o'clock and sometime in the day, I send up a prayer for [my daughter's] safekeeping and comfort and courage for the poor souls in the concentration camps and occupied countries. For the poor things that have been bombed and those that are possibly being bombed at just that minute [...] prayer cannot mean anything if it is prayed in selfishness. We do not need to pray for ourselves except for the strength and courage for what we have to face, but if a force of strength could go from you through God to a suffering Pole as a great warmth can enter a starved body that would count. Prayer can do that. Only by our constant thought for those who are suffering the brutalities and tortures can we hope for some of them to come out of their ordeals sane. Dear God how you must be weeping. [Later] The night is weeping the same as the day. I have sent many, many miles away a message of hope and faith through God [...] I'll never know who gets my messages, but they give me comfort, and to another who has no future to look to perhaps they have comfort [...] Life goes on, how small we are.[80]

---

78   Interview with Betty Jones, March 2002.
79   Mass-Observation Diarist DR 5420, 17 August and 26 August 1940.
80   Mass-Observation Diarist DR 5420, 21 March 1941.

Jean Cuthbert remembered the sheltering routine

> was kind of a ritual. You came home from school, you helped to do some sandwiches up and then you got ready to shelter [...] and we were there for hours; you came home and you went to bed. You really kind of tried to find out if everyone was alright, everyone that you knew [...] I had an uncle in Grange Road and somebody used to nip up to see if he was alright [...] my grandmother used to take her bag with her money in [to the shelter], Gran was a bit superstitious, she took luck charms, she was very superstitious [she took] family documents and things like that.[81]

In addition to the traditional means of 'protection' such as prayer, the reliance upon amulets and rituals, and various attempts at managing the unknown, were clearly in evidence in the population at large. Mass-Observation found, in a report of 1941, that 86% of women and 50% of men admitted to some kind of superstitious belief or practice. These superstitions ranged from, more popularly, dealing with spilt salt, to the fear that if the *News Review* were read during an alert it increased the likelihood of a bomb being dropped in the vicinity.[82] Moreover, Geoffrey Gorer, in his post-war study, *Exploring English Character*, based on a questionnaire to readers of *The People* newspaper, found that resort to a lucky mascot for protection during the war was admitted to by some 14% of the population.[83] Such recourse to superstition in wartime was strongly criticised by Clement F. Rogers, Professor of Pastoral Theology at Kings College, London. To him such an approach to understanding reality was, plainly, not 'sensible'.[84] He described the ways in which resort to superstition was being made during the blitz: 'There are stories of how by mere thought power one of these gifted people watched a bomb fall and ordered it to fall where it would do the least harm.' In his judgement, 'the most powerful corrective of superstition [...] lies in right belief about God.'[85]

---

81 Interview with Jean Cuthbert, March 2002. For First World War examples see Wilkinson, 1986, p.277.
82 Mass-Observation Topic Collection Religion 3/B, December 1941.
83 Gorer, 1955, p.265.
84 Rogers, 1941, p.9.
85 Rogers, 1941, pp.15 and 59.

Spiritualism, a movement which had burgeoned during the inter-war years, based upon the desire of many to be in contact with their deceased loved ones, continued to appeal in the Second World War.[86] One significant aspect of this movement was the 'Cross of Light' campaign, the origins of which were explained thus by one of its proponents:

> The Poster of Light, which we had during the war years, was a wonderful source of strength to so many people. It was inspired by an address that White Eagle [a spirit guide] gave us. He spoke of the cross of light in the circle of light [...] it would spread across the whole country and protect us. I was sitting on a tube one day and I remember seeing with my inner eye a poster with the cross of light and the rays shining down with the words 'May the Forces of Darkness Halt Before the Cross of Light'. I had a strong sense that we had to have this poster made [...] So many people related subsequently the experiences they'd had about how they'd put the poster up and their house had not been bombed [...] One person said how they'd been walking with the poster rolled up in their hand and a bomb had fallen not far off, but they'd come to no harm. They were even in the underground stations where people slept at night and we heard stories from there about how they were lying under that poster and the feeling of help it gave them.[87]

Alongside the offering of predictions of when and how heavy the next blitz would be, some mediums said that they could protect people from death.[88] Likewise, for a minority whose spiritual practices and beliefs were not of the Christian mainstream, an alternative narrative circulated explaining why, in the darkest days of the war, the expected invasion didn't happen. Paddy Slade, a witch living on the south coast of England, recalled:

> Round about the early part of September 1940 it was becoming obvious that England was going to be invaded if the German Luftwaffe could get supremacy over the RAF and the witches, all the way around the coast, wanted to make sure that this didn't happen. A couple of days before this invasion was supposed to happen [...] my mother and grandmother and various other old grannies – there were about a dozen of them – all went down to the beach right on the tip of Kent. As the tide turned so that it was ebbing, they threw what we call Go Away

---

86   Mews, 1994, p.451; Hazelgrove, 2000 and 1999.
87   Ylana Hayward in Akhtar and Humphries, 1999, pp.88–89.
88   Ylana Hayward in Akhtar and Humphries, 1999, p.88.

Powder into the tide with such invocations as 'You Can't Come, Go Away, Bugger Off' over and over again. And the invasion never happened.[89]

It is interesting to note that this narrative of witches defending the nation from invasion further found its way into the popular mindset in the form of the film of the children's story *Bed-knobs and Broomsticks*. The mythology that the spiritual realm was key to the defence of mainland Britain mutated in variant forms and proved a resilient and all-purpose motif.

For the nation as a whole, as in wars stretching back generations prior to this one, the monarch's periodic call to prayer summoned churchgoer and non-churchgoer alike to the nation's churches. Interestingly, and this fact says much of the character of the faith of the majority of the populace, attendance at such events often out-stripped church attendance at major Christian festivals. As a case in point, at Birmingham's cathedral, St. Philip's, on the National Day of Prayer, 3 September 1943, not only was the cathedral full but an additional service was held by the cathedral clergy in Lewis's department store, with some 1,150 staff in attendance. By comparison at Easter Sunday services in the cathedral in wartime there were, on average, approximately 100 communicants. Similarly, services held for peace or thanksgiving attracted large numbers.[90] In another parish, St. Peter and St. Paul, Aston, figures for national days of prayer were double that of usual Sunday attendance.[91] It seems that, in Birmingham at least, people at large may have been more in sympathy with the religious rhetoric attached to the nation's cause than with the Christian religion *per se*. However, this sentiment may have been more widespread, for on Easter Sunday 1941 attendance at churches in Paddington was a third less than at the National Day of Prayer of 23 March 1941.[92] Consequently, the religiosity in evidence during national days of

89   Akhtar and Humphries, 1999, p.46.
90   St Philip's Cathedral Register 1936–1949.
91   Register of Services, St. Peter and St. Paul, Aston. E.g. 26 May 1940, 168 attended the National Day of Prayer and on 23 March 1940, 97 attended: average Sunday attendance was approximately 80. Easter Sunday communicant figures here, however, were significantly greater.
92   Snape and Parker, 2001, p.403.

prayer received a mixed assessment from clerics, and the genuineness of such religiosity met with some critical disdain. Canon Salter, in the entertaining tone of his published radio broadcasts, observed:

> Radiators of prayer are needed in these days. I do not mean people who just go to church or chapel when we have a national day of prayer, but those who master the art of waiting upon God. Prayer, it has been truly said, is not asking God for favours, but waiting on God for orders. If your time for prayer begins and ends with a civic parade or an isolated service, it is bound to be a failure […] It is right that we should seek God's blessing on our country and on all the world in days like these, but our primary aim in prayer must be to find and follow His will for all mankind […] A nation on its knees is a sign not of weakness but of wisdom. To pray to God for help is not a confession of failure but a determination to be worthy of victory […] we need thousands of prayer radiations in this, our day of destiny.[93]

Whether such disparities between attendance figures were indicative of a general disillusionment with the Church, but not with matters of civic or national religion, is a moot point. In Birmingham at least, civic religiosity proved vibrant. For instance, in 1941 some 45,000 people attended the outdoor services hosted in Birmingham's parks under the auspices of the summer 'Brighter Birmingham' campaign.[94] The success of such events was reported in the Ministry of Information's periodical *The Spiritual Issues of the War*:

> The Lord Mayor of Birmingham spoke at a recent church service in Handsworth Park, one of a series which has been running since midsummer. 'We have been running these services in the parks since the end of June. They have been extraordinarily successful, not only on account of the large numbers who have attended them – congregations of a thousand have been common – not only on account of the good singing or the inspiring messages delivered, but because of the large number of people who have been helped, encouraged and inspired in these somewhat depressing days. As Lord Mayor, I want to pay my tribute to the good work the Churches have done […] It matters little where the message of the Church is delivered — whether in a great Cathedral or in a city park. This year the parks have been used to a great extent. I hope they will continue to be

---

93 Salter, 1942, p.40.
94 The Birmingham Christian Social Council: Annual Report and Accounts, 1942.

used in succeeding years, and that, as a consequence, the spiritual life of the city will be extended, strengthened and deepened.'[95]

However, the responses of the clergy to such displays of piety varied. Some clergy were happy to exploit the opportunities that the national call to prayer provided; others were cynical of the genuineness of the devotion, as William Connor, the columnist 'Cassandra', wrote in his *The English at War*:

> Even the well-drilled cohorts of priests, ministers, parsons and other men of God who guard the National Soul could not agree as to whether these days of prayer were induced by true spiritual fervour, or by the growing uneasiness that comes from adversity and the gregarious humility that breeds in tragedy and fear of the Unknown. The Reverend W. Rowland Jones, Vicar of Denton, with welcome candour and unusual courage denounced them as a sham! 'Out of fifteen people you meet, only one of them has even a passing interest in God. It means that the overwhelming majority of our nation must be deemed irreligious. It is not a pretty thing to see these people who, in days of peace, utterly ignored even the existence of the Deity, coming grovelling to His feet because they are now in a spot of trouble. If you can get along nicely without God when the sun is shining, then, literally for God's sake, keep away from Him when the storms come.'[96]

In a sermon at St. Philip's Cathedral on 14 September 1941 Bishop Barnes took the opportunity to warn of the ill effects of war upon people's spirituality. Pointedly, he observed the 'coincidence' between the timing of the National Day of Prayer a week previously and the heaviest raid yet upon Berlin carried out that same evening. There is in such services, he cautioned, a whipping up of the 'remembrance of evil [and the] desire for revenge: the primitive "eye for an eye and tooth for a tooth" [is encouraged to] rise to the surface' by them.[97] National days of prayer not only promote nationalistic fervour, he warned, but they are akin to other forms of reassurance, such as astrology, in the popular mindset. These forms of piety, he argued, diminish Christian morality and by them 'Christian good sense yields to superstition.'[98] Similarly, perhaps it was national days of prayer that Barnes had in mind when,

95 *The Spiritual Issues of the War*, Number 148, September 3 1942.
96 Cassandra, 1941, p.57.
97 Barnes Papers EWB 12/1/591. Sunday 14 September 1941.
98 Barnes Papers EWB 12/1/591. Sunday 14 September 1941.

at his Diocesan Conference in 1943, he claimed that 'for the time being Christianity is prostituted to what is termed "aiding the national effort."' [99]

National days of prayer, though often significantly better attended than even the major Christian festivals, were still felt by some to be wearisome reminders of the unattractiveness of institutional religion. One woman felt the artificiality of the religion that seemed to be on offer in these staged events: though even she was given pause for thought when the apparently miraculous seemed to happen as a result of such days, as in the Dunkirk evacuation shortly after a day of prayer in May 1940:

> Yesterday was the day of prayer I did wonder if I would go to church. They strike me as so cold and sombre and we have so few churches left standing [...] After the Dunkirk affair and its amazing climax I have more faith, perhaps, in collective prayer. Up to then I had looked on an order for a day of prayer to amount to just nothing, but if Dunkirk was a direct result of concentrated prayer I shall become convinced that there is something in it. [100]

Because of the scale of the evacuation, and the apparent link made in many people's minds between the people's prayers and the decisive events of May 1940, such sentiments were widespread. As another Birmingham citizen, E.A. Platt, a worker at Snow Hill station, surmised: 'everyone must have said their own silent prayer to God for the miracle.' [101]

Hymns and communal singing also played an important part in the collective and personal devotion of the civilian during the Second World War, just as it had done for many a 'Tommy' during the First World War. Memories of hymns sung in childhood at home and in school served as a emotional link with loved ones and provided an associated sense of security as a result. Additionally, singing together served to increase the bond amongst the sheltering folk. [102] Strong indications of the familiarity and importance of hymnody are to be

99   Barnes Papers EWB 12/1/640. Diocesan Conference. Thursday 4 November 1943.
100 Mass-Observation Diarist DR 5420, 24 March 1941.
101 Imperial War Museum, MISC 185, Item 2772, May/June 1940.
102 Williams, 1999, pp.148f.

found in the diary of one Birmingham woman, Vere Hodgson,[103] an Anglican and a Spiritualist. Heading each page of her published wartime recollections are lines from famous hymns. These are not arbitrarily chosen lines, rather they are phrases that for her seem to catch the mood of the moment, in terms of national events as well as her personal state of mind. Thus, in June 1940, during the aftermath of Dunkirk, when invasion seemed imminent, she selected the phrase 'See how our foes their banners are unfurling.' Likewise, during the month in which the Battle of Britain began she chose the words 'We are not divided – all one body we.' Likewise, a central Birmingham resident of the time recalled that, after the bombing of a church where many were sheltering, the vicar roused the people there by his rendition of 'Roll out the barrel': eventually all joined in and defiantly proved they had survived the attack.[104] Some of the most popular hymns of the sheltering masses seem to have been: 'Nearer, My God, to Thee', 'Lead, Kindly Light' and 'Abide With Me'.[105] Vere Hodgson's application of hymnody to national events and the many occurrences of communal hymn singing suggest that there was a general familiarity with religious language and ideas and a spiritual vocabulary (probably because of upbringing and schooling) to be drawn upon in times of crisis. It also implies a tendency amongst many to assume that the nation's role in this conflict could be likened to the experience of Israel or to the Church in persecuted times.

Many sheltering night after night were reassured by the popular ditty and Sunday school song which was to be found on countless public shelter walls and widely published in parish magazines around the country:

> God is our refuge
> Be not afraid
> He will take care of you
> All through the raid
> When bombs are dropping
> And danger is near

103   Hodgson, 1976.
104   Interview with Beryl Keith, April 2001.
105   Barber, 1946, p.30.

He will be with you
Until the all clear.[106]

However, not every display of such familiarity was welcomed by their contemporaries. Penny Keel recalled singing such apposite hymns as 'Onward, Christian Soldiers' and 'Fight the Good Fight', whilst sheltering with her family, only to be told, 'shut up [...] we can't hear the bombs dropping.'[107]

It was widely believed that the burdens and sufferings of wartime were being borne with stoical pragmatism, and many attested to this. Arguably, such courage was sustained by faith, as in this exemplary story related by Canon Salter:

A few months ago a man stood in the street and gazed at his wrecked home. It was not a pretty sight. Nothing was left but a heap of ruins. Yet there was a whimsical smile on his face as he surveyed the scene. No wonder people sometimes ask if the English are really crazy! His wife arrived shortly afterwards, and looked at him with a puzzled expression in here eyes. 'John,' said she, 'why are you standing there like that?' [...] He paused for a second, and then replied: 'It's all right, my dear. I'm just counting our assets and, in spite of everything that happened last night, I really believe we've still got much more than we've lost. [...] This morning [...] some one came into our dug-out and told me that we had lost everything. It's a lie. Thank God I've still got health and strength to carry on with my job. I still have you, my dear, and the children. Thank God you're all safe. Hitler hasn't smashed my faith in the love and wisdom of God, nor my faith in the ultimate victory of Right. I still have hope for the future. [...] So I reckon that you and I ought to thank God that we have saved more than we have lost. Houses and buildings may be wrecked and ruined, but you and I can still hold on to things which can never be shaken or destroyed – our religion, our comradeship, our ideals, our faith in the decencies of life. Yes, I've counted my assets, and I still find we are on the right side.'[108]

---

106 Mass-Observation TC/47/1/I and *The Messenger*, magazine of Lozells Congregational Church, Birmingham, October 1940. References are made to this song elsewhere also.
107 Interview with Penny Keel, March 2002.
108 Salter, 1942, p.34.

The Spectre of Death

Day to day, during the blitz, civilians had to live with the prospect of their own death or that of their kindred. People coped with the possibility of this in various ways, and often they did so very pragmatically. Interestingly, the practicalities of preparing for the likelihood of death were often left to women, who in many families were responsible for planning in case of death, becoming organisers and custodians of the household life insurance. As Joan Evans recalled: 'I had to go out [to the air-raid shelter] first because Mom was so busy getting her bag with the policies in.'[109] Betty Jones' grandmother did the same, and she remembered: 'the neighbours that we was in the shelter with […] her daughter had got a panda with a zip up the back and she used to keep all her policies in that.'[110] For families with children an uncertain future made it doubly important to plan ahead for the security and care of progeny. Joan Evans remembered her family's particular plans and their sad outcome:

> The man who lived […] four doors above us, his name was Billy Hopkins. He was going to have me in their home and eventually adopt me […] that was not written down, it was a gentleman's agreement. On 11 December when this landmine came down he thought it was a German on the end of it and of course he wanted to go and capture him. So, he saw this parachute in a tree, and he was going over people's gardens […] the thing went off […] he was hit pretty badly. In 1948–49 [he] died of cancer and we always said it was through that landmine.[111]

In the opinion of another interviewee, not only was wartime Birmingham an assumedly Christian context in which 'you believed everyone else believed in God', it was also one that brought people closer to the reality of the divine.[112] Penny Keel asserted from memory of the time that 'I don't think there would have been people in the war

109   Interview with Joan Evans, March 2002.
110   Interview with Betty Jones, March 2002.
111   Interview with Joan Evans, March 2002.
112   Interview with Penny Keel, March 2002.

who did not believe in God because they lived so close to death [...] they say you never find an atheist on a battle field and I think that is true. I think it was a time when we needed religion.'[113] Another woman, echoing this, indicated that prayer and the proximity of death were companions amidst the fears of the sheltering experience:

> It came as second-nature that you prayed that things would work out well [...] I never thought once, ever, that we should go under [...] I think we all prayed to ourselves [...] There was once when we all felt we were going to die, we were all together, the four of us, and we heard this unusual sound; it was like a train [...] it was getting nearer, and nearer [...] and we all felt this was it.[114]

The character of popular religiosity was shown by the type of language and concepts drawn upon to explain, understand and mitigate events. As such, in the case of one of Birmingham's worst nights of bombardment, parallels were drawn between the tragic fallout of events and the sufferings of Christ,[115] especially when the aftermath happened to coincide with Passiontide. Thus, C.J. Rice, an employee of the Birmingham department store Lewis's recorded the events following a heavy bombardment, the morning of Maundy Thursday 1941:

> On Maundy Thursday 1941 Birmingham suffered its severest blitz [...] I arrived at the store on Good Friday morning expecting a relatively quiet day. The already battered city showed the usual post-raid rubble and general untidiness, with here and there a dead body under tarpaulin [...] I went in through the staff entrance [...] the basement [...] was crammed from side to side with blood soaked clothing. I went to a place from where I could look down on the unfortunate people of Birmingham, row on row, the air raid victims [...] I took another route where I crossed the stretcher filled floor. Only the faces of the people lying there were showing. All the faces bore the same reddy-brown colour, caused by the brick-dust from demolished houses [...] here and there a doctor or nurse was bending over a maimed body but medical attention was minimal. I thought of the wrecked houses, and the families anxious to distraction as to the whereabouts of so many of these victims. Many of them were children, I found the eyes of one face, that of a boy, looking towards me. I went over and

113   Interview with Penny Keel, March 2002.
114   Interview with Beryl Keith, March 2001.
115   Contrary to Wilkinson's view that such parallels were almost unknown in this war (Wilkinson, 1997, p.159).

96

spoke to him. He asked faintly where he was I told him and said I would come back and see him later. Many died that Good Friday [...].[116]

Even in less extreme circumstances people testified to the importance of religious faith in helping them to cope with what the war confronted them with. Penny Stephens recalled that

Inwardly I felt safe because of my faith [...] I didn't worry, I expected that everything would turn out right for us [...] I prayed a lot more then than I do now [...] I didn't think that anything would harm us really [...] my faith didn't falter.[117]

Signs, Portents and Visions

The nation appeared to draw great consolation and a degree of moral fortitude from the image of St. Paul's Cathedral standing relatively unscathed amidst the ruins of London at the height of the blitz.[118] Photographed and dubbed by *The Daily Mail* as 'War's Greatest Picture', a *Mail* reporter described how

[Through the] glare of many fires [...] a wind sprang up. Suddenly the shining cross, dome and towers stood out like a symbol in the inferno [...] it symbolises the steadiness of London's stand against the enemy: the firmness of Right against Wrong.[119]

Though smacking of the 'superstition' otherwise disapproved of by clerics, none less than the Dean of St. Paul's, Canon W.R. Matthews, wrote of the event: 'Who shall say that the unceasing prayer which went up from St. Paul's had no part in its preservation from such a multitude of perils?'[120] In the midst of such general devastation, it

116   Imperial War Museum, recollections of C.J. Rice Miscellaneous 22 (388).
117   Interview with Penny Stephens, March 2000.
118   Calder, 1991, p.250.
119   *The Daily Mail*, 31 December 1940.
120   Matthews, 1946, p.51.

seemed remarkable; even indicative, when churches survived, that God was smiling on the British.[121] Of course, in actuality, many of Birmingham's churches were damaged or destroyed by bombs, though when buildings were preserved this did not go unnoticed. For example, one Birmingham diarist recalls his experience of walking home through Birmingham town centre after a blitz-night dance:

> The long walk home that night was unforgettable [...] the centre was literally on fire it was reminiscent of 'Old Chicago' – arcades, shops, multiple stores – everything seemed to be burning – except the Cathedral![122]

Birmingham had its equivalent 'St. Paul's' in addition to the cathedral's noted preservation.[123] Birmingham's historic parish church, St. Martin's, received only minor damage on the same night that the market area around it was flattened; its spire still stood and, for some, this was considered miraculous considering the general devastation.[124] This phenomenon was similarly photographed, heightening its appeal as a defiant and hopeful symbol. Moreover, Birmingham's Lord Mayor later recognised the significance of the church's deliverance to the city's morale:

> The Parish Church is a fine symbol of the triumph of freedom over tyranny; for although it suffered badly from enemy damage, it continued its fine work courageously through the years of war and will, I hope, for all time hold the warm affection and devotion of the people of Birmingham.[125]

Preserved churches were seen as signs of hope, bolstering the sense of the righteousness of the national cause; but even where churches were damaged congregations defiantly went on worshipping, meeting in bomb-damaged buildings if necessary.[126] At St. Martin's,

---

121   Indeed, images such as these were reproduced by cinematographers, as in the film *Mrs Miniver* (see below). See also Humphrey Jennings' considered ending for *The Heart of Britain*, referred to in Smith, A. (2003), p.137.
122   Imperial War Museum, MISC 185, Item 2772, Diary of E.A. Platt, August-September, 1940.
123   However, the cathedral was badly damaged in October 1940.
124   Butcher, 1999, p.151.
125   Rogers, 1956, p.181.
126   As in the example of Rocky Lane Mission, Nechells, Birmingham.

services continued despite the considerable damage inflicted on the building of the night of 9 April 1941. On Easter Day, Handel's 'Hallelujah Chorus' was sung in the church, its sound floating out to passers by through the glassless windows.[127] Even where damage occurred a positive spirit prevailed, parallels often being drawn by local Christian communities with the experience of others through Christian history:

> And after all why should we be depressed? The early Christians again and again had their churches destroyed, their possessions confiscated and their books burned; but they triumphed over all their difficulties, which were far greater than ours are. They had no sympathetic government to promise compensation, but only a tyrant to torture and kill them. We are far better placed than they were, and this calamity shall make our zeal the keener, our hearts braver and our devotion warmer.[128]

Akin to the First World War soldier's wonderment at the way in which wayside crucifixes remained unscathed, people often marvelled at the seemingly miraculous preservation of statues and other religious artefacts amidst widespread devastation.[129] For instance, the statue of the Virgin Mary in the Roman Catholic St. Dunstan's Church, Kings Heath, remained intact despite the corrugated iron building's destruction on Maundy Thursday, 1941 causing many to comment.[130] People's perception of similar events led them to assume God's favour upon the British people. Sometimes people emerged from sheltering in the crypts of such churches only to kneel to pray in thanksgiving for another night's grace. The seeming protection of religious buildings and artefacts led people to construe a providential patterning to indiscriminate bombing. Popular religion thus fed popular defiance.[131]

---

127 Rogers, 1956, p.181.
128 *The Fiery Cross*, the parish magazine of St. Agatha's, Sparkbrook, Vol. XV, No. 12, December 1940.
129 Wilkinson, 1997, p.151.
130 Correspondence received from Mr George Parsons and Miss M. Shepherd of Kings Heath.
131 Author Unknown, *Ourselves in Wartime* London: Odhams Press, undated, p.115.

As well as the reassuring physical evidence of churches remaining relatively unscathed, some claimed to have received explicit personal assurance from God that they would be protected; on occasion this led them to a resistance to normal air raid precautions, as one Birmingham Mass-Observation diarist recorded:

> Mrs Bland […] is crippled and disfigured with arthritis, she had to have one eye out and the other is nearly blind […] she is afraid of the war, they had a bomb drop off and their windows out yet she never flinched and she can only remain in bed in the front downstairs. I asked her how she could feel like that (her life hangs on a thread). She told me that one day she wasn't asleep but everything was quiet about her, her own words were 'Our Lord came before me, just by the door, he looked beautiful. He had on a white gown and his beautiful hair but no crown, no crown.' He said to her, 'I will protect all your loved ones, fear not,' and he faded as he had come.[132]

In accordance with Jennifer Hazelgrove's observation[133] that it is women rather more than men who were susceptible to visions, on 3 September 1942, the third anniversary of the war, and a National Day of Prayer, the same diarist received a reassuring vision of her own:

> This is the day of prayer […] each night at 9 o'clock […] I pray. [Tonight] I looked out of the window after my special prayer, the sky was marvellous, a very, very deep blue and three very large searchlights crossed like this [a picture is drawn] the ends looked like long burning torches then round and round went a series of little torches the clouds in the sky making them appear like torches instead of the usual blob. I stood at the window for 10 minutes and the large searchlights remained steadfast and while the little ones kept revolving like a merry-go-round. I know it was only a demonstration, but to me it was symbolic. The large ones made a complete cross and symbolised our steadfastness of purpose, the small ones were restless and urging us on, and do you know it may sound daft but I can almost imagine Christ descending the beam of the searchlight.[134]

Similarly, many people were affected by reported sightings of crosses in the sky in eastern England. The significance of these sightings was variously interpreted, but the Reverend Harold Green of Ipswich

132 Mass-Observation Diarist DR 5420, 6 May 1941.
133 Hazelgrove, 2000, p.80.
134 Mass-Observation Diarist DR 5420, 3 September 1942.

interpreted them, amongst other events, as a sign of God's favour on the British people, sightings akin to the ones of the 'Angel of Mons' during the First World War.[135] How widespread such visions as those of Mrs Bland were is difficult to determine. However, what these examples suggest is the tendency to interpret the commonplace wartime events (such as a searchlight scanning the sky) religiously. War, it appears, honed people's intuitiveness (especially, it appears, women), sometimes encouraging a religious reading of events.

Similarly, the Dunkirk evacuation of the British Expeditionary Force during May/June 1940 was recalled by individuals as reassuring, because of the seemingly miraculous nature of the rescue implied. As has already been said, some churchmen had few qualms in interpreting these events as miraculous, as Beryl Keith recalled:

> A lot of our young men were involved at Dunkirk. I can remember being in church and messages coming through while we were there and they'd announce; so and so is safe [...] I think we looked on Dunkirk as a miracle because although it was a defeat we did get all those many men back [...] I know our vicar made it sound a triumph rather than a defeat.[136]

Fatalism, the sense that events did not happen haphazardly but had a mysterious meaning and guiding hand behind them, gave some a sense of personal reassurance, consolation when danger was averted and meaning when things went wrong. For some, persistent belief in fatalism, coupled with a degree of stubborn pragmatism, led to a refusal to enter an air-raid shelter, choosing instead to stay indoors: occasionally tragedy followed.[137] For others, particular events were explicable in terms of fate or a degree of pre-determination. Jean Cuthbert remembered:

> I lost my aunt and cousin in an air raid in October. I had been there the day before, and [...] I'd never ever come back the same day. She'd always let me stay [...] but she wouldn't let me this time; very funny that was I think. I came

135 Snape and Parker, 2001, p.402.
136 Interview with Beryl Keith, March 2001.
137 One example of this stubbornness was presented in the interview with Joan and Norman Oswald, March 2002.

back and they were killed the same night. She was ten, my cousin, and my aunt was thirty-three. I just couldn't believe it.[138]

As the same woman recalled, this prevailing fatalism could be tinged with a degree faith in providence. This admixture of beliefs is characteristic of the expediency of wartime popular religion:

A lot of people [found religion reassuring] they used to say 'thank God we have survived this one.' I don't think as a nation we talk about religion that much. If you were religious, you were religious [...] you did what you wanted to do as far as religion was concerned; well at least in my family.[139]

Another child of wartime, Penny Keel, recalled that her presence during a bombing raid was regarded somewhat as a jinx:

I spent some of the time through my childhood at Lickey End, Bromsgrove, where they sent me as soon as the war broke out, and we did not get bombed. I came home and we were bombed. So, I was sent back again. I came home again and we were bombed. [It seemed like] they were in touch with the Germans when I was at home.[140]

Similarly, Martin Ryland remembered how he prayed as a child for the war to end. His reminiscence depicts an eclectic conceptualising of prayer, in which chance could be manipulated by will or personal sacrifice. Of a wartime family holiday he recalled: 'I went to a wishing well [in Weymouth] and threw a farthing in and prayed, at least hoped for the war to end as a wish.'[141]

Betty Jones spoke of the death of her grandparents in an air raid. Although its circumstances were undeniably tragic, for her there appeared to be logic in the loss, which seemed to explain its occurrence and alleviate the worst of the pain:

My nan and granddad always used to say they wouldn't even go in the shelter because they had a long walk to their shelter, so they'd always said they'd remain in the house, that if they were gonna die they would die together: and

138   Interview with Jean Cuthbert, March 2002.
139   Interview with Jean Cuthbert, March 2002.
140   Interview with Penny Keel, March 2002.
141   Interview with Martin Ryland, March 2002.

one night there was a thirteen hour raid and the RAP [*sic*] men went round knocking the doors telling people to go into their shelters. So, they fetched my nan and granddad out of the house. They had to come up their garden path, along the top of their yard, up an entry and at the bottom of the entry they were told to wait 'cos they'd got to cross a road [...] Also at the bottom [...] lived my aunty Daisy, she'd got little Jimmy [...] as they went across a bomb dropped. Nan and granddad pushed Aunty Daisy and Jimmy to the floor and nan and granddad got killed [...] Their house still stood, and the dog lay by the fire. So, if they hadn't gone out the house they wouldn't have been killed.[142]

The human desire to find explanation for and a sense of order within events, which concepts of fatalism provided on a personal level, also had parallels at the communal level. Canon Roger Lloyd of Winchester wrote an incisive attack on these in an article entitled 'The Heresy of Fatalism' published in *The Expository Times* of April 1942. In this, he portrayed the way in which people's social and psychological mindset may be manipulated by stirring up fatalistic sentiments. By fostering fatalism, he admitted, people can be encouraged to endure: 'To believe that one's death, in date and manner, is inexorably predetermined, and that no amount of caution or playing for safety can alter one's fate by a hair's breadth, does demonstrably lend courage to the faint-hearted and endurance to the weary.'[143] What is more, promoting a sense of collective fatalism, of national destiny, is eminently serviceable to the propagandist. By instilling in people the belief in the ultimate destiny of their cause and the inevitability of victory, the methods and means of reaching victory, he argued, may go unquestioned. Lloyd, though arguing that this form of fatalism is 'Fatalism in its most majestic form', fell short of applying the same critique to British propaganda.[144] It is dictators, he claimed, who 'call history by the name of Destiny' and by so doing manipulate ordinary people's morality making them far more brutish than they would otherwise be.[145] Moreover, the civilian who believes in such forms of fate, destiny or history, synonymous terms according to Lloyd, is potently influenced to accept suffering. Even atheism, he observed, is not immune to a belief in fatalism. The

142 Interview with Betty Jones, March 2002.
143 *The Expository Times*, Vol. LIV, No. 7, April 1942, p.229.
144 *The Expository Times*, Vol. LIV, No. 7, April 1942, p.229.
145 *The Expository Times*, Vol. LIV, No. 7, April 1942, p.230.

fatalist and the Christian, Lloyd went on, are dealing with the same difficulty, how to explain the unfolding nature of the universe without recourse to chance as the only explanation. The only Christian response to fatalism, Lloyd urged, is predestination. In his understanding, ultimately nothing that happens falls outside God's plan, nothing is irrelevant to it, though there can, of course, be accidents and there can be 'defiances of His love'.[146] However, the envisaged ends do not justify the means, according to Lloyd. The will of God is the goodness of human beings, and this is only served in the interim by moral action: 'any idea that God's plan can be best served by methods which are clearly in opposition to the best that human beings can know' is anathema to the Christian world view.[147] Thus, there arose for some serious questions about the kind of blind fatalism catalysed by war.

146   *The Expository Times*, Vol. LIV, No. 7, April 1942, p.231. Lloyd mentions the
       Nazi concentration camps as an example of such defiance.
147   *The Expository Times*, Vol. LIV, No. 7, April 1942, p.231.

The Parish Magazine and Popular Religion

Circulation figures are not available for this usually monthly publication, which was a highly popular way of communicating news and publicising clergy opinion during wartime. However, what is clear is that the church or parish magazine was viewed as an integral part of Church life, for its distribution was given priority, even in the face of a shortage of quality paper. In practice, magazines were circulated well beyond the confines of the churchgoing congregation, and its delivery was often coupled with a visit from a Church worker.[148] Thus, the magazine and its distribution were a critical means of keeping in touch with parishioners as well as the dispersed flock (those displaced by bomb damage or in the armed forces) and thereby demonstrating care in adversity. It seems that the continued publication of the church magazines was another means of showing defiance in the midst of difficulty, and representative of the people's determination that life would go on as normal.

Almost every issue of the parish magazine contained the minister's reflections upon current affairs, with their characteristic and quotable spiritual slant. Furthermore, many of Birmingham's parish magazines occasionally contained inserts, which were nationally published organs similar in tone to their parish counterpart. These inserts, and, the stories recounted within them, reflect the brand of piety favoured in wartime. One such insert published inside the Birmingham Oratory's parish magazine of 1944, told the story of 'The Lady of the Woods'.[149] This story has an airman recounting to a fellow flier a vision which he had had whilst in action in France, a vision of a woman 'with golden hair in long tresses and wearing a long dress of dazzling white', clearly redolent of the Virgin Mary. The airman who experiences this vision is later shot down over the place where he had seen it. News of this comes to the other airman as he is listening (significantly) to the nine o'clock news, causing him to exclaim: 'the Lady of the Woods will look after him.' The story underlines the

148   Cox, 1982, p.65.
149   *The Oratory Parish Magazine*, May 1944, p.76.

reality of the supramaterial protection afforded to the combatant, for the comfort and benefit of loved ones at home. Similarly, *Home Words,* the regular digest of more evangelical Anglican parishes, adopted the prevailing conditions as a means of conveying to its readers the continuing truths of its brand of Christianity. The author Canon Salter is quoted in the circular's May 1942 edition (and inserted, amongst others, into the parish magazine of St. James's, Ashted). Whilst wandering around a blitzed town, Salter describes encountering the wreck of a church, an apparent 'dim and distant relic of the past.'[150] Upon entering the church he discovers people kneeling at prayer and is drawn to the conclusion that, in fact, 'the Church is alive and active.'[151] As well as being a sign of the vitality of wartime religion amidst adversity, this story may be interpreted as attempting to reassure readers of the persistence and priority of personal piety as opposed to the outward and visible signs of institutional Christianity. Accordingly, the war provided novel contexts in which to frame and popularise the familiar tenets of Christian orthodoxy, whilst at the same time shoring up British morale by recourse to them. In wartime, piety was able to adapt itself, utilising current experiences as means of communicating particular religious beliefs.

Faith on the Airwaves

Radio had already begun to be an important aspect of home life well before the outbreak of war. Indeed, some of its repertoire, judged by the testimony of one interviewee, was deemed unsuitable Sunday material:

> There were certain things you could do and certain things you couldn't do […] it
> might sound silly to you now but we weren't allowed to listen to Radio

150   *The Parish Magazine of St James's Ashted,* May 1942.
151   *The Parish Magazine of St James's Ashted,* May 1942.

Luxembourg on a Sunday. If we had the radio on, it was mainly churches and church music and church services.[152]

Radio had its heyday in 1940s Britain: arguably, in wartime, it came into its own.[153] In Birmingham, it can safely be said that given the numbers of wireless licences in the possession of Birmingham's people, some 286,995 by the late 1930s, most of its citizens lived within earshot of a radio set.[154] The potential for influencing the majority of the populace by this medium was recognised early on. So, when war came, radio assumed the role of propagandist, as well as entertainer; of attitude and opinion former, as well uplifter of the spirits. Likewise, religious broadcasting, still in its infancy at the time, served to enlighten, evangelise and envision in its attempts to deal with spiritual and moral questions thrown up by wartime events. Just as radio informed the masses of wartime's news events, bringing distant happenings into the home with greater immediacy, affecting the mood and morale of the home and private world of the majority, religious broadcasting also had the power to shape the frame of mind of the people.

The power of this relatively new medium was clear from the war's outset. For instance, most people heard the broadcast of the Prime Minister, on the morning of 3 September 1939, and can recall the solemn mood that met the declaration of war. Many churches even installed speakers on that Sunday morning so that people could be sure to hear the broadcast. Such was the power of this medium to influence that Neville Chamberlain's broadcast words inadvertently prompted religious devotion amongst Christians across the religious spectrum, as one Birmingham diarist recorded:

Now we know. We heard the Prime Minister at 11:15. At last the suspense is over […] I found my friend about to go to Church for Exposition (we are both Roman Catholics). I went with him. There were a dozen people in Church, and a

---

152 Interview with Jean Cuthbert, March 2002.
153 The role of radio broadcasting in wartime Britain is explored in Nicholas, 1996.
154 Hopkins, 1990, p.140.

steady stream were coming in. Afterwards we went back to his home, and I helped in the blacking some of their windows.[155]

Another Birmingham diarist wrote:

> In the evening I went to Carrs Lane church here in Birmingham, to hear what is considered the most outspoken pacifist Non-conformist church in the Midlands had to say about the war–peace question. There was an atmosphere in the building which suggested these words to me; 'It is upon us, the church is powerless.' The sermon concerned St. Paul, and the way he maintained his faith even in the darkest of his days [...] Coming out of the church we were in twilight which was quickly deepening into the war's first black-out.[156]

The Churches recognised the potential of radio for religious purposes and determined that the function of religious broadcasts in war should be subtly different to that in peacetime. Religious broadcasts were aimed at strengthening the nation's resolve in its cause; that of defending Christian values, avoiding controversy and subversiveness at all costs. Moreover, religious broadcasting should further Christianise a Christian nation, not only through its broadcast services, but also by an increasing number of broadcast talks. The aim, however, was not to stir up hatred of the enemy.[157] In the words of Canon Guy Rogers, Rector of St. Martin's, Birmingham, and a member of the Religious Advisory Board of the BBC, wartime religious broadcasts should function to provide 'a prophetic interpretation of our situation [...] some measure of consolation [and the] creation of hope and expectation in the language of reconstruction after the war.'[158] The search was on to find personalities, regardless of denomination, who were able to 'speak with an exceptional simplicity, and [in] theological concepts in common speech rather more ably than most clergy.'[159] One clergyman considered to have these qualities was Leyton Richards, who, prior to the war, had been minister of Carrs Lane (where in wartime broadcasts were often hosted). Richards, a co-founder of the

155   Mass-Observation Diarist DR 5064, September 1939.
156   Mass-Observation Diarist DR 5228, 3 September 1939.
157   Wolfe, 1984, p.212 and p.157.
158   Wolfe, 1984, pp.154–155.
159   Wolfe, 1984, p.211.

pacifist Fellowship of Reconciliation, was now warden of Woodbrooke College, Birmingham, having resigned his pastorate of Carrs Lane because of his pacifism. Broadcasting on 11 February 1940, Richards preached an explicitly pacifist message causing a minor uproar amongst listeners and a revision of the BBC's policy with regard to the censoring and selection of its speakers.[160] Despite his clear gifts as an orator, because of his pacifist views Richards was never asked to broadcast again.[161] In this way, two prominent Birmingham clerics helped to determine the shape of religious broadcasting at a formative time.

More attuned to the mood of the authorities, and extremely popular with the listening public, was Ronald Selby Wright, dubbed 'the Radio Padre'. The audience figures for Selby Wright, a Senior Chaplain in the army with considerable experience of working in slum parishes as a Church of Scotland minister, reached the 10 million mark, making them at least as popular as the most popular of wartime programmes, 'ITMA'.[162] Sometimes, Selby Wright even made short broadcasts in the middle of comedy programmes themselves such as 'Ack-Ack, Beer-Beer'. Selby Wright's broadcasts typically consisted of a discussion between the Padre and two or three soldiers on a number of topical moral issues. By his conversational, pragmatic and authoritative style on such themes in personal ethics as wartime weddings, as well as the more explicitly religious themes such as heaven and hell, Selby Wright seemed able to interrogate and to communicate the Christian faith to the satisfaction of his audience and within the bounds of acceptable wartime rhetoric.

The oft depicted, and somewhat idealised, cameo of the British family huddled around the wireless set to hear the evening nine o'clock news became, in fact, a necessary ritual of wartime. This almost liturgical routine, which meant for many the chance to keep abreast of the progress of war, developed an increasingly religious significance as the chimes of Big Ben came to 'symbolise the heart of the nation [...] and indeed of the free world fighting the Nazis'; for some the chimes

160   Wolfe, 1984, p.178.
161   Richards, 1950, p.89.
162   Mass-Observation, Ronald Selby Wright, 8859/2.

were even felt to summon the nation to prayer.[163] Hearing of this idea, Percy Pierce, Vicar of St James's, Ashted, Birmingham, urged his people to make use of this 'minute a day to think and pray' adding that 'before darkness falls we [should] make it our practice to pray for all the people in this city [...] to be kept safe from the ravages of air-raids.'[164] The opportunity of having the nation's prayerful attention for a few moments each night was seized upon by an interdenominational group that came to be known as the 'Big Ben Minute Association'.[165] This movement to keep a silence, or to say a prayer, won widespread support, though there was much disagreement as to how the time signal could best be used. One commentator urged that: 'the mass of our people should realize that this war is on a spiritual plane as well as the material.'[166] The Bishop of Lincoln suggested that people be encouraged to say the Lord's Prayer at the sound of the chimes. Others wanted this 'dedicated moment' to be promoted by the use of the song:

> When Big Ben chimes, he seems to say; be silent all and pause and pray; O Lord our God make strife to cease, In thy good time grant us thy peace.[167]

In the end the BBC, the Churches, and the Big Ben Minute promoters could not agree about either the theology of prayer suggested by the 'minute' or its function in the broadcast schedule; and so it was left to the discretion of the public how the time should best be used. Thus, on Sunday 10 November 1940 the Radio Times rather open-endedly announced that:

> The minute it took Big Ben to strike the full hour of nine before the 9 p.m. news would henceforth be considered a special moment for listeners, for consecration of the land they love [...] thoughts of their dear ones [...] and [...] other individual needs [and thus] 'The Big Ben Minute' became a fixture of radio schedules.[168]

---

163   Wolfe, 1984, p.158.
164   *The Parish Magazine of St. James's, Ashted*, December 1940.
165   Longmate, 1971, p.428.
166   Wolfe, 1984, p.159.
167   Wolfe, 1984, p.164.
168   Nicholas, 1996, p.128.

Despite the controversy over the exact usage of the time signal, and the refusal of some to invest it with religious meaning, this particular opportunity for collective prayer caught on overseas, so much so that British soldiers would often conclude their letters: 'Give my love to Ben'.[169] Such a moment of consecration therefore provided an additional spiritual and emotional link with home and loved ones for those overseas. Additionally, it reinforced the idea that war against the Nazis was being waged on the home front by spiritual means as much as abroad by military ones.

As listening figures for more formal religious broadcasts for the wartime years demonstrate, radio was utilised by many as an effective medium of spiritual sustenance during times when many were distanced from traditional means of such succour. Audience figures of 7% on average for the Daily Service, and some 12% on average for the Sunday morning service, figures that declined significantly and rapidly in the post-war years, prove the potency of radio religion in shaping the British popular religion.[170]

Religion at the Cinema

The Birmingham Christian Social Council, the ecumenical body representative of all mainstream Protestant Christian denominations in Birmingham at the time, and chaired by Bishop Barnes, had as its major bugbear of the 1930s the Sunday opening of Birmingham's cinemas.[171] Its opposition to Sunday opening was threefold. Firstly, it was seen as a direct violation of the Sabbath. Secondly, the council recognised and deplored that 'cinemas do more than any other single

169   Hoover, 1999, p.111.
170   Averages calculated from Currie, Gilbert and Horsley, 1977, p.235.
171   Barnes Papers, EWB 9/1/11; Richards, 1983, pp.37–43.

agency to mould the thought and feeling of the nation',[172] believing, in particular, that it was 'both immoral and demoralising' to the working classes.[173] Thirdly, in the Churches' perception, the success of Sunday cinema placed it in direct competition with Sunday religion. Despite the case against Sunday opening of cinemas being forcefully put by the council, the Sunday opening of cinemas debate was concluded locally in favour of cinemas, and in February 1933 Birmingham cinemas opened for the first time on Sundays: Churches reported no consequential decline in attendance.[174] However, there must have been brief cause for celebration amongst the cinema sabbatarians when at the outbreak of war all cinemas were closed for fear of air raid attacks. In fact they reopened a few days into the conflict, for it was generally agreed that 'going to the pictures' lifted people's spirits and 'took them out of themselves' during the blackout.[175] The significance of the reopening of Sunday amusements was met with indignation by a number of clergy despite some wartime performances beginning with a service led by local clerics.[176] The Rector of Edgware Parish Church strongly feared that just as the closing of cinemas at the start of the blitz drew down God's blessing so their reopening might forfeit it.[177] Bishop Barnes likewise read into the Sunday opening of cinemas a significant foreboding, believing that the Church would, as a result, finally lose its moral influence upon the young, gloomily predicting that:

> We shall get a truly pagan England [...] Sunday schools, religious observance, the quiet thoughtfulness of 'the day of rest' may easily seem to an outside observer to have constituted a quaint but unimportant peculiarity of Great Britain. These elements of our social life were, in fact, the 'still small voice'

172 The words of Bishop Barnes in an address to the Birmingham Rotary Club. Barnes Papers, EWB 12/1/596 'Reconstruction', The Rotary Club, Birmingham, Nov. 3 1941.
173 Richards, 1983, p.40.
174 Richards, 1983, p.43.
175 Chapman, 1999, pp.40f.
176 Wilkinson, 1986, p.279.
177 A. Briggs, 1975, p.199.

keeping our youth and our leaders firmly wise. That voice silent, we are set on uncharted seas.[178]

Perhaps to a degree that attending Church never had, people were able to find a comfort and escape from the privations of war by going to the cinema. Cinema-going figures soared from 19 million in 1939 to 30 million in 1945, despite the dangers of going to the cinema during the blitz.[179] In fact, increased wages in wartime made cinema the most popular leisure activity of the war.[180] The same people who had been going to the cinema in peacetime went even more regularly to the cinema in war.[181] Based upon national statistics, it is possible to assert that the people of Birmingham went more regularly to the city's 98 cinemas during the war than they had done previously.

However, despite clerical qualms, the populace could not escape religion even at the cinema. Though the cultural historian, Jeffrey Richards, in his major work on cinema and the construction of British national identity[182] downplays the significance of the religious in films, choosing to only focus upon those with explicit religious content (such as *Pastor Hall* (1940), telling the story of Pastor Martin Niemöller, and *The Great Mr Handel* (1940), concerned with Handel's composition of the *Messiah*) in fact the visual diet people consumed at the cinema was replete with implicit as well as explicit religious imagery, motif and subject matter deployed (deliberately or unconsciously) by filmmakers and propagandists precisely because such themes resonated with the cinema-going public. Such filmic representations often characterised the cultural and religious virtues of the British, allying these to particular personality, gender or national traits. The fact that such discourses were being circulated (in particular those containing religious allusions) demonstrates the continued sway of religious protocols over national life. That cinemas were so well attended proves the likely relevance and influence of the discourses they contained.

178   Barnes Papers, EWB 12/1/586 'A Changing England', March 10, 1941.
179   Chapman, 1999, p.40.
180   Machin, 1998, p.118.
181   Chapman, 1999, p.41.
182   Richards, 1997, pp.100f. and p.110.

For instance, several wartime films strongly enunciated the message that this was a Christian nation fighting in defence of its Christian heritage supported by Christian spiritual means, whilst at the same time characterising the way in which one needed to be in order to prosecute the cause of war successfully. Whether produced in Britain or Hollywood, filmmakers constructed, or reflected, a notion of Britishness in which the Christian faith was allied to national identity, subtly and indirectly claiming divine mandate for Britain's cause thereby. Additionally, filmmakers depicted the heroes and heroines of such films as stoically resisting the evils that war brought, often being strengthened in their cause by the British Christian tradition. A very good example of this is the very popular wartime film *Mrs Miniver*.[183] A box-office hit in 1942, and the recipient of many awards, *Mrs Miniver* is, in essence, about a mother who holds her family together around the time of the post-Dunkirk blitz and the Battle of Britain, and is a mixture of social comment and myth-making concerning national identity. Significantly and evocatively, the film's beginning and ending are set in church. At the outbreak of war the characters are found worshipping together; the implicit message being that 'the parish church unites all Englishmen under the roof of God' and that, whatever their social class, churchgoing is the norm for the British.[184] The wartime task is, so the film's clergyman preaches at the beginning of the picture, to unite in the cause of the defence of freedom: this said, he dismisses the congregation. The combatant's sacrifice is not the focus for the film; instead, it is the civilian sacrifice and experience, especially that of women. The film utilises the symbolism of the English rose (qua all that is good about Englishness) personified in the character of the wife and mother Mrs Miniver: it is she who personally disarms a Nazi airman, acts as a moral force in village life, and watches over the vicissitudes of her airman son and the contribution her husband makes in the 'miraculous' recovery of the B.E.F from France. The implicit message of the film is that all that is good about England will endure beyond the suffering because Mrs Miniver (the

183   For an alternative discussion of the religious and social connotations of this film, see Brown, 2001, pp.83f.
184   Koppes and Black, 2000, p.227.

ideal English woman) and all like her will do their utmost to preserve it. Moreover the lead character of Mrs Miniver may be understood to be a type for that other motherly ideal, the Mary of Christian devotion, who similarly watched over the sufferings of her son and rejoiced in the promise of the resurrection. Mrs Miniver, who observes the sufferings of others, bears her own distress in a determined and patient manner. She embodies, the film implies, how women in particular need to be in wartime.[185]

The film concludes powerfully with a depleted group from the village meeting in the parish church, this time after it has been severely bombed. Defiantly the people worship on, counting the cost of their initial endeavours. The clergyman asks why these people had to suffer the loss of their loved ones, and explains: 'this is not only a war of soldiers in uniform. It is a war of the people – of all people – and it must be fought not only on the battlefield but in the cities *and in the heart* of every man, woman and child who loves freedom [...] This is a people's war.'[186] The camera then pans away from the clergyman to the view through the damaged church roof of fighter planes flying over, the people singing 'Onward, Christian Soldiers'. Given real-life accounts of similarly defiant continuance of worship in the face of damaged church property, as well as the recognition of the spiritual dimension of this conflict, it is clear that this fictional portrayal matched reality closely enough in many people's experience to make it all the more powerful. An abiding image, therefore, of this film and others, such as the Ealing film *The Bells Go Down*, is of a religious service in a bombed-out church.[187] Not only does this image contain the powerful identification of religion with the nation's cause, its defiance especially resonated with the lived experience of many of the faithful in Birmingham, and elsewhere, making it truly symbolic. The church in this context is used as a vehicle for the message that in war class distinctions are obsolete; the nation is being called to the altar of its national faith, and upon this altar sacrifices have to be made.

185   Brown, 2001, pp.83f.
186   Koppes and Black, 2000, p.229; my emphases.
187   Richards, 1997, p.110.

These themes of 'class-levelling' and 'sacrifice' are similarly depicted in the wartime film *Millions Like Us*. Supported in its production by the Ministry of Information, in a conjunction of documentary and fictional narrative forms, and filmed in an aircraft factory in Castle Bromwich, Birmingham, *Millions Like Us* follows the experiences of one woman's conscription to labour in an alien environment (a common experience which would, once again, have resonances with many of the cinema-going public). The lead character adapts to it and is portrayed as recognising that personal sacrifice is necessary if the war is to be won.[188] With an eye to the potential post-war social and political rewards of victory, the film exhibits the national readiness to recognise that a hoped-for good can only come by suffering, a notion which is identifiably Christian in origin. Like the aforementioned films, many others contained similar storylines depicting the sacrifices made in the war by people from a range of social classes. Films such as *In Which We Serve* propagated the notion that this was 'A People's War'; in reality, sacrifices were, of course, more unevenly borne.[189]

A Canterbury Tale, a relatively unsuccessful film at the box-office, consciously concerned itself with the values that were being fought for in this war. In the words of the filmmaker it was about 'explaining to the Americans and to our own people, the spiritual values and traditions we were fighting for'.[190] Its storyline depicts a series of tensions between the old and the new, between rural and city life, between the England of the past and the England of the future. The central characters, an American army sergeant, an English army sergeant, a land girl and a member of the landed gentry, wrestle via the storyline with the meaning of Englishness. Two important themes emerge, first that the spiritual is linked to the land and to the ordinary and everyday as depicted in the rural idyll. Secondly, that English identity is inextricably linked to religious identity; the journey of the film is the journey to this truth as depicted in the film's final shots of a service in Canterbury Cathedral, where the pilgrim characters meet and

188   Chapman, 1999, pp.56–59.
189   Calder, 1969, p.351ff.
190   O'Shaughnessy, 1995, p.42.

find the resolution of their dilemma. At Canterbury, the characters find themselves together at a cathedral service to consecrate a group of combatants and it is their consecration too. One, whose Sunday attendance at church has lapsed, plays the organ; all three end their 'pilgrimage' having clarified their futures in the self-discoveries made. Somehow, the future lies in a return to the past, a rediscovery of traditional values. This realisation has been facilitated by the war, as the film's director stated: 'Canterbury Cathedral itself can now be seen clearly as bomb damage has opened up new vistas.'[191] A national religion transports them to understanding things at a new level and in a renewed way, providing them with the spiritual *nous* to move on; hence, a heavenly choir of angels provides the background music for the end of the film. Mirroring such services as that broadcast on Palm Sunday, 2 April 1944, from St. Martin's, Birmingham, in which Jesus' triumphal entry into Jerusalem, 'God's Marching to Calvary', was likened to the expected invasion of Europe, and at which the hymn 'The Son of God goes forth to war' sounded like a battle cry, this film must have resonated with the actual experience of many of the populace.[192]

The 1942 Ealing film *Went the Day Well?* based upon a Graham Greene story, depicts the thwarted invasion of the fictional but idyllic English village of Bramley End.[193] In the film, Bramley End is infiltrated by a 'fifth columnist' squire who conspires with a Nazi invasion force to hold the village captive prior to a planned full invasion of Britain. The film is a classic portrayal of the bravery of civilians and of the brutality meted out equally at the front and on the home front in this war. Christianity is significantly shown to be at the heart of (English) village life, its day-to-day calendar and routine governed as they are by the Christian festivals (in this case Whitsuntide) and sacraments (in the film a marriage). Contrastingly, the invading forces are represented as irreverent (for example, by being

191 O'Shaughnessy, 1995, p.44.
192 Broadcast service from St. Martin's, Birmingham: 'God's marching to Calvary', 2 April, 1944. Service conducted by T. Guy Rogers and the address given by Alderman L.G. Alldridge.
193 For further comment see Calder, 1991, p.259.

prepared to operate on Sunday), disrespectful (for example, by writing notes whilst resting on the village's First World War memorial), and brutal (for example, by killing the elderly vicar of the village first, when he refuses to kneel to the German commanding officer). Moreover, the vicar's defiant last words are telling: 'you ask me to bow down before the forces of evil in the house of God [...] I will take no orders from those who are the enemies and oppressors of mankind.'[194] Thus, the film described a particular understanding of English character, intertwined this with Christian idiom, and projected it onto the cinema screen for the audience to see, imbibe, and be motivated by.

Humphrey Jennings, co-founder of Mass-Observation and war-time documentary filmmaker of the Crown Film Unit, also sought to encapsulate British identity in his films, and project the ideals being fought for. The predominant message of his documentaries was the nobility of the nation's cause as reflected by the efforts of the working classes in the service of the cause. This message was communicated using biblical language and Christian symbolism, thereby further reflecting the fact that wartime Britain regarded itself as 'identifiably and self-consciously Christian' and articulating its self-understanding by the religious resources it felt at ease in using.[195] For example, his short documentary of 1941, *The Heart of Britain*, showed ordinary people across the land coping with the ravages of the blitz. The closing shots of the film juxtapose several images underscored by a choir singing words from Handel's Hallelujah Chorus 'the Lord our God omnipotent reigneth'; shots of bombed-out Coventry, with defiant spires pointing upwards; the hills of England equally pointing to the skies, and a bomber taking off on its vengeful but righteous flight. The narrator determinedly booms, echoing the words of the Psalmist: 'people who sing like that in times like these are not easily beaten [...] a people slow to anger, not easily wrathed [*sic*], these people have the power to hit back'.[196]

---

194 *Went the Day Well?* (Ealing Studios, 1942): from the film's script.
195 Snape and Parker, 2001, p.400.
196 Psalms 86:15. *The Heart of Britain,* London: The Imperial War Museum/Central Office of Information, 1991.

In many ways then, the cinema both constructed and reflected the spiritual and religious values of British (more properly, English) society during the war. Many films' content and underlying motifs depicted the conscious and unconscious cultural self-understanding that Britain was a Christian nation, fighting a Christian cause, by Christian means. Thereby, not only were the cinema-going public engaged in escapism when 'going to the pictures', they were having a mirror of their own lives held up to them, thus perpetuating their cultural myths. How many people adhered to, or were taken in by, this mythology is hard to discern: probably, however, the Churches had less to fear from cinema than they realised, for many of the messages people were being offered were similar to those offered by clerics.

As well as being inspired and uplifted by films, the people were often comforted by what they saw. A Mass-Observation report of 1940 showed that films that dealt with the afterlife optimistically, and which presented loved ones as continuing their interest in living relatives, were a great success.[197] Just as many people had turned to Spiritualism during and after the First World War,[198] and some Protestant clergy had made recourse to praying for the dead in their pastoral ministrations,[199] so now films such as *Smilin' Through* and *The Three Comrades*, in which life goes on after death, provided a source of comfort and hope to the bereaved.[200]

Conclusion: Religion and Civilian Morale

J.G. Fuller, using Marshall's definition of morale, argues that it is

> The whole complex body of an army's thought: the way it feels about the soil and about the people from which it springs. The way it feels about their cause

---

197   Hazelgrove, 1999, p.415.
198   Hazelgrove, 2000, pp.13–41; Hazelgrove, 1999, p.408.
199   Wilkinson, 1978, pp.176ff.
200   Mass-Observation FR 2190E, *Spiritual Trends in Films*, December 1944.

and their politics as compared with other causes and other politics. The way it feels about its friends and allies, as well as its enemies. About its commanders [...] About food and shelter. Duty and leisure. Payday and sex. Militarism and civilianism. Freedom and slavery. Work and want. Weapons and comradeship. Bunk fatigue and drill. Discipline and disorder. Life and death. God and the devil.[201]

Translated to the civilian context, morale is additionally understood by Noakes to be 'a belief in the justice and necessity for the war effort, reflected in a willingness to undertake and continue to fight until victory is won, even in the face of great hardship'.[202] During the Second World War by various means religion informed the majority of those aspects identified by Fuller and Noakes as influential to morale. Popular religion shaped and sustained wartime spirits and, ultimately, bolstered morale in support of the war effort. Further evidence of the character and extent of Christianity's influence upon civilian life and wartime culture will be explored in what follows.

201   Marshall, S.L.A. quoted in Fuller, 1990, p.29.
202   Noakes, 1992, p.15.

3: The Churches' Ministry in Wartime Birmingham

> The life of the home clergy in war-time is subject to a new and ennobling condition. It is more like that of the Padre at the front. Instead of being called upon to help the anxious parishioners whose husbands and sons have gone to war, visiting and sustaining them and offering daily prayers for and with them, they may suddenly be called themselves to take a leading part with doctors, nurses and all good people in facing danger and calamity in their own neighbourhood, heartening and helping the stricken.[1]
>
> It is not for Christian clergy, either from patriotic or from social motives, to advocate military enterprises. Their duty is to minister to the suffering and to the bereaved and to pray for peace.[2]

> Only by turning to God through penance and prayer shall we be able to stem the flood of ruthless barbarism which has burst over the world and to win the victory of right over might [...] There is no one who cannot wield the weapon of prayer; as individuals and as a nation we must first put ourselves right with God and pledge ourselves to be more loyal to Him.[3]

By the end of the Second World War, the blitz on Birmingham had resulted in some 2,241 fatalities. On one night alone, which turned out to be the city's worst, that of the 19 and 20 November 1940, there were over 1,353 people killed or injured.[4] As well as coping with civilian casualties on a scale unknown in modern conflicts prior to this, Birmingham's people had endured the trauma of severe bombardment and incendiary fires, the stress and disruption brought on by war work, the privations of rationing, and the loss of loved ones to 'safer' areas and to the armed forces. What were Birmingham's Churches and Church workers doing during this time of crisis; what involvement did the clergy have in wartime events, and how did they rationalise these events for the people they sought to serve? How did the Churches

1   Woodward and Blackburne, 1939, p.10.
2   Bishop Barnes to the Diocesan Conference of 10 June 1942: Barnes Papers, EWB 12/1/603.
3   *The Parish Magazine of St Alban's, Bordesley*, June 1940.
4   Black, 1957, p.88.

respond to the perceived needs of wartime and how did they exercise pastoral care?

Padres on the Home Front

The experience of First World War chaplains informed to a considerable extent the ministerial responses of the Churches on the home front during the Second World War both in Birmingham and elsewhere. The deployment of patterns of ministry learnt in the Great War to the civilian context in the Second depended upon a number of factors. Amongst these were the extent to which the lessons learnt by First World War padres were disseminated in the interwar period; it also depended on the post-war careers and influence of padres, and the degree to which they became role models for more junior clergy. *The Church in the Furnace*, the collected reflections of seventeen Anglican chaplains published towards the end of the First World War, exemplarises the desire of a considerable core of chaplains to shape the Church of England's future ministry, taking into account the epiphanic insights gained by them at the Front.[5] 'When the Priests Come Home', wrote Kenneth Kirk, a Senior Chaplain to the Forces in 1917 and bishop of Oxford by the time of the Second World War, few could 'be content [...] to fall into the old grooves again'.[6] Indeed, many clergy did return inspired by a new perception of the nature of British religion as they had seen it exemplified by the soldier, and with an enhanced sense of how the Christian religion could best be communicated.[7] There were lessons to be learnt by the Church across the gamut of its life and it was imperative that the Church of England's worship, theology, mission, ministry, and the training of its clergy be shaped by the wisdom gleaned from the chaplains' furnace-like trial. Naturally, the impact of their garnered wisdom was particularly influential when

5   Macnutt, 1917.
6   Kirk, K.E., *When the Priests Come Home,* in Macnutt, 1917, p.409.
7   Kirk, K.E., *When the Priests Come Home,* in Macnutt, 1917, pp.410ff.

it was embodied in the post-war ministries of particular clerics. Many First World War chaplains found themselves in influential positions during the interwar period and in the years of the Second World War, and were therefore in a position to remodel the ministries of others according to their own. For example, F.R. Barry, a Great War chaplain and, during the Second World War, bishop of Southwell, led an experimental initiative at Knutsford in Cheshire during the interwar years, which trained ex-soldiers for ordination.[8] Initially this work took in 200 ex-servicemen as candidates for ministry, thus relieving the Church of its immediate shortage of ordinands and responding instantly to the post-war demand for a recognisably different kind of cleric.[9] Similarly, B.K. Cunningham, chaplain and trainer of chaplains in the First World War, became principal of the Anglican theological college Westcott House in 1919.[10] Writing later of the future of clerical training in the Church of England, he lauded the efforts of those First World War padres who saw it as their duty to deal with the recreative and educational as well as the spiritual needs of the soldiers, arguing that in future the Church 'must strive to bring into its service the best of English manhood', and that the characteristic 'English Gentleman in Holy Orders' had proved of little use as a chaplain and would have no place in the church of the future.[11] Thus, by the direct influence of individuals such as these, the wisdom and experience of First World War chaplains was diffused among a younger generation of priests of the Church of England. Significantly, one of the many padres who came home altered by their experiences at the front was Guy Rogers, rector of Birmingham during the Second World War. At the end of his time as chaplain at the front, he resolved to 'put into practice what I believed the Spirit of God was teaching me' in his future theology and ministry.[12] Another exemplary cleric with regard to the application of his chaplaincy experiences was Francis Drinkwater, whose hard-won

---

8   Bullock, 1976, p.80. For the careers of some other First World War chaplains see Wilkinson, 1978, p.276.
9   Wilkinson, 1978, pp.277–280.
10   Wilkinson, 1978, p.276.
11   Cunningham, 1926, pp.84 and 76.
12   Rogers, 1956, p.130.

lessons as a Roman Catholic padre were fastidiously applied to his parochial duties as parish priest of the Holy Family, Small Heath, when the 'blitz' on Birmingham came. These clerics, and many others, senior in age as well as stature and influence by the outbreak of the Second World War, modelled wartime ministry for their less experienced ministerial colleagues in Birmingham. As this chapter progresses it will be demonstrated how they, and others, were influenced, directly and vicariously, by the pastoral context of the First World War: how they sought to pattern their wartime ministry second-time-around according to the functions and practices of the padres of the Great War.

The qualities of character and the necessary activities of the Great War padre gradually emerged as they were shaped by the painful realities of trench ministry. When it came to the second conflict, the clergy had a pattern to work from in defining their role. As the civilian wartime context was rapidly recognised to be effectively another front line, so parallels could be drawn between these two environments. Thus, Harry Blackburne's book *The Clergy in War-time* typified the drawing out of these parallels. In his book Blackburne, an Assistant Chaplain General in the First World War and Dean of Bristol in the Second, outlined the envisaged pastoral priorities and the ideal persona of the cleric in the predicted conditions of blitz ministry. Interestingly, they echo B.K. Cunningham's assertion that effective ministry in such situations depended upon a meeting of practical as well as spiritual needs. Blackburne's ideas describe eminently the wartime ideal, and thereby set the scene for the actual examples of pastoral practice that follow. Firstly, Blackburne stressed the need to combine a concern for the spiritual wellbeing as well as the physical needs of one's flock. It is not sufficient to be a jolly stalwart:

> For the first time in the history of our country, the whole of the clergy are on active service […] the part we are called upon to fulfil […] can be best summed up in two words: 'Good Samaritan' […] to render thorough service, personal service and unselfish service […] Our work is spiritual [not] being merely a cheerful soul [nor] being so absorbed in purely spiritual concerns that everything material is ruled out […] know how to sterilise a wound or apply a tourniquet […] make ourselves acquainted with all the ARP services.

Secondly, Blackburne urged upon the minister the need to be visible, and to be a known, familiar and affable presence.[13] He recommended the enlistment of helpers and the use of the resources of the local Church. He advised about the tone of preaching. He goes on:

> know and be known [...] a friendly visit to the posts allotted to wardens would be in nearly every case warmly welcomed[; give] the free use of our parish rooms and halls [...] find time to visit [the] lonely souls and give them the encouragement they need [...] we should enlist the help of a few trusted lay folk in making this visiting regular and widespread [...] tell them all the good news possible [...] In our preaching and in our ministrations the note of courage and confidence in the Spirit of God must be paramount, though the note of penitence will not be forgotten.

Finally, Blackburne provided explicit guidance concerning ministry during and after an air raid. He not only suggested how the minister might help, but said that he ought to:

> [During air raids] go as soon as possible to the scene of any disaster [...] give a clear and definite lead in checking any signs of panic [...] by our own behaviour and demeanour. The quiet and efficient manner in which we go about our work will do more than anything to preserve the morale of the people all around [...] act calmly [without] haste or fussiness [...] keep silent [be] a quiet, self-effacing man of God. [At times] what will be welcomed will be [...] certain suitable and short passages of Scripture and simple prayers [...] the allay[ing of] fears [...] be ready to cheer and console [in a] quiet, unhurried way [...] be serene [...] pray silently for the passing soul. [Amongst the duties of the clergy will be administration of] the Blessed Sacrament [...] to break the news [of death] to make the necessary arrangements for the funeral [become] a familiar and trusted friend.[14]

As this chapter progresses it will be demonstrated that in Birmingham the qualities and practices urged by Blackburne upon wartime clergy

---

13   A recommendation echoed in advice given by 1940s psychologist Fred Bennett Julian that the presence of a familiar authority figure helped to calm people. Cf. Bourke, 2005, p.243.

14   Woodward and Blackburne, 1939, pp.11–29.

(those of meeting the priestly – spiritual and sacramental – and the diaconal – physical and material – needs of people) were epitomized.[15]

Despite Christianity's arguably anti-war message, clerics were often complicit in boosting the wartime morale of Birmingham's people.[16] Just as the role of the chaplain was recognised to be crucial in sustaining morale amongst the soldiers at the front in the First World War, so it became clear that the activities of the Churches and the daily rounds of its clerics were effectual in galvanising a positive frame of mind amongst the civilian populace during the Second World War.[17] Morale, that somewhat insubstantial quality of communal psychology, was partly influenced by religious and quasi-religious sentiment. It was also determined by the clergy's direct practical, and indirect ideological, interventions during the different stages and events of the war. Morale, argued the Methodist Sidney Berry, was intimately connected to people's spiritual wellbeing. Therefore, the minister's role was critical in order to 'keep the spirit of triumph indomitable through the warring tests [and maintain] a deep faith that the things for which we strive are of eternal value'.[18] Hence, it is unsurprising that, amongst the many official Government documents reporting on the state of civilian morale in Birmingham during the war years, the conduct of the clergy and the Churches is often reported as significant.[19] Moreover, the Government set out to exploit any influence clergy might have on morale via its Ministry of Information [MOI], which established a Religions Division at the outset of war, the purpose of which at home was to impart a 'real conviction of the Christian contribution to our civilisation and of the essential anti-Christian character of Nazism'.[20] Throughout the war, the Religions

15   Wilkinson, 1981, p.254 mentions the tensions that chaplains sometime felt between these two aspects of their role.

16   Wilkinson, 1981, p.254 explores the paradoxical character of the clergy role here.

17   My thanks to Michael Snape for giving me sight of an unpublished manuscript detailing the extent to which the First World War padres were deemed to influence morale by the military hierarchy of the period.

18   Hoover, 1999, p.105.

19   See, for example, Public Record Office, HO 192/1205.

20   McLaine, 1979, p.151.

Division of the Ministry of Information churned out its weekly publication *The Spiritual Issues of the War*. This organ officially informed the clergy of the situation of European Christianity vis-à-vis the Nazi regime. It reported the views of the clergy and the Church press on these matters, especially where the clergy favoured the war effort. The stated purpose of this publication was outlined early on as 'supplying [the reader] in convenient form [...] items of news, bearing on the moral and spiritual issues of the war, which may be of special interest to you [the clergy], and may be useful to you in your work'.[21] Anything quoted was obviously viewed as profitable to the purposes of the MOI and therefore published to promote a particular brand of clerical thinking. Accordingly, the Birmingham Quaker H.G. Wood was cited as someone who not only recognised the influence that the clergy had on morale, but saw it as the clergy's responsibility to sustain it.[22] Additionally, it produced such starkly ideological tracts as *Put Ye on the Armour of God*, a publication aimed at Catholics which represented the Second World War in clear-cut tones as an out-and-out spiritual crusade. Nazism is the devilish enemy of Christianity, it urged, which Catholics on the home front can only defeat by a whole-hearted effort:

There is no time for dalliance amidst the roses of our personal interest, only for the Cross and the rosary round the sword hilt. We must fight [...] a holy fight [...] with a clean heart and in the spirit of our religion [...] The acceptance of sacrifice [...] cheerfully borne [...] for those who cannot fight for God with the sword [...] it is by prayer and service that we must justify our faith. As the hosts of paganism pour against us [...] so should our prayers storm Heaven [...] Our passion should be more, not less than [...] paganism [and its] mechanistic gods [...] There will be dangers from bomb attack [...] fears to conquer [...] It is for us [...] to use them to temper our spirit and to purify us so that we can add them to the total sacrifice and effort. Let our daily lives [...] be as complete a sacrifice as those of our fighting men [...] Let us bear our troubles cheerfully and willingly for the sake of God's cause.[23]

21   *The Spiritual Issues of the War*, No.7, 18 Nov, 1939.
22   *The Spiritual Issues of the War*, No. 33, 15 June 1940.
23   MOI, July 1940.

In a similar vein, the government projected the importance of the blitz ministry of the clergy and the critical import of religion to the British way of life in two propaganda films circulated by the Ministry of Information during the bombardment. This was no doubt meant as a stimulus to national morale, by implying that the character of British religious life was qualitatively different to that of the enemy. In *Neighbours Under Fire* and *Religion and the People*, religiously-motivated practical help is depicted as a spontaneous and implicit part of the British way of life. *Neighbours Under Fire* described itself in its opening frames as 'a record of human kindliness during the first weeks of the Blitzkrieg'.[24] In the film we see the patriarchal figure of the parson orchestrating an impressive caring operation. He greets the people made homeless by the bombing, whilst his helpers welcome them with tea and sympathy, guiding them through the mass of bureaucracy which leads to official help and eventual rehousing. The people are naturally, in the director's portrayal of them, deferential and grateful for the help offered. The final scenes of this brief film see the parson conducting the people in a spirit-lifting chorus of 'Down at the Old Bull and Bush'. Moreover, he prays with them, Moses-like, as a Passover of bombs drowns out his words and the people sleep protected by his presence and blessing. The important, morale-sustaining message is that this people are protected from harm by the fatherly and sacred presence of the parson and by the morality of the nation's cause. The implication of the film is that this is a Christian nation fighting a Christian cause with the full support of the Churches. A second MOI film *Religion and the People* reinforces these points. This film examined four situations of practical religious service from contrasting denominational and religious positions: Anglican, Free Church, Roman Catholic and Jewish. The promoted notion is that, for the British, religion and its attendant moral implications are natural and instinctive. The film's message is that the mutual care shown stems from what may be described as a patriotic faith, a faith that exists as an intrinsic part of the rest of the British way of life. Religion is interwoven with British culture, natural to the British mindset; not forced, but spontaneous; not persecuted, but encouraged; it is popular,

24   From the film's narration.

diverse, widespread and flourishing. In itself, it tolerates diversity, encourages human growth, especially fostering physical activity and welfare. According to the film, British religion cultivates mutual care, especially the nurture and care of the vulnerable. In the context of the war effort the hidden message is, of course, that this good is worth preserving and worthy of the fight in which the population is engaged.

Away from the propaganda portrayals, what can be said of the realities of the caring ministry offered by the clergy and the Churches of Birmingham in wartime? In what ways did their ministry mirror that of their First World War predecessors, and how can it be said to have shaped the mood of the people of the city at this critical time? Certainly, by the time that the worst for the city was over, clerics had won admiration for their efforts. For instance, the Anglican bishop of Birmingham, Ernest Barnes, thought that his clergy had done their pastoral duty. In an address to the clergy of June 1941 he lauded their efforts: 'during last winter the clergy, with very few exceptions, set a fine example of courage and endurance. The way in which clergymen, often no longer in the prime of life, lived and worked in heavily bombed parishes, deserves warm admiration.'[25]. Likewise, archbishop Williams, the Roman Catholic archbishop of Birmingham, expressed his gratitude in a circular letter to the clergy of the archdiocese: 'We gladly take this opportunity of thanking the clergy for the bravery and self-sacrifice they have shown and are showing during night raids, not only in looking after the people, but also in protecting the diocesan property entrusted to their care.' [26] What actual incidents of service lie behind the praise offered by bishops Barnes and Williams?

Before proceeding, it is important to remember two things. Firstly, that the pastoral task of the Churches and of Christian organisations in wartime was not exercised exclusively by clerics. Hence, evidence of the laity's involvement in these wartime acts of care is interwoven with the service offered by clerics. Secondly, whatever the lofty ideals of Blackburne and others, it is to be remembered that clerics are subject to the same sentiments of fear, confusion, panic and boredom as anyone else. The mood of the country

25   Barnes Papers, EWB 12/1/588, 11 June 1941: 'Address to the Diocesan Clergy'.
26   Archbishop Williams' Papers, *Ad Clericum*, 19 March 1941.

at the outset of the conflict was an amalgam of gloom and foreboding. The government had extrapolated from the experience of the First World War, and had envisaged that during the early months of another conflict deaths would run into millions.[27] The authorities had calculated that the worst would come from bombs and gas attacks and taught the people to prepare for this by issuing them with protective masks and blackout instructions. These pessimistic statistics proved, thankfully, to be a gross overestimation and the prospect of gassing did not come to fruition. However, the sense of apprehension brought on by these necessary preparations affected all. Uncertainty invoked fear, which later gave way to a sense of resignation and then realism, amongst broad swathes of the populace. In the event, incendiary bombs did much more damage than high explosives in Birmingham. The frame of mind of people at the time was captured and recalled by a clergyman sixty years on, his words demonstrating the intensity of emotions felt and the sense of unreality into which the war erupted:

> We felt [at the outset], that all the cities would be blown up together [...] Our ideas were in many ways uncertain and ill informed. And so we just went on with our ordinary life as far as we could [...] whereas up till then you felt 'Well I've got certain control over my life I can decide': in many ways, in many little ways, it was decided for us, even what we did to help people [...] Half of you felt that Chamberlain can go and pull this off [...] I remember that night when he came back it was 'peace for our time'. We were having a beetle drive [...] and everybody turned up [...] the atmosphere was terrific, a sort of emotion of relief, war can be avoided; half of you knew it couldn't, half of you knew it had been bought at a price [...] I remember the first raids [...] we'd been thinking all this Armageddon and [they were] only small. Of course, that didn't last very long [and] then we were into the big raids.[28]

Notwithstanding the lessons to be drawn from the previous war, the context of the Second World War on the home front was to prove in many ways unique, and the particular wartime eventualities were to make for a steep learning curve for the particular individuals involved.

27   Harrison, 1976, p.24.
28   Interview with Canon William Edward Brooke, May 2000.

Evacuation and Dispersal

> Father Joseph Degan of Swadlincote, and Father Cyril Horspool, of Staveley, Derbyshire are appealing for prayer books, hymn books and rosaries for some 300 Birmingham children evacuated to villages in South Derbyshire. 50% are weekly communicants and may walk two and a half miles from their new homes to Mass at 8 a.m.[29]

On 1 September 1939 and the days following, some 42,000 of those considered the city's most vulnerable were evacuated from Birmingham by train to the 'safer' areas of rural Warwickshire, Worcestershire, Gloucestershire, Herefordshire and Leicestershire.[30] It was the hope of the authorities that by shipping women, children and those most frail away from the enemy's attack the population would be spared the worst of the envisaged holocaust. The expected did not arise and gradually, throughout the early months of the war, which came to be known as 'the Phoney War', many of the evacuated drifted back to their homes and families. The clergy played a limited part in the shepherding programme that took place, and this was to their later regret, for the episode threw up a number of issues and challenges. Locally, evacuation depleted congregations, leaving a vacuum within which to exercise their ministry. If one were to care, to whom was this care to be directed? In the circumstances, the clergy went on ministering to the remnant, keeping services going, as a defiant symbol of the objective of preserving what was of value; keeping life as normal as possible. Secondly, the evacuation of women and children presented Church communities with the wartime duty of caring for those either detached or semi-detached from them. Thus, Benjamin Clarke, during the war years curate of Erdington and then vicar of St. Matthias, Birmingham, remembered that when 'many of the children and the headmaster of the school were evacuated [he wrote] letters enquiring about the children whose parents had not heard from them.'[31] This

29 Notice in *The Universe*, 10 November 1939.
30 Chinn, 1996, pp.47–56.
31 Questionnaire Response: The Reverend Benjamin Blanchard Clarke, March 2000.

obligation to keep in touch with those scattered abroad was acted upon by a number of Birmingham's Churches. Many sent their parish magazines to servicemen and kept up a constant flow of correspondence with the dispersed flock, reporting news, whenever it was known, to folk at home. Sometimes, this correspondence acted to reassure those in the forces that stability of life was being maintained at home. A letter from E.H. Hardy, Methodist Minister at Coventry Road, instances this:

> Dear Fred [...] recalling my own experience in the last war, I know how much one can feel cut off from the old associations and almost forgotten [...] I think of your wonderful wife, for instance. When the day's work is done and dear little Philip is gathered in, there's the housework to do. I called one evening before Christmas and she was almost spring cleaning the kitchen. How cheerful she was and contented and I wished you could have been there just to know. Your funny little chap made me draw aeroplanes, ships, cars [...] As I go about I am humbled by the brave hearts that carry on, buoyed up by their hopes, their love and prayers. Family life means more than ever before and if that deepens and develops we may well build better than our parents did.[32]

It was occasionally the function of the ordained minister to insist upon marital fidelity, and to reassure husbands and wives separated by the war that distant partners were remaining faithful. John Jackson, curate of Bordesley, then of Sparkhill, in wartime recalled:

> One of the fears when we went to see certain wives was were their husbands behaving themselves properly? They had certain information given to them in one form or another which I think in many cases was complete rumour. They had fears that their husbands may have been playing a bit truant and we then had to get in touch with the men concerned and give a reassuring message to their wives that everything was perfectly alright.[33]

Despite clerical interventions, British divorce rates due to adultery rose by 100 per cent each year of the war.[34] In the stressful conditions of

---

32   Letter from Rev. E.H. Hardy, of Coventry Road Methodist Church, 11 January 1944.
33   Interview with Prebendary John Jackson, April 2000.
34   Machin, 1998, p.114.

wartime, peacetime sexual mores were sometimes, unsurprisingly perhaps, suspended.

Sometimes correspondence with the distant flock deliberately
conjured up images of home and reminded the combatant of the land
that was being fought for. For example, the minister of Erdington
Congregational Church wrote in one of his numerous circulars to those
in the forces:

> As you will see form the address [sic], I am on holiday and enjoying it
> immensely. The country round here is very beautiful – rich and rolling land,
> running up to a fine ridge of hills […] The little villages lie placid and at peace,
> with their quaint red cottages and Norman or early English Churches, built of
> local red stone. This is rich country, and beautiful too, and mellow with history.
> It is the England we are fighting for, and you who are on the high seas, or in the
> blistering heat of the Middle East or Tunisia, or Sicily, let me tell you that this
> England is still here, still secure, as lovely as ever, and the plums are ripening
> and the apples hanging on the trees. You may keep your figs and lemons and
> melons and oranges. We have our fruit in England now […] When 'C.L.100'
> was written, we were just nicely through the blitz […] We ought to be (and I'm
> sure we are) very thankful to God for the great change in our conditions and
> prospects […] One day, please God, you will come back to us and put all your
> initiatives into the building of a better world.[35]

For those Christian communities whose distinctive identity and
future numerical security most depended upon the nurturing of the
young in the faith, for example the Roman Catholic community,
distance from the flock was of gravest concern. In a circular letter to
schools at the beginning of the evacuation Archbishop Williams
recognised that evacuation was 'unavoidable' but he feared that
children might be billeted with non-Catholics leading to 'some
difficulty in the observance of the Sunday obligation and Friday
abstinence, and [that] there may be danger of our children going to
non-Catholic places of worship'. It was the duty of teachers and clergy,
he stated, to 'guard the children against these dangers […] seek[ing]
guidance and counsel from the priest of the place in all matters
affecting the spiritual welfare of the children'.[36] Williams's fears were

---

35 Erdington Congregational Church, July 1943, C.L. [circular letter] 200.
36 Archbishop Williams's Papers, *Ad Clericum*, 1 September 1939.

justified, for the sensibilities of the authorities were clearly not awake to the diverse needs of religious communities, as was shown elsewhere in the country also.[37] In a further letter to clergy of 8 June 1940 Williams urged that if children could not be billeted close to a Catholic community then evacuation should be resisted.[38] Father Charles Heurtley, a Roman Catholic priest of the Birmingham Oratory, complained in January 1941 of the specific difficulties encountered: 'our evacuated children are distributed in three villages near Ashby [...] they are happy and well cared for. The trouble is that the foster parents try to take them to a Protestant Chapel on Sunday evenings.'[39] In a similarly insensitive way, Jewish children were often lodged with non-Jewish households who had little concept of the particularities of the faith. As we have seen, one Birmingham Jewish man recalled that when he and his sisters were evacuated to rural Leicestershire, their first meal was one of roast pork.[40] These blunders on the part of the host families and the authorities indicated a lack of planning, foresight and consultation with the religious communities of Britain in the lead up to the evacuation. There appears to have been a general assumption of uniformity, both social and religious, amongst the general population: and it turned out neither was the case.[41] Commenting upon the survey *Evacuation and the Churches* published in 1941, S.M. Gibbard, Chaplain of St. Boniface College, Warminster, wrote that the 'chief defects' of the evacuation procedures were in the sporadic consultation of the local Churches and the Churches' uneven response: there needed to be a more 'thorough survey of the reception areas.'[42] There was, he noted, little thought given to a suitable match between the home and host families and the moral and spiritual welfare of the

37   Machin, 1998, p.113.
38   Archbishop Williams's papers, circular letter, 8 June 1940; Calder, 1969, p.41 (which notes that spiritual dangers were often considered greater than the physical dangers of wartime).
39   *The Oratory Parish Magazine*, January 1941.
40   Interview with Martin Davies, October 1999.
41   Angus Calder explores the apparent clash of cultures that occurred during the evacuation period when social differences between city and rural areas were uncovered: Calder, 1969, pp.35–50.
42   Gibbard, 1941, p.42.

children had been disregarded.[43] The overlooked possibility, he continued, is that 'the most serious ill-effects of the evacuation will be psychological.'[44] Yes, there were some notable examples of hospitality on the part of the host Churches, but he deplored the fact that 'a third of the Churches in reception areas made no real attempt to welcome evacuees.'[45] Gibbard's article implied that religious communities felt estranged from evacuation measures, seeing the resultant blunders as resulting from, and emblematic of, the rift between Church and society. Consequently, the report was insistent that the Christian faith be returned to its proper status: 'A British victory will be useless without a rebirth of Christianity at home and abroad [...] the Church must press for a genuine recognition of this by the State in its legislation and administration.'[46] Arguably, therefore, Gibbard's wishes prefigure the sentiments of the legislation in relation to Religious Education in the 1944 Education Act, of which more will be said later.

Ministry to the Air-raid Shelters

It is lamentable that in this twentieth century after Christ we should have to take refuge from the ferocity of our fellow-men by burrowing into the earth.[47]

One of the most demanding tasks of wartime ministry was the care of those who sought safety from aerial bombardment in air-raid shelters. Sheltering was a new and distressing experience endured by the majority of people, either in a purpose-built public shelters, converted basements, or with family and neighbours in an Anderson outdoor shelter or a Morrison indoor type. Being hurriedly crammed into dark,

43   Gibbard, 1941, p.43.
44   Gibbard, 1941, p.44.
45   Gibbard, 1941, p.45.
46   Gibbard, 1941, p.46.
47   *Carrs Lane Journal*, Vol. XXXVII, No. 9, September 1939.

sometimes damp places, with strangers as well as neighbours, for indefinite periods of time, with time to kill, as well as the prospect of being killed, and the seemingly unending noise of anti-aircraft fire and exploding bombs, could not have been anything except distressing. Responding to the impact of these adverse conditions was primarily the responsibility of the civil defence, though more often than not lay Christian and clerical figures were present in official and unofficial capacities. Though Bishop Barnes did not encourage his clergy to be air-raid wardens, some undertook ARP training and were issued with armbands to identify them to other workers and to the needy.[48] The leading London Methodist minister, Leslie Weatherhead, brought the work of the minister in the conditions of the blitz to life in a book that helped encourage sympathy with Britain's cause in the United States:

> Last night my elder son and I went on duty for the local air-raid warden in order that he might get what chance there is of a night's sleep. The siren [...] wailed its melancholy message at dusk, and the 'all clear' sounded just before six the next morning. All through the long, hideous night the din went on. In my neighbourhood, five people were killed near one end of the road and three near the other. Thousands are homeless [...] every evening multitudes take a three-penny ticket on the underground railway, and [...] stay there all night [...] they lie down [some] stand up all night, and then, hollow-eyed and weary, go to work the next morning [...] The work of the minister of religion can be easily imagined. He must 'carry on' as far as possible, though daily his difficulties increase. People need God as never before [...] people are so starved of sleep, so tired of journeys, that who can blame them if they stay at home [...] Many ministers are doing splendid service in air-raid shelters. Some of the shelters are beneath Churches, and ministers have found that they have a resident congregation after the early afternoon! [...] All ministers find their visiting heart-breaking. I recall an afternoon in which I visited a paralysed boy, a family of ten with hardly a room left to them by the fires that raged all round them, two maiden ladies whose little business has almost come to an end through the war, and a girl with both feet trapped by her falling house. Another girl from my Church, bravely doing her duty as an A.R.P. warden, had her arm blown off by an explosion outside the warden's post [...] My telephone [...] rings [...] A doctor [...] asks whether I will go to such and such hospital [to see a] badly injured girl. Her sister was killed last night. Her mother has not yet been found [...] Her father is dead also. I must try to comfort her [...] day follows day in

48   Barnes Papers, EWB 8/29/476. Wilkinson, 1986, p.234. See also Williams's Papers, *Ad Clericum*, 24 August 1939.

agony, sorrow and suffering [but] Hitler will never beat the spirit of the British people [...] And though the price they are asked to pay is hard and heavy [...] they would rather lose their dear ones [than live in] a land impoverished [under] a mad tyrant [...] I believe in Britain's cause. [49]

Moreover, Mass-Observation recorded the typically chaotic life of one shelter in London in the early part of the war. This description provides an illustration of the kind of conditions people endured in the shelters themselves and the tension which those engaged in pastoral care had to deal with:

At 8:15 [...] Already about 35 people have crowded in. Some are sitting on stools or deckchairs, some standing [There is] a colossal crash [...] the shelter itself shaking [...] an ARP helper, a nurse, begins singing lustily [then] Three more tremendous crashes. Women scream and there is a drawing-together physically [...] a feeling of breath being held: everyone waiting for more. No more [...] Here the ARP helper tries once again to start some singing. 'Shut your bleedin row!' shouts a man of 50. 'My God,' says a young artisan, 'I want to laugh!' Around midnight, a few people in this shelter are asleep but every time a bomb goes off, it wakes them. Several women are crying [...] Two men are arguing about the whereabouts of the last bomb [...] Suddenly a girl cries out [...] 'It's no good! I'm ill! I think I'm going to die!' [...] women with deck chairs are lying back [...] rocking and groaning. Woman of 60: 'If we ever live through this night, we have the good God above to thank for it!' Friend: 'I don't know if there is one, or he shouldn't let us suffer like this.' When the all-clear goes, about 4:30 a.m., there is a groan of relief. But as soon as the first people get outside the shelter, there are screams of horror at the sight of the damage [...] People push and scramble out of the shelter [...] there is a wild clamour of shouting, weeping, and calling for absent relatives [...] Others sob and cry and cling to one another. One woman throws a fit, another is sick.[50]

Though an extreme example, this report is illustrative of the wide range of reactions to the experience of the grim realities of sheltering. Amongst the range of reactions were, more surprisingly, the ones that found shelter life preferable. People who came from 'solitary bed-sitting rooms [...] found that they could spend their evenings [...] surrounded by company [Some] shelters [...] maintained [...] a family

49   Weatherhead, 1940, pp.vi–xii.
50   Harrison, 1976, pp.59–61.

atmosphere' and therefore people were reluctant to leave these communities behind after the war.[51]

Churches were often used as air-raid shelters, not only because of their structural strength but also, perhaps, because of the religious reassurance of sheltering in a place deemed to be sacred, apparently made secure by providential oversight. Of course, in practice, bombs fell upon the righteous as well as the unrighteous, and many of the churches of Birmingham were badly damaged or obliterated during the blitz.[52] One converted church was the so-called 'Tin Tabernacle', Dyson Hall, a mission church in Aston. During the war its facilities were used extensively, though on two occasions it suffered damage from 'near misses.' Its basement became a public shelter and rest centre, serving food and refreshment to people in the local community. Its rooms were used to train first-aiders and by the education authority as a schoolroom.[53]

Ministry to the shelters, dubbed by some as 'Parsons' Particulars', does not appear to have been centrally organised by the denominations of Birmingham, though it was in other cities.[54] Instead, the city relied upon the initiative of clergy and lay volunteers to respond as each local Church saw fit. However, Archbishop Williams did attempt to organise the work of his priests by allocating particular clergy to particular first-aid posts dotted around the city to minister to injured and dying Catholics during air raids.[55] Many clergy gave ministry to public shelters priority, especially those clerics who ministered in areas that suffered most from the enemy's attention. In these, mainly central, wards, living and working conditions were amongst Birmingham's worst. Here, factories combined with tightly packed terraced properties to create lethal bombing conditions, and amidst this the populace relied upon public shelters in the main for their safety. The importance of the clergy's ministry in these conditions was widely recognised, and later

51 Calder, 1969, p.338; Wilkinson, 1986, p.276.
52 Some 15,000 ecclesiastical buildings nationally according to Wilkinson (1986, p.275).
53 Mass-Observation, TC 66/1/C.
54 Ziegler, 1998, p.202; Woodward and Blackburne, 1939, pp.14–15 for the example of Bristol, whose Churches organised care together.
55 Archbishop Williams's Papers, *Ad Clericum*, 18 September 1939.

138

celebrated. The rector of Birmingham, Guy Rogers, as well as being an air-raid warden, had a regular shelter-visiting routine, and was a well-known presence in the public shelters in the market area of central Birmingham. In a photograph accompanying the official history of the 'blitz' upon St. Martin's Church, he is depicted conducting the watch night service in the Market's air-raid shelter on 31 December 1941.[56] The people have song sheets and Union Jack bunting adorns the space. In another case, the ministry of 'Tommy' Bevan of the Digbeth Institute became legendary amongst his colleagues and the wider community. His dedication to shelter duty was exemplary, though it led to the eventual failure of his health. An ARP warden recalled his efforts at a memorial service in Bevan's honour:

> He was always to be found amongst his flock doing his duty night after night, never stopping one moment to think of himself and what the strain of such labours might one day mean to his own health. When the blitz was at its worst and bombs were falling a few yards away sounds of laughter could be heard, in response to his jokes; and later the strains of familiar hymns coming up from the cellars as he held his evening service. He was a true watchman of the night and never relaxed until the 'all clear' sounded.[57]

Such dedication, though not regularly eulogised or made noteworthy, was typical across the denominations. For instance, as an ex-military chaplain Father Francis Drinkwater, Roman Catholic parish priest of The Holy Family, Small Heath, remained with his civilian 'troops' throughout the worst of Birmingham's trial. Just as he might have done at the 'Front', he refused to abandon his position even when the presbytery and the church were badly damaged on the night of Friday 22 November 1940. This did not keep him from returning to his parish duties once essential repairs had been completed. As the blitz on Birmingham continued, the church became a target once more. When the presbytery became uninhabitable, Drinkwater took instead to sleeping in the vestry. In a letter of August 1941, Archbishop Williams

56   Birmingham Parish Church: *St. Martin's, Bull Ring. Blitz, April 10, 1941.*
57   Recollections of an air-raid warden from *Rev. T.J. Bevan 1919–1944: A Tribute.*

pleaded with Drinkwater to think of his own health; after all, a church could be repaired, but: 'what about repairs to the Parish Priest?'[58]

The clergy and Church workers of Birmingham's Churches were a regular and visible presence in the city's air-raid shelters and during the daytime respite. Percy Pierce, the vicar of the city-centre parish of St. James's, Ashted, recorded the breadth of duties undertaken by its Church Army and ministerial staff in his parish magazine of December 1940:

> Captain Nichols has been on duty as shelter warden every night with hardly a break since August 8th. Captain Gray, who is fully qualified as an ambulance worker is on duty most nights at the casualty clearing station [...] Sister Murdoch is we know, a very welcome visitor at the homes of the aged and invalids every morning after an air-raid, at the same time carrying on her work amongst the girls and women. We have difficulty preventing her from overwork, but she works very hard indeed [...] and she is always bright and cheerful. The vicar makes a nightly round of various shelters taking with him his portable harmonium, pushing it about on the little truck. He takes with him his Community Song Music Book and leaflets. At one large shelter the light was insufficient for reading so we sang all the old songs we knew and volunteers sang solos [...] Everybody joins in and it is surprising how it helps the evening pass.[59]

More often than not, it was the provision of liquid refreshment as much as spiritual sustenance that people relied upon. Such service in the midst of adversity gave rise to many humorous anecdotes. John Jackson, an Anglican curate in wartime, recalled that his church bought an old ambulance to carry himself and his clergy colleagues about the parish ready to help with an urn of tea. His vicar's driving, however, was notoriously bad, he being described by Jackson as: 'one of the worst drivers in creation'. John Jackson recounts:

> And I well remember, on a wonderful moonlit night we set off and he never gave us a chance to close the doors with the result that, first of all, one of my colleagues [...] fell out of the ambulance into the middle of the street in St. John's Road. I saw him there in the pale moonlight wondering what on earth had happened to him. We carried on but by that time, all the urns had fallen [over]

---

58   Francis Drinkwater Papers: letters, 14 August 1941.
59   *The Parish Magazine of St James's, Ashted*, December 1940.

140

and we were absolutely up to our knees in tea and coffee, and when we got to the end of the road where we were supposed to be the vicar got out and said: 'Where is John?' [...] I said, 'Oh he's in the middle of the road up there if you want find him.' 'What is the incompetent fool doing there?'[60]

Sometimes the help that was on offer from clerics was not met as deferentially as the propaganda portrayal of *Neighbours Under Fire* would have it. Another occasion recalled by John Jackson occurred in a public shelter near the Birmingham City football ground:

There were hundreds of people in those places. But we did our best to supply them with drinks and a few refreshments if we had them. And I always remember one night when I'd been down there and returned almost under fire from what was coming down, [I] went to the vicarage to replenish my flagons (whatever it was we used!), and there was a loud knock at the door, and I thought, 'Oh that's the warden come to tell me that our lights were shining in the vicarage.' There was a man there, a tall man, very tall indeed and he said: 'Are you the little "fella" who's been to us tonight to bring our tea and coffee?' I said 'Yes' [...] he put his mug up to my hand, [and] he said: 'Where's the bloody sugar?'[61]

Generosity amidst austerity characterised much of the day-to-day life and ministry of many Christian communities. As well as leading the singing of hymns such as 'What a friend we have in Jesus' and other 'hymns that the people knew', the minister of Wattville Chapel, Handsworth, often queued for food to distribute to people in the locale; boiling up remnants of food as sandwich filling for the church's shelter rounds.[62]

Not only were individual clerics and their lay assistants to be found in and around the shelter environment; other Christian organisations also assisted in the caring operation. For example, the Birmingham Salvation Army's central citadel paid regular visits to the city-centre shelters, including that under the department store 'Grey's' on Bull Street, to lead communal singing. They also provided canteen services in blitzed areas for those bombed out and for the emergency services. Later in the war the Salvation Army provided over 100,000

60   Interview with Prebendary John Jackson, March 2000.
61   Interview with Prebendary John Jackson, March 2000.
62   Interview with Laura Evans, May 1999.

meals for the troops based around the city.[63] In a situation of dire shortage, such acts of genuine generosity were gratefully received. As well as this, the presence of the Salvation Army band often uplifted, reiterating the feeling of hope amidst adversity and defiance of the enemy. As the journal of the citadel records, such defiance was particularly symbolic on Easter Day 1941:

> Parish Church and Shops in Bull Ring badly damaged in recent raids [...] We manage to hold our usual open-air Sunday night, our triumphant playing, singing, and declaring of the Easter message, 'I am the resurrection and the life' sounding out as a challenge to the dislocation around us, and of a joyous hope of the better things which are to be.[64]

As part of a co-ordinated caring campaign across many bombed cities, which included the distribution of hymn sheets and prayer cards to enable people to join in shelter services and pause and pray in the silence before Big Ben struck at nine, the Church Army operated a military hut in Birmingham, which in one legendary week served some 41,000 sandwiches.[65] In addition, the YMCA offered vital Christian service in Birmingham throughout the war. Its mobile canteens went from five in number in 1940 to eighteen in 1941 and were allotted to particular areas of the city where they toured public shelters, gun positions, searchlight and balloon barrages, serving as many as 5,000 teas to the firewatchers, civil-defence operatives and the public in one night. As well as this, the YMCA had a number of 'static canteens' in Dale End, Bristol Street, Erdington, Hall Green, Handsworth, Harborne and Stechford, offering as many as 30,000 meals a week, in addition to hostel accommodation for those in temporary need, and a range of recreational facilities. In this context, many citizens earned a reputation for conspicuous and unstinting aid, oftentimes in dire and dangerous circumstances. One such citizen was a certain Mrs Beech (later Mrs Stephenson) who was reputedly 'as strong as a horse and as brave as a lion [having an] ability [to handle] the most awkward and,

63   Birmingham Salvation Army Citadel Journal, 1944 entry
64   Birmingham Salvation Army Citadel Journal, Easter Day, 1941.
65   Barber, 1946, p.49.

142

on occasions, the most dangerous men'.[66] Moreover, the young people of Rocky Lane Methodist Church developed a reputation for their service during the bombing. In an interview conducted on behalf of the Home Office, the Rev. R.A. Holtom, the minister, witnessed to a variety of acts of bravery and community service by the young people of the Church:

> We came in touch with some young men of the Friends Ambulance Unit anxious to provide warm drinks in public shelters. We came to their aid, and our Girls and Boys Club started boiling water and making cocoa, and taking it out – 1500 cups in eight days – not bad for a beginning. These young people are working hard every night from six until ten, on this. Later we hope to do more for the thousand people in Newtons, Wrights, Giles, Billiard Hall and our Chapel Shelters. It is good work this by our gallant young folk.[67]

Likewise, a member of Rocky Lane Church recalls the extraordinary bravery of one of the young people, behaviour out of character until his contact with the Christian faith and the onset of war:

> Everyone [in his family] bar Norman had been in prison [in fact] Norman's mother came up to Randolph Holtom (the minister) and said: 'You've spoilt my lad, he's the only one that hasn't been in prison' [...] I was on fire watching with him that night when the church got bombed, we was only 14 [...] right here in the entrance was an escape hatch, when that got bombed under here was stacks of people [...] they couldn't get out [...] as they opened the lid [...] shrapnel come down and Norman threw himself over the first one and saved her from shrapnel and he had ribs cracked and all sorts of things, that was the sort of bloke he was.[68]

During the blitz, Birmingham's clerics, like many chaplains in the First World War, put themselves at enormous risk to ensure that people were being cared for and that they received some sustenance, spiritual or otherwise, that would get them through. They bravely took to the streets to do their duty whilst others lay in relative safety in the shelters. One Roman Catholic lay person recalls sheltering with her family during a raid upon Liverpool. The family heard a shuffling

---

66   IWM Dept of Documents, Cadenhead, W.G. 85/51/1.
67   Public Record Office, HO 192/1205.
68   Interview with Alfred Brinkworth, February 2000.

sound outside their Anderson shelter. It was later discovered that their parish priest, recognising that some of his 'flock' might very well meet their deaths that night, was wandering around the parish pausing outside each home and shelter to absolve the people inside.[69] No doubt, this kind of meticulous care would have been typical in other places, as priests sought ways to accommodate the pastoral theology and requirements of peacetime with the peculiarities of conflict. Indeed, evidence suggests that a carefully thought through theological justification for particular practices such as this was sought and obtained.[70] Certainly, and with air raids in view, Roman Catholics were urged to consider the fate of their souls and to examine their consciences by a handy card distributed to the faithful by the Catholic Truth Society, entitled *Air Raids: Five Spiritual Commandments for Protection Against Air Raids*. The reader was exhorted to go to confession 'if your conscience is not in order [for] once the enemy planes are overhead it is too late.' Similarly, they were advised to sprinkle holy water when an air raid sounds, for 'whatever this water touches may be protected [...] Remember that your fate is in the hands of God [...] Further, keep your soul free from mortal sin, as air raids urge Christ's warning: "Be ever ready".'[71] Moreover, the faithful of the Birmingham Oratory were exhorted 'to look round for special patrons to pray to amidst the trials, difficulties and even dangers of the blackout', the writer suggesting the Three Kings or St. Genevieve as appropriate intercessors.[72] Sometimes the peacetime patterns of ministry dovetailed with the pastoral needs presented by war. Hymn singing and preaching, for example, central to

---

69 With thanks to an assistant archivist (anonymous) at St. Chad's Cathedral for this recollection.

70 See for example the argument put that in an air raid, numbers of people could be considered to be 'in periculo mortis' and therefore absolution might justifiably given to a whole populace. However, the line was drawn at the case for giving absolution to the whole country in an air raid (Anon., 'Absolution in Danger of Death', *The Clergy Review*, Vol. XXIII, No. 3 (1943), pp.130–131).

71 Card seen in St Chad's Catholic Cathedral Archive.

72 *The Oratory Parish Magazine*, January 1940. 'The Three Kings' were invoked to lead the people through the darkness of the blackout, and St. Genevieve, no doubt because of the sense of feeling hemmed in as if under siege. The people of Paris similarly invoked her during the siege of city in 1870–71.

Nonconformist worship, mission and ministry, fitted well into the context of sheltering, because here, as in church, it uplifted and brought people together. However, when the stresses were greatest and people were panicky and fearful, the clergy were often ill fitted to cope. Amongst the little advice they were given was the need for extreme treatments for panic (such as kicking the hysterical person or dousing them with cold water), advice which was more often than not eschewed.[73] William Brooke, one Birmingham cleric trained at West-cott House by B.K. Cunningham, the First World War padre, recalls having to deal with such situations:

> At the sort of crossroads at St Agatha's with Stoney Lane and Stratford Road and Walford Road, there was a big underground shelter. It was about the first big raid on the district and people were coming in, some of the women came in hysterical, screaming, clinging to anything and any body they could. The prescribed treatment was to slap them and say 'stop it'. I never did that – you'd try to bring a little sanity into it.[74]

Clergy had received little or no training, beyond the basics of first aid, for the demands presented by shelter work. In the words of Benjamin Clarke, 'there was no training; we had to feel our way from day to day.'[75] Consequently, they often needed to react instinctively to demands as they arose, only able to draw upon the example of their role models and the limited knowledge provided by their theological training. Despite their lack of expertise, clerics were often called upon to lend a hand to deal with some horrific circumstances and to assist as best they could. The wartime rural dean of Aston, Canon W.S. Power, recalled one incident after an explosion, when he was called upon to help a doctor deal with a woman who had been badly injured in a blast. Despite the horrendous nature of the injury, Power described dealing with it in a relaxed tone:

> One victim presented us with a problem. She was a woman, but whether young or old I could not say. Her face was ashen white; her right hand, or what was left of it, was bleeding profusely. As soon as we put on a new bandage, it became as

---

73   Bourke, 2005, p.250.
74   Interview with Canon William Edward Brooke, May 2000.
75   Questionnaire response from the Reverend Benjamin B. Clarke.

red as the one we had just taken off. At last I said to the Doctor, 'Doctor, isn't this a case for a tourniquet?' He agreed and soon the tourniquet was applied. After about half and hour the bleeding had ceased.[76]

Power mentions that his pastoral involvement with the woman continued in a more conventional way after the war, presiding at her wedding and at the baptism of her child.

Sometimes, clerics and Christian organisations were the first on the scene after a bombing. The activities of Norman Power, the curate of Christ Church, Summerfield, provide an example of this, and were captured in the parish popular history of the war years:

> He made his way to Coplow Street to seek out Mrs Virgin. She was a remarkable woman suffering from arthritis in arms and legs but a spirited wonderfully cheerful person. She used to sit by her window with a mirror to watch the passers by and give then a cheerful smile. The curate found her as cheerful as ever. She had been buried by a wall and her windows had been blown in but she had protected her face with the curtains. Her remark at the time demonstrates her spirit. 'Fancy Hitler wasting a bomb on me. Couldn't even kill me!' Leaving Mrs Virgin in good hands the curate joined the team of rescuers toiling over the piles of bricks and shattered timbers digging their way down to the trapped and injured.[77]

Naturally, despite an eminent psychologist's recommendations that only those who had conquered their own emotions were able to capably assist others,[78] the clergy were as fearful as any other citizen as the bombs rained down around them; their behaviour, though often enormously brave, was similarly reflective of panic and folly, as well as of courage. For instance, William Brooke, curate of St. Agatha's, Sparkbrook, recalls:

> I also remember a night, Canon Tilt, I don't know why he did it, it was well on in the war, there was this raid going on, shrapnel was falling round and he insisted on lying in the gutter, lying in the gutter you were a much better target

---

76   Power, 1970, p.147.
77   While. [n.d.], p.11.
78   Bourke, 2005, p.243.

146

for shrapnel than standing up with a tin hat. I remember this semi-argument as to which was the right posture.[79]

Equally, John Jackson remembers:

> The vicar and myself were out one night and we heard one of these cluster bombs coming down and we knew it was going to be a pretty horrible business. We'd heard one or two before and so James, my vicar, hearing this whining its way down to earth, suddenly got hold of me and threw me under his stomach and both of us lay on the ground. And he said to me 'Cheerio John, we shan't see each other again', cause we were quite convinced this thing was coming right on top of us. I don't know which was worse, the bomb coming down or me being underneath the vicar's tummy because he was a very heavily built man.[80]

However, the ministry offered was not only that of an ambulance type, keeping people's spirits up, or mopping up the physical and emotional debris resulting from the bombardment. Norman Power's efforts to find billets for those made homeless by the blitz meant that his bicycle was a familiar sight around his parish:

> This cycle came to an untimely end during the blitz. Whilst cycling across Summerfield Park the curate was flung headlong from his saddle by the blast from a bomb that fell on the children's playground and he landed in the bushes. That was the last he saw of his precious bike. He searched high and low for it without success.[81]

Some clerics were also engaged in challenging the authorities with regard to the adequacy and quality of air-raid shelter provision. Guy Rogers was a regular visitor of the large shelter in the city centre called the Toll Market, in which during the heaviest nights of the blitz several thousand people took cover. He deplored the conditions in which people had to seek safety, later writing:

> It was horribly damp and dismal and the scenes by night incredibly pathetic. If children were not actually born there, we had to hustle expectant mothers away

---

79   Interview with Canon William Edward Brooke, May 2000.
80   Interview with Prebendary John Jackson, March 2000.
81   While. [n.d.], p.11.

at the last moment by ambulance. The spectacle of hundreds of people bedding down for the night in such discomfort was one never to be forgotten.[82]

Such protestations that Rogers made with regard to sheltering conditions received the attention of the Home Office, for in a report deemed secret at the time and which openly criticises the civic authorities for their recalcitrance, Guy Rogers' name features as a chief protagonist.[83] Rogers clearly had the respect of his bishop in this and other matters and the evidence he provided Barnes with led the redoubtable bishop to enter the fray. In an infamous statement made by Barnes in the House of Lords on December 1940, which led to a lengthy libel case against him, he argued that it was the deliberate connivance of the cement manufacturers, and their keeping back the supplies of cement for advantageous reasons, which led to the unsatisfactory and unsafe conditions of many air-raid shelters. The bishop's pronouncements are indicative of his propensity to outrage and his underlying desire to dissent against the war in subtle ways reflective of his pacifism. However, his involvement may be more generously viewed as a prophetic and vocal defence of the people's welfare, proving the care he took to deal with the fallout of total war upon the wider populace. Barnes described the terrible conditions endured by the sheltering populace thus in his address:

A fortnight ago, I visited a vast underground shelter in Central Birmingham. The drainage from the latrines that had been erected was inadequate. The shelter stank. Almost everywhere, there were drops of water on the roof. People in one corner had brought their beds and – it was a pathetic sight – had tried to protect them from wet by stretching sacking above. In one part of the shelter, where the water lay half an inch deep on the floor, I asked a workman the cause of the dripping on the floor. He replied: 'The water lies above there: the Corporation has not been able to get cement to finish it off.' 'Crouch under the stairs while the raid is on' has actually been given as official advice. Now it is one thing for those who live in solidly built houses so dispersed that bombing, save as spasmodic terrorism, is not worth while – it is one thing for such persons to accept the risk of remaining at home, it is quite another thing for a worker to

82   Roger, 1956, p.282.
83   Public Record Office HO 192/ 1205.

148

remain in a fragile home crowded near a munitions factory likely to be heavily bombed.[84]

Whatever may be said of the prudence or motivation for his statements, his bravery in defence of the rights of the citizens of Birmingham was surely commendable as a critical piece of pastoral oversight.

Thus, it can be seen that the clergy's and the Churches' ministry during Birmingham's air raid experience was dictated by the needs of the sheltering public. It was reactive rather than planned, but it was nevertheless deliberate in its methods and shaped, in particular, by the lessons of the previous war. The clergy and Christian congregations cared where they could, and with all the means, spiritual and otherwise, at their disposal.

Keep Praying Through

> On Moseley Road there was a big Methodist Church [...] early on in the blitz it was bombed; it was obliterated and its shell remained. The shell had a gigantic notice board that said, 'The City of God Remaineth' and that stopped on all through the war. Nobody ever tried to rip it off.[85]

An important dimension of the clergy's ministrations was the preservation of patterns of religious observance, and the protection of places of worship and sacred objects, so that spiritual resources endured. This was almost certainly intended as a sign of defiance, as well as reflection of the commitment to the ideals that were being championed by the war. As the Methodist Minister of Kingstanding, J.J. Whitfield, put it:

84 Barnes Papers, EWB 12/1/582, Speech to the House of Lords, 15 December 1940.
85 Interview with Winifred Harrison, December 1999.

Dear Friend [...] our church buildings remain undamaged, [and] none of our members have been lost by 'enemy action'. We have suffered the general inconvenience with which everyone is familiar, and some dislocation of our work [...] The Sunday school has been greatly reduced in numbers, both of scholars and staff: but as far as possible we carry on. Benjamin Franklin once said in a time of crisis: 'Though the sun has gone down and it may be long before it rises again, let us make as good a night of it as we can: we may still light candles.' That is just what we try to do, surely the task of every Church in these dark days: whatever other candles go out, ours must be kept burning, that by the light of the Gospel men may find and follow the way of truth and love and peace. Our witness to the spiritual values that are fundamental and eternal is needed today more than ever: the Christian fellowship must be maintained: the Church must make contact with the people in the areas where they reside: though some opportunities may be lost to us, others have been created. Soldiers stationed at the Pheasey Camp have found fellowship in our services, and friendship in the homes of our people. A.R.P. Wardens and others have been welcome visitors to our clubs. And most significant of all, we have been able to open up during recent months, two new centres of Methodist activity, one on the Pheasey Estate and one at Perry Common. In both places, vigorous Sunday school and youth work is being carried on [...] the future in full of promise: both places depend [on] the ministerial oversight [of] Deaconesses appointed to this new work. In days when so much of the world's resources are being devoted to destruction, we rejoice in being used of God [sic] in work that is constructive and uplifting. We believe that a better world can only be made by making better men and women and that [the] work of the Church, directed as it is toward the transformation of character, is the highest form of national service.[86]

In some quarters this determination that life, in this case religious life, would continue unabated led to the liberation of the gifts of women to undertake roles otherwise occupied by men. A case in point was that of Olive Young, wife of the Baptist minister O.D. Wiles, who occupied a leadership role in her husband's absence as an armed-forces chaplain.[87] The gifts of Winifred Harrison, a young Methodist Sunday-school teacher, were demanded even after she was 'bombed-out'. Nevertheless, in a similar way to those women conscripted for war work, she too remained subordinate in authority to a man:

---

86   Kingstanding Methodist Church, April 1941.
87   Cf. obituary of O.D. Young in *Baptist Union Directory* (London: Baptist Union, 1980), p.306.

> One night, it was during a snowstorm, the bell went and I went to the door, and it was the Pastor from the Maypole Methodist Church, and he'd walked an hour to get to me in the snow [my] Minister had said that I was living with my sister temporarily and he thought I might be useful to him starting a Sunday school; so on the Sunday I trudged all through the snow [...] when I got there there were 12 children and the gentleman who was going to be the Superintendent [...] I found a pianist [...] we also started a women's class.[88]

The first ordination of a woman to the ministry had occurred in 1917, that of Constance Todd to the Congregational Kings Weigh House.[89] No doubt, therefore, women's ministerial gifts were increasingly being utilised by the time of the Second World War. Indeed, in a similar way to those women conscripted to secular occupations to replace male workers conscripted to the Forces, it is likely that those women who were engaged in additional Church work to replace male ministers similarly absent accrued expectations of greater responsibility in the post-war world. Moreover, amongst those Churches where women were yet to be ordained, perhaps their wider participation in roles which traditionally belonged to men added weight to the case for their ordination.[90]

All of these activities, the practical ones and the idealistic, have to be set against the backdrop of the people's sense of their own mortality in the midst of conflict. The people worked for the preservation of what was important from the past, undoubtedly, but very much within a context of an uncertain and insecure future:

> The ordinary aim to was continue the life of the church as we understood it. The second was to minister to the needs of the people [...] it wasn't dictated by theory, we couldn't say this is what we think is right and this is what we're going to do. You were presented with a situation you've got to deal with [...] so it was very much more intuitive [...] dealing with people; people where families were broken up or where certain key members were called up into the forces, where they had anxiety or bereavement that sort of thing [...] you just had to deal with what was there [...] take the short view sort of things, we don't know if we shall be alive tomorrow. I remember days, mornings where Canon Tilt

---

88   Interview with Winifred Harrison, December 1999.
89   Hastings, 1987, p.44.
90   The degree to which the war acted to free women of their traditional roles in non-ecclesiastical life is explored by Dorothy Sheridan (1990, p.32).

came down and looking for people [...] he'd come down [...] meet us in the hall and embrace us and say: 'Thank God we're all here'; [Moreover], the war seemed to threaten all the sorts of foundations of what we understood as Christendom. [We were] hoping that we could do something to ensure the continuance of the Christian witness, Christian way of life and Christian civilisation in its broadest sense. So, along with the immediate aim there was the further aim, which probably kept us going.[91]

The Bruges Sisters at Harborne Hall Convent recounted their wartime experiences in their journal. Not only does the account of their war show a determination to continue to live and worship according to peacetime patterns, it records how the sisters kept in contact with those of their community in Belgium and Switzerland, including a number who were sent to concentration camps.[92] The way in which this war was experienced, by these sisters of a Birmingham religious community with a European perspective, is typified by the journal extract of 12 December 1940:

> Mass 6:45. It was a dreadful night. The alert sounded at 1:30 and was sounded again at 1:45. The all-clear did not go until 7:25 am [...] Between 8:30 and 8:45 whilst the Community was at Night Prayers a number of Incendiary Bombs were dropped on our house and in the garden. Two fell on the chapel roof [...] We put out most of the bombs ourselves but the A.R.P. men quickly came to our help. We phoned the fire-brigade but by the time they arrived all – practically all – were extinguished.[93]

Where churches were damaged or destroyed, Christians worshipped on regardless, very often recovering what precious items they could from the debris. For instance, when St. John's, Harborne was bombed, two women, a Mrs Hedges and her sister, members of the Church, rescued, amongst other things, the church Bible.[94] Likewise, when St. Anne's, Moseley was bombed for the third time, on 3 December 1940, a party of women salvaged hymn books, prayer books, hassocks and furniture from the ruins.[95] Congregations were

91   Interview with Canon William Brooke, May 2000.
92   *Harborne Hall Journal*, 14 March 1941.
93   *Harborne Hall Journal*, 12 December 1940.
94   Correspondence from Penny Carter of Edgbaston, March 2002.
95   Correspondence from Graham Underhill of Moseley, March 2002.

also forced to worship in other places, as in the case of St. Mary's, Acocks Green, who after their church was rendered unusable on 10 December 1940 worshipped in the Warwick Road Cinema.[96] Other homeless congregations were offered space to worship in the buildings of a different denomination, so enhancing ecumenical understanding and goodwill during wartime and later. When the corrugated iron Roman Catholic Church of St. Dunstan's, Kings Heath, was destroyed by a 'time bomb' on Maundy Thursday, 1941, the neighbouring Anglican church offered the use of its school hall until alternative arrangements could be made. Differing theologies were, it seemed, subsumed for the duration beneath a sense of Christian and national camaraderie.[97] In a similar vein, congregations came to share buildings for Sunday worship albeit at different times of the day, as they did when members of the Congregational Digbeth Institute worshipped at St. Martin's, a practice which later led to an annual joint communion service.[98] Similar interdenominational cooperation, through the Birmingham Christian Social Council, led to the establishing of a 'factory padre' scheme in a number of the largest of Birmingham's factories, and, in 1942, to a United Mission.[99] Such acts of goodwill added to, as Hoover calls it, 'the ecumenical fallout of the war'.[100] After the bombing of St. Martin's on the night of 9 April 1941, Guy Rogers, the Rector, set about defiantly ensuring that religious life continued, whilst taking time to climb onto the roof of the local YMCA to commiserate with its secretary about the damage done there.[101] In a similar vein to the famous images of St. Paul's Cathedral towering above the debris of the London blitz, so too, the Parish Church of Birmingham took on a symbolic status and this was recognised by Rogers and other senior clerics:

96   Correspondence from Eileen Dingley of Acocks Green, March 2002.
97   Correspondence from Miss M. Shepherd and Mr George Parsons, Kings Heath, Birmingham, February 2002.
98   Driver, 1948, p.87.
99   Sutcliffe and Smith, 1974, p.263.
100   Hoover, 1999, p.111.
101   IWM Dept of Documents, Cadenhead, W.G. 85/51/1.

I did not want the continuity of the services to be broken, so every one we could get hold of was roped in to tidy up. The bishop and Leyton Richards might have been among the debris [...] We got some part of the church into useable order before Dr. F. W. Howard, Principal of the Methodist Theological College, Handsworth, arrived to preach, after difficulty in getting through the cordon placed as a precaution against delayed-action bombs. Although his congregation consisted of eight, I insisted on his going to the pulpit [...] As soon as [his address was given] we rushed round to the offices of the Birmingham Post and Mail so that the report of it could appear in the Press immediately [...] People were astonished to read the midday service had been held, and it stopped the wild rumours going round the city that the Parish Church was flat on the ground [...] eventually we were rewarded by a message of congratulations from the Lord Mayor at the close of the V Day celebrations.[102]

Many congregations organised special prayer services for the families of those in the armed forces. Laura Evans of Wattville Chapel spoke of the moving and efficacious nature of these events:

There was a long roll call read out every month [...] it was wonderful how they all came back, except one [...] On those Sunday nights when the roll was called it was absolutely packed [...] we sort of moved so that people could come in [we stood] while the names were read [...] it was quite a long list you know [...] we was all glad to stand in reverence really and you'd see some of the mothers wiping their eyes [...] when their lad or daughter was called.[103]

Similarly, many churches remained open during the blackout and many people, churchgoers or not, took the opportunity for solitary prayer. Likewise, 'even in homes when you went in [...] you'd just lead with a prayer – especially if people knew you went to church; they'd just ask you.'[104] It seems that, for a great many people, wartime events engendered a revision of priorities and that a call to defend family, home and nation and all that it stood for had a great resonance. These sentiments often embraced the defence of Church buildings and the 'national' religion.

Even when Church buildings were destroyed, clergy and congregations found a theology of hope to deal with the loss. Indeed,

102   Rogers, 1956, pp.180–181.
103   Interview with Laura Evans, May 1999.
104   Interview with Winifred Harrison, December 1999.

154

'many church-goers only began to appreciate what their church had meant in their lives when it was destroyed [...] oddly enough, when a church was bombed the result was often a larger and more dedicated congregation.'[105] The Church, they defiantly reminded one another, is a spiritual body, not one made of stones. Thus, despite the destruction of buildings, such as Coventry Cathedral on 14/15 November 1940, their religious significance was retained and even somewhat strengthened. In the case of Coventry this meant that it could still be utilised for propaganda purposes (Coventry Cathedral was the setting for the Empire broadcast of Christmas 1940, which had as its theme the slaughter of the innocents), causing people, at the very least, to ponder the relative importance of the material as opposed to the spiritual.[106] Indeed, recognising the power of such symbolism the Director-General of the Ministry of Information sent a verse from a poem by Anna Wickham to the official artist of the bombed-out Cathedral, which characterised the message sought from the artist's commission:

> Thank God for war and fire, to burn silly objects of desire; that from the ruin of a Church thrown down, we see God clear and high above the town.[107]

When St. James's, Ashted was all but destroyed in December 1940, the Vicar, Percy Pierce, boldly and hopefully recounted that: 'some of us were in the shelter [beneath the church] singing words that we can still sing, "So long Thy power hath blessed us, sure it will still lead us on".'[108] Later on, the new incumbent, John Preston, chided those parishioners who had not achieved a proper sense of proportion about their lost building, likening the spiritual state of those who cling to the need for buildings to the materialism that led to the downfall of France, and urging the recent sacrifices of Russia as the correct spiritual attitude:

> There is one thing which is not healthy in the life of the wartime Church life in Ashted. It is a concern, a mourning for a ruin [...] the best that St. James' stood

105   Longmate, 1971, pp.388–389.
106   Campbell, 1996, p.9.
107   Campbell, 1996, p.9.
108   *The Parish Magazine of St. James's, Ashted*, January 1941.

for [was] the real cement [...] of Christian love and friendship [...] the Church does not stand for a burnt out shell, but a living faith and a fellowship. Wherever faith is vital, the war has shown that it has been something which has been willing to sacrifice. Russia burnt her factories and fields. Russia now lives, though the cost of it [was great]. France wavered, and thought to preserve her cities, and is in chains. London risked her all, and still stands [...] this is Easter [let us give thanks] because the Christian way of life is kept alive among ourselves.[109]

It seems that the preservation or destruction of churches could alike be replete with spiritual meaning and effectual in influencing morale.

The metaphors used to describe the experience of sheltering bespoke the theology and self-understandings of particular Christian communities. Often, they harkened back to religious trials of the past. Some Christians likened the 'blitz' experience to the Passover that preceded the people of God's exodus from Egypt. Laura Evans, lifetime member of the Wattville Chapel, Handsworth, recalled that the text: '"When I see the blood I will pass over you" [...] really helped. In those days people thought they was safe, you know, because the Lord was there protecting them [...] I always felt safe really.'[110] Many implicitly believed such sentiments, trusting that the nation was providentially chosen and thereby assured of the protection of God. Others held that the people may perish but the faith itself would, ultimately, be preserved and persist. The congregation of Carrs Lane, sheltering near the church itself, equated the experience of sheltering to the early Christians' lives in the catacombs; they too were hiding from destructive forces, living to perpetuate the mysteries of the faith for the future:

[On] Sunday [...] the 'alert' signal was given during a service [...] We finished the preliminaries [...] and then most people went down to the Catacombs – a public shelter in Moor Street – [...] On this occasion we achieved a full house and standing room only [...] we sang a verse of 'All people that on earth do dwell' [...] Nearly everyone had lost windows and tiles and had other much more strenuous experiences to make great demands on faith in the enduring things which transcend material damage [...] The sermon on 'Faith' was preached in a cellar crowded to capacity [and those there] showed by the calm of

109   *The Parish Magazine of St. James's, Ashted*, April 1942.
110   Interview with Mrs Laura Evans of Wattville Chapel, Handsworth.

their faces that with their faith in the eternal love of God and the ultimate decency of human nature they could withstand the 'Blitz'.[111]

Clergy Roles and their Leadership

For many clergy, as well as having to deal with the novel circumstances presented by war, there was also the difficulty of negotiating their role and sense of purpose in a context in which their parish population was reduced by evacuation, or dispersal by the effects of bombing. John Jackson summarises the shape of such a ministry and the need to be adaptable in a wartime parish ministry:

> The ministry of the blitz was primarily to help people in their homes to come to terms with what was going to be and proved to be a very difficult situation. But of course, many of them in any case had already taken flight and evacuated themselves to other parts of the city. Most of my people left, a lot of our congregation [...] When I went with Canon Jenkins to Sparkhill [...] they went up to what they called the 'safe area' of Hall Green [...] We lost [...] about a hundred people because of that [...] they got settled there, although a few came back, many of them decided to put their roots down. The next job of course, was to minister to people in whatever capacity we could. Now one of those [...] was to go into the factories and try and bolster up their morale [...] We were always, both my vicar and myself, very courteously received and very often in the lunch break, providing circumstances were all right, there was no raid on or anything like that, they would invite us to say a few words to the people [...] It was a tremendous challenge to go to those places and of course terrible sadness when one realised that the places to which we went some of them were bombed unmercifully and of course a terrible loss of life. One must remember that you could hardly move but a few yards before there was a factory.[112]

Contemporary experience and the statistics at the time seemed to bear out the view that the make-up of British society in 1939 was tending to a gradual decrease in the population's affiliation to and

111   *Carrs Lane Journal*, Vol. XXXIII, No. 12, December 1940, p.3.
112   Interview with Prebendary John Jackson, March 2000.

sympathy with organised religion and it was therefore not possible for clergy to assume that people would have the language, concepts or will to be involved in such things as religious worship in public air-raid shelters. Much as armed-forces chaplains had found in the First World War that the average soldier was relatively ignorant of formal religiosity, similarly the home-front clergy nervously supposed that the sheltering public were, on the whole, religiously illiterate and, indeed, scarcely interested in such things. Consequently, the clergy often demonstrated uneasiness in pressing their ministrations upon the people.[113] However, their reticence was unfounded, for, as we have already seen, the people were perfectly capable of participating in worship: indeed, such occasions were often well-attended, momentous and poignant. Despite religion having a significant place in the sentiments and daily life of working-class communities, the Church at times felt ill at ease with the masses. In a sense, therefore, the social and cultural conditions of the public air-raid shelter epitomised the Churches' missionary dilemma: how could one meaningfully minister to a people one believed to be alienated from the idiom, ritual and ideas of the Christian tradition? When the people and the Church were thrown together in the shelter, how clergy and Church workers coped with the challenge thus became a critical test, one which was, in many notable cases, memorably responded to. William Brooke, however, recalls the tentativeness of his own approach to air raid ministry:

> We aimed to go about the parish, during the raids [...] So we went to the shelters and did what we could, it was always a little difficult with a very mixed people who don't want to be where they are, to force too much religious observance on them, without the opportunity or requests as it were.[114]

Pastoral care was usually offered without partiality, to people within and beyond the confines of the minister's own flock as 'social

---

113 This was true for Dr. W.E. Sangster at Westminster Central Methodist Hall, who established all kinds of non-religious activities because he did not want to assume the people's need of more specific religious help. Cf. Wilkinson, 1986, p.273.
114 Interview with Canon William E. Brooke, May 2000.

and religious barriers were eroded by the air raids.'[115] More widely, there was opportunity to offer hospitality to the exile and to the 'enemy'. For example, the community of the Birmingham Oratory gave shelter to the Austrian theologian Monsignor Johannes Messner, whose presence was remembered long after; so much so that the room he stayed in is still known as Messner's room.[116] Similarly, the vice-rector of Oscott Seminary, Frank Davis, regularly travelled to Colchester to teach a group of P.O.W. student priests.[117] Likewise, Harborne Methodist Church's hospitality was rewarded by a group of German P.O.W.s at the end of the war when they presented the congregation with a hand-carved cross made from wood gathered from the grounds of their camp.[118] However, the breadth of sympathy was not always as consistently felt beyond the confines of one's own religious community. For instance, John Power, parish priest of Our Lady of the Rosary, Saltley, writing to Archbishop Williams on 9 January 1939, enclosed his parish's donation to Cardinal Hinsley's refugee appeal. He commented:

> Enclosed find £3-0-4 refugee collection + £2-4-1 for the African collection. I am sure that as a Parish Priest yourself you realise the refugee fund collection was launched at the worst possible moment for us – the week before Christmas – I hope however that the poisonous Jews get none of this collection and that it is really devoted to the Catholic victims of the 'strafe' in spite of the article in the Universe this week.[119]

The ministry of clergy is often recalled with pride and affection as, when 'our minister' stood with us in 'our trial'. One such was Randolph Holtom, Methodist minister of Rocky Lane in Nechells. Alfred Brinkworth, a lifelong member of the Methodist mission at Rocky Lane, recalled the personal qualities which won the minister such respect:

115 Wilkinson, 1986, p.272.
116 Information from Mr Gerard Tracy, archivist at the Birmingham Oratory.
117 Obituary of Mgr Henry Francis Davis, *Archdiocese of Birmingham Directory*, 1987.
118 Allen, 1989, p.25.
119 Papers of Mgr John Power, St. Chad's Cathedral Archive.

He was that sort of man, he wouldn't mind going into pubs [...] preaching in there, he was a man's man, you know. He didn't drink but he'd go in there and have a word with them [In the shelter] some people was really scared, I mean there was one family I don't think they ever saw their house, they was down there all the time [...] Holtom [...] used to go down the shelter in church as well in turns, they'd have a little service, they used to love it [...] Holtom was the bloke for the job at the time, he really was, he lifted people.[120]

Contrary to this, those ministers who themselves sought safety away from the bombing are recalled with a degree of bitterness and a little shame, as poor shepherds of the flock. Enfys Jones, a migrant who came to the city in the 1930s remarked of her minister:

He used to come back for different functions and he was a lovely man really [but] because his wife and his son had gone, been evacuated I suppose he wanted to be with them. I suppose it was a natural thing, I don't know [...] but we always felt as young people that he wasn't there for us [...] he was a refined kind of man and perhaps that was [it], he should have been more rough and ready [...] we did feel he lacked what was needed during the war to keep us together and if we could have felt that he was there, as the head of the Church [we might have felt differently].[121]

Clearly, as in the First World War, clerics were judged by the degree to which they were prepared to brave circumstances in order to exercise their ministry. Just as in the First World War there were some who were rarely seen at the front, now in the Second World War there were clerics who felt it impossibly bold or foolhardy to remain in dangerous circumstances with their civilian flock.[122] Estimates of clerical competence rested as much upon their continued presence with people in adversity as upon their particular personality, temperament and social skill. It is obvious that the stresses upon clerics in the wartime context must have been greater than those in peacetime. Not only were there different and unpredictable circumstances to respond to, but the leadership expectations upon them were clearly greater also.

120   Interview with Alfred Brinkworth, February 2000.
121   Interview with Mrs Enfys Jones of the Welsh Congregation, Birmingham, April 2000.
122   Contrast this, for example, with Studdert Kennedy who was often seen at the front, much to the surprise of the soldiers. Wilkinson, 1978, p.122.

The clerics who did not retreat from the strains that the rest of the populace were called upon to endure were the ones later eulogised. The Church hierarchy, however, seems to have deemed it unnecessary to try to reduce the pastoral burden upon clerics. It was left to clergy locally to support one another in their endeavours, to take turns over shelter duties, for example, whilst other colleagues caught up on sleep out of the area: 'we did take it a bit in turn to be in or out [...] Canon Tilt, [and] Mrs Tilt would go away for a night, have a nice rest. I'd be on duty at St Agatha's, my friend Ron often came in to be with me and go round the shelters. Another night I'd go to Yardley and they'd be on duty [...].'[123] There is scant evidence that senior clerics supported their juniors practically with these challenges. Indeed, in one instance, Bishop Barnes refused to allow one of his clergy access to charitable means whereby he could escape a badly bombed vicarage for a much-needed holiday in order to recover from his ailments.[124] Neither were the routines of religious observance in wartime significantly eased to lighten the burden upon the laity for whom sheltering at night was often coupled with arduous war work during the day. The desire to maintain normality had its own tensions, and clergy still expected much of their remaining flock by way of commitment and attendance.

Theological Themes of Wartime Rhetoric

Let your happy heart and your smiling face be a daily advertisement of your faith in God and Right [...] Let's all smile when we can and chase away the war blues.[125]

123 Interview with Canon William Brooke, May 2000.
124 Barnes Papers, EWB 7/3/24; of the Rev E. Lewis Blood (St Stephen's, Newtown Row).
125 Salter, 1942, p.11.

At the outbreak of war, the Anglican Bishop of Birmingham, Ernest Barnes, wrote in the Diocesan *Monthly Messenger*, giving advice to clergy about the content of their wartime sermons. This advice might equally have applied to their other orations, for the essence of it is reflected in much that Birmingham clerics wrote and spoke about in relation to the war. His guidance contrasted the tone of teaching in this war with the occasional bellicosity of certain notorious clerics, such as the Bishop of London, Arthur Winnington-Ingram, in the First World War.[126] Barnes's advice won him wide regard for its measured wisdom.[127] He managed to advise the clergy on their wartime conduct whilst maintaining his own pacifist integrity; recommended that they should:

> Never belittle our best achievements [...] or fine qualities [...] Do not cast doubts on the sincerity of our aspirations and ideals [or] our right to be indignant over known wrong; do not acquiesce in a self-righteous patriotism [...] Do not speak as though we had no responsibility for the creation of the temper [which] led to war; Emphasise the character and purpose of God [...] goodness may lead to a cross but it triumphs in the end [...] Remember that the Church of Christ should be a fellowship of [...] all nations; Speak of [...] the value of prayer, undeserved suffering, the problem of evil [...] be honest; frequently and strongly teach that evil [cannot] be conquered by force [but] must be overcome by good [...] evil [...] can only be destroyed by moral victories [...] we can only build peace by international justice and goodwill; urge [...] clean living [and] the quiet confidence [...] of trust in God; [teach people] to entrust [their] loved ones – in life or death – to God; preach as little as possible: pray as much as you can [...] before beginning to prepare a sermon put down your newspaper [consider] the mind of Christ. You are His minister.[128]

In the end, Barnes's advice to clerics was, in reality, epitomised in the character of the published clerical reflections. The majority of clergy managed to maintain the even-handedness that Barnes recommended. Few, if any, doubted and wrote that the war was unjustified. In contrast with the First World War, few, if any, certainly in Birmingham, can be accused of warmongering. Clerics, overall, managed a level-headed

126 Hoover, 1999, p.99.
127 Barnes, 1979, p.354.
128 *The Monthly Messenger: The Official Publication of the Birmingham Diocese*, No. 117, October 1939.

patriotism: they were able to combine repentance for the nation's complicity in the creation of the circumstances giving rise to this new conflagration, whilst not losing faith in the nation's uprightness and the justice of its cause. The change in the tenor and tone of clergy statements, between the Second World War and the First, seems to stem from several interwar developments; not least, closer working relationships between British and German Christians (for example, between ordinands of Queen's College, Birmingham and Tübingen); a decline in the theological dominance of liberal idealism, and the gradual supplanting of it by a Niebuhrian political realism.[129] The tone of clerical pronouncements in the Second World War was characteristically sombre, calm, and resolute. Amongst non-pacifist clergy, Nazism was regarded as an evil to be opposed.[130] However, in addition, within the various fora of clerical thought and thinking – books, journals, pamphlets, sermons, parish magazines, correspondence and the like – it is possible to discern particular theological themes which predominated. Some of the dominant themes of clerical thinking nationally were common to Birmingham's clerics also. The principal theological themes cluster around notions of the purpose and causes of war, ideas about the spiritually regenerative quality of warfare and particular understandings of God's providential activities amidst events. On the whole Birmingham's clerics eschewed references to the war as a crusade, though they sometimes repeated the widely felt sentiment that this war was being fought for Christian civilisation, or at the very least, as Archbishop William Temple argued, for the possibility of it in the post-war world.[131]

This war, according to many clerics, was not the fault of one man or one nation alone, though Nazism was occasionally characterised, at the extreme, as the Antichrist.[132] The British were not blameless, and thus it was not as simple as praying for victory of right against wrong;

---

129   For a description of the burgeoning interwar ecumenism see Wilkinson, 1986, p.67. Likewise, for the decline of liberalism and the rise of theological and political realism see Wilkinson, 1986, ch.7.

130   Except for some notable bishops e.g. Headlam of Gloucester; cf. Wilkinson, 1986, pp.145ff.

131   Hoover, 1999, p.98.

132   Hoover, 1999, p.57.

this was not simply a holy people pitted against the unholy, whatever was thought to be the real character of Nazism.[133] For example, Alan Richardson, a biblical scholar of some renown, refused to indict Germany without also demanding that Britain examine its own conscience:

> Is it not apparent that we are fighting within ourselves – both in our national life and in our own hearts – those things which we say that we are fighting against in others – aggressiveness, acquisitiveness, selfishness, bad faith, oppression and so on? Only when we recognise these things in ourselves are we spiritually fit to fight against them in others: 'Then shalt thou see clearly to pull out the mote that is in thy brother's eye.' (Luke 6:42).[134]

This war was brought about by a much deeper malaise than the identifiably political one, clergy argued. The real reason for this second world conflict was the malignant spiritual state of British and European civilisation.

> We have to remember that the root cause of all wars is the greed of gain and lust of power, and that the whole of our western civilisation has been infected with this poison [...] the achievement of a just peace can only come by the output of immense human endeavour and by a willingness to suffer and sacrifice [...] yet no peace, that is worth calling peace, will come from all this service and sacrifice unless there is a deep movement in the hearts of men towards the reassertion in our common life of the things of the spirit.[135]

This spiritual malaise was linked in the minds of clerics with a rampant paganism and with the sins of materialism, which could only be healed by a Lenten-like purging of the West.[136] This was an opportunity, they urged, for individual and national reconversion, a time for penitent service and stoical self-sacrifice.[137] To many clerics, this was a spiritual war, every bit as much as it was a military one. The prospect of imminent invasion made such sentiments even more urgent, 'altar

---

133   Keith Robbins overlooks this nuance of thinking in his piece on 'Religion' in Bear and Foot, 1995, p.937.
134   Richardson, 1940, p.14.
135   Thompson Elliott, 1939, pp.47 and 49.
136   Bevan, undated, p.17.
137   Longmate, 1971, p.398.

calls' to conversion being found in the most surprising of places, such as in the evangelical tones of *The Times* in July 1940:

> The enemy is at the gate. A time of testing has come to this nation more severe and searching than ever before in the long story of its life. How shall we meet this test? […] in the last resort it is upon the spirit of the whole nation, of every man and woman within it, that the issue will depend […] It is in prayer that we thus lift up our hearts. We must 'pray without ceasing' […] To this end we who send this message ask that daily at noon our fellow citizens who believe in God should in the midst of their work whatever it may be make a momentary act of remembrance and prayer […] penitence […] for our failure to be a Christian nation in fact as well as in phrase.[138]

In Birmingham, as elsewhere, this war was likewise often spoken of by clerics as a time of spiritual purgation. In terms similar to those spoken to the generation of the First World War, clergy once again asserted war to be an opportunity for national religious and political renewal, calling the nation to repentance.[139] For instance, the vicar of St. John's, Sparkhill declared in his parish magazine in October 1939:

> Whatever the immediate causes of the conflict may have been, when we reflect on the past two decades, there must come from our hearts an expression of utter penitence, because we have not striven harder to establish the will and ways of God among men […] this [is the] stupendous task that confronts us as individuals and as a nation. First, our penitence; a plea for pardon, and then, a prayer for strength to rebuild the world on a foundation which cannot be shaken, on the foundation 'which is Christ Jesus' […] Come regularly to church and join with others who commit themselves, their loved ones, their country and their cause to God, and ask for strength and wisdom to persevere faithfully day by day […] let us dedicate ourselves to fulfil the will of God.[140]

Similarly, two further quotations serve to illustrate the widespread notion amongst Birmingham's clerics that the Second World War was fundamentally a spiritual opportunity of critical import. Firstly, H.R. Chaffer, Vicar of St. Nicholas, Lower Tower Street, wrote to his parishioners in October 1939:

---

138   *The Times*, 2 July 1940.
139   Thompson, 1983, pp.344–345; Crerar, 1995, p.192.
140   *The Parish Magazine of St. John the Evangelist, Sparkhill*, October 1939.

Dear Friends [...] The forces of evil have broken loose violently in the world. The struggle into which we have entered is, above all, a spiritual struggle. We have put all our spiritual and material resources at the disposal of the Cause of Righteousness, Liberty, Justice and Truth [...] We are far from being free from blame that it has been possible for evil so to raise its head; The high ideals which we have embarked on in the struggle must be living things, and things which will survive all the stress of war. We must do all that we can that God may be able to use us to bring good out of evil [...] Repentance and Self-dedication to the Service of God must go hand-in-hand. Our prayers must be for the triumph of Right, and for the establishment of Righteousness on Earth [...] We are called to faith, calmness and patience, and to a quiet observance of the rules and regulations which will be made from time to time for our protection and wellbeing. Here the Christian can be of great help to the world; for the calm courage and obedience necessary can spring from faith in God alone.[141]

Dudley Clark, Vicar of St. Alban's, Bordesley, wrote of the practical spiritual opportunity presented by the keeping of a wartime 'Lent':

The war makes its own appeal [...] to us all to fulfil the three great Lenten precepts of self-denial, almsgiving and prayer [...] in many cases self-denial has been forced upon us, self denial in the matter of food and drink, sacrifice of leisure and amusements [...] Almsgiving too, the war with its necessary accompaniment of relief funds has brought this duty into startling prominence. And most of us have probably begun to realise more than ever the need of prayer [...] we must be prepared to sacrifice [...] if we are to suffer hardship as good soldiers of Jesus Christ.[142]

Moreover, sermons were preached then published in the local press, which sited the war in the spiritual realm as much as on the battlefield, inciting victory on the home front by spiritual devotion, as much as by civilians' material contributions.

If this war is really to be won on the spiritual battlefield, then the deliberate weakening of our spiritual forces is surely the best way to defeat [...] We are having warship weeks by the thousand; I have yet to hear of a single town in the country which has [organised] a worship week [...] If the Cross is the sign by which we hope to conquer, might [we not make] Good Friday a day of national

141 *The Parish Magazine of St. Nicholas, Lower Tower Street*, October 1939.
142 *The Parish Magazine St Alban's, Bordesley*, February 1940.

166

spiritual mobilisation [...] If everyone would cut one hour a week out of sleep to watch with the Master, a mighty national prayer force would be released.[143]

Many others were quick to seize the opportunity for national spiritual self-appraisal, which the war seemed to present. For example, the editors of *The Christian News-Letter*, a significant Christian periodical that had its genesis in wartime, published a series of books on the war from various perspectives aimed at intellectuals amongst the Christian audience. One book in the series, by Alan Richardson, was *The Message of the Bible in Wartime*. This title and others were written with a consciousness of the resonance of the fundamental themes of Christian theology with the events of the conflict, encouraging lay people to meet together in small discussion groups or 'cells' to discuss wartime events, and to reflect and rationalise them in the light of the pillars of Protestant orthodoxy. In a similar vein, Roman Catholics, initially with their Protestant Christian brothers and sisters, met to do the same under the aegis of the Catholic *Sword of the Spirit* movement, an ecumenical discussion forum for the lay Christian.[144] Likewise, the wartime book by the Vicar of Leeds, W. Thompson Elliott, entitled *The Spiritual Issues of the War*, revealed the same kind of thinking. This war, Thompson Elliott claimed, elevates itself to that described by St. Paul in Ephesians, 'a spiritual wrestling against principalities and powers, against the rulers of darkness'. The cosmic battle between good and evil goes on, he wrote; now it has broken out into war:

> For us it is a war against evil things [...] we are fighting against Germany because of the evil things which have been expressing themselves in the ruthless policy of their leaders [...] it is what happens in men's hearts while they are subject to the sufferings and cruelties of war which will determine the issue. We have, therefore, to begin with our own hearts.[145]

Such sentiments as these often resonated with political rhetoric that also sited the conflict in the moral arena: Chamberlain himself said

---

143 Sermon preached at St. Martin's Birmingham, at its regular Thursday lunchtime service, by Mr. Hugh Redwood, then reproduced in *The Birmingham Post*, Friday 27 March 1942.
144 Mews, 1983.
145 Thompson Elliott, 1939, pp.8–9.

that the nation was fighting against 'evil things'.[146] Moreover, a wartime poster of Winston Churchill depicts him symbolically in a Kitchener-like pointing pose urging, not a challenge to arms this time, but a pseudo-spiritual challenge to: 'Deserve Victory'. Even the pacifist Bishop Barnes warmed to such sentiments. When asked by Archbishop Temple to pray in the House of Lords he used the words 'make us worthy of victory'.[147] Repeating the oft-heard belief of the First World War, that 'the living owed a debt to the fallen', *The Spiritual Issues of the War* emphasised a similar call to spiritual and moral fortitude.[148] Its editor wrote: 'Deeper than the prayer for victory must be the prayer that we be made worthy of it. "Deserve Victory" must be our battle-cry.'[149] Canon Jenkins, vicar of Sparkhill, urged a similar spiritual recollection upon his flock:

> I sometimes wonder if in these days of stress, when God is invoked and His guidance and strength sought, whether we are really worthy to gain from Him all we seek and desire. Are our spiritual exertions comparable with our efforts in other directions? The evidence afforded at present does not seem to indicate that we are turning to God in real earnest [...] I should like each one of us to examine his own life and give answers as far as we are concerned personally [...] Am I, in prayer and Christian practice putting my trust, my hope, my life into God's hands? Am I expecting much from Him and giving Him little of what He expects of me? Am I witnessing to the fact that above all else I believe that He is the ultimately the giver of all victory and that without Him we cannot succeed? [...] it is unreasonable to expect God to rule among the nations unless we are prepared for Him to rule in our life [...] 'Blessed is the people, O Lord, that can rejoice in Thee; they shall walk in the light of Thy countenance.' [...] If our cause is God's cause, we must be God's people, and if we are to be quite honest about this, then it will mean a change of heart for many of us. If God is to defend the right, then we must be right with Him and give to Him his place in our life, He must come first not last.[150]

---

146   Cassandra, 1941, p.31.
147   Barnes Papers, EWB 9/13/144.
148   Brown, 1994, p.102; Crerar, 1995, p.151; Wilkinson, 1997, p.157.
149   *The Spiritual Issues of the War*, No. 36, 3 July 1940.
150   *The Parish Magazine of St. John the Evangelist, Sparkhill*, January 1940; the words of the Vicar, the Revd. A.T. Jenkins.

Clearly, the clergy understood this war to be in the purposes of God. However, in this conflict the war effort was not as directly identified with 'the earthly realisation of the Kingdom of God' as it had been in the First World War.[151] Birmingham's clergy reinforced, again and again, the rationale for the conflict to their readers. It was impossible to escape the message from many quarters that the events unfolding before people's eyes and in which their efforts were significant were nothing if not momentous in human history. Nonetheless, for some, there was no guarantee of victory, only a conviction that ultimately, in this battle between good and evil, good would win the day.

> Whatever God has in view, whatever His purpose for this world so torn and distorted by the ruthless power of men, that purpose will be fulfilled. His purpose may be thwarted by their acts of aggression; they may possibly delay the fulfilment of his plans. But ultimately the Purpose and plan will be brought to final conclusion and fulfilment [Just as the] coming of Jesus into the world was no chance happening [...] In Jesus [...] will be the fulfilment of God's purposes [when] the Son of Man sits in judgement over the nations.[152]

Again, the influence of the thinking of Reinhold Niebuhr, and of others like him, is clear. It is erroneous to claim that God will defend particular nations or institutions. It is the cause of God that is inviolate, not this or that temporal medium of it. Indeed, claimed some wartime Christians such as Leslie Weatherhead, Methodist Minister of the Temple, London, and Nathaniel Micklem, Congregationalist Principal of Mansfield College, Oxford, defeat and suffering may actually benefit the spiritual state of peoples and nations. Neither did defeat in this battle between good and evil mean the end of the war.[153] As the journal *The Spiritual Issues of the War* put it in mid-1940, at a time when the threat of invasion loomed large:

> The impact of tremendous events is forcing us to face two religious issues which we must clearly distinguish. The first is whether our faith in God is sufficient to

---

151 Crerar, 1995, p.187.
152 Sermon first preached at Harborne, December 28, 1941 by Mr H. S. Cull, Local Preacher at Bournville Methodist Church.
153 Hoover, 1999, p.15.

stand any strain, even that of defeat [...] If Christianity means anything at all, it is the message about what is eternal and unchanging through all the vicissitudes of this mortal life [...] I cannot doubt that the God whom we worship in Jesus Christ is also the Lord of history, and that the growing meanings which are built into the fabric of society and wrought into tradition, custom and institutions by the toil and sacrifice of successive generations are part of His plan for human life. It does not follow [that] God must give us victory [...] The righteous, even if they are righteous do not always triumph.[154]

Moreover, this nation was not immune to the judgement of God, concluded Alan Richardson, in his *The Message of the Bible in Wartime*. The prospect of imminent invasion did not deter him from concluding that, in judgement, God may well indeed let Britain be invaded by her enemies: Britain's destruction however, should not be equated with the defeat of God. In a parody of Jeremiah's prediction of the judgement and invasion of Israel (Jeremiah 8), and with a sense of wryness, Richardson wrote: 'there shall be no butter in the shops or bacon on the breakfast-table [...] the sound of his aeroplanes is heard from John O'Groats; at the roar of his bombers the whole land trembleth.'[155] Any sufferings borne because of the war, argued Richardson, resulted from a common guilt in its causes: suffering should be seen as the loving chastisement of God.[156] However, God is not impassible; he 'does not remain unaffected by the spectacle of human suffering'.[157]

No matter what the outcome of this war, victory or defeat, many Christians saw its events in the context of eternity. Some notable figures, such as William Temple, deviated from this line, preferring instead to believe with hindsight the portentous nature of events as indicative of the intention of God to preserve this nation. He declared:

We may and must believe that He who has led our fathers in ways so strange and has preserved our land in a manner so marvellous, has a purpose for us to

154 *The Spiritual Issues of the War*, No. 36, 3 July 1940.
155 Richardson, 1940, p.19.
156 Richardson, 1940, p.31.
157 Richardson, 1940, p.30.

serve in the preparation of His perfect Kingdom [...] Thanks be to God Who preserved us from destruction.[158]

Some Birmingham clerics preferred the confident beliefs of Temple to the open-ended prospect of the Niebuhrian thinker. John Jackson's sermon to the Parade of Wardens and Fire-fighters of 24 August 1941 explained God's actions through wartime's purgations in positive and forthright terms, reassuring people of the evidence of God's providential care:

> Surely we have to admit first of all that there is a God, and secondly that He is very active in this troubled world, that He is intimately connected with the cause for which we have taken up arms and that but for His providence we should never have been in the position we are today. If you doubt this, then let me recall three incidents which to my mind form conclusive proof of the truth of this fact. Sir Neville Henderson revealed in a speech at Ipswich on November 1940, that on 28 September we possessed no Spitfires, we only possessed 1 or 2 experimental Hurricanes and only 7 modern A.A. guns for the defence of London out of 400 estimated as the minimum necessary [...] Surely Hitler knew to some considerable extent the position of our unpreparedness in this island. Why then didn't he strike? [...] God kept back the enemy when all things were in Hitler's power to crush us [...] who can deny that the hand of God was plainly discernible at Dunkirk, when the B.E.F. was in so grave danger. You may remember that a few days before that evacuation the Germans had announced that the B.E.F. was 'encircled' [...] God again heard and answered our prayers, and that memorable and historic evacuation took place constituting what Mr. Churchill called a 'miraculous deliverance' [...] this island was wide open to Nazi invasion [...] Truly, good friends, GOD HAS BEEN ON OUR SIDE, or we might today be under the heel of a cruel, ruthless, tyrannical foe. Yes, God is actively engaged in this titanic struggle with us; [tell those] you will come across in the course of your duties [...] who are sceptical about God's activity, that they are not alone in their sufferings, that God *is* here with us all, sharing in it all, lifting our hearts to a new brave hope and clearer vision.[159]

The more reassuring was surely this latter way of thinking. To many its empiricism was to prove alluring, perhaps because it was explicable to the ordinary mindset, and, thereby, it bolstered the British wartime mythology of a people remaining unconquered despite the odds.

158 *The Spiritual Issues of the War*, No. 204, 30 September 1943.
159 John Jackson: sermon to 'Parade of Wardens and Fire-fighters', 24 August 1941.

Certainly, in the midst of the impossible circumstances of the early years of the war, to believe other than in the certainties of God's protection might have proven fatal to morale. It must therefore have been necessary to believe the comforting words printed by one parish magazine, that all was under the Divine eye:

> The patrol of the angels passes along over the whole world. All is under survey, nothing happens anywhere at any time unseen by those strong and tranquil ministers of the divine purpose [...] It is just what we are sometimes tempted to doubt – the universal providence of God. The world seems to be at the mercy of evil, lawless forces, which have broken away from all control. In truth God is on His throne; the patrol of the angels marches everywhere, the providence of God stands over all, supreme and sure. Tranquil and unconquered the patrol of angels moves over the world, along the vast battle frontiers they keep watch and ward – amid the great ships on the seas; through the ranks of hospital beds, over the resting places of the dead they pass. They move along the broken cities and the wasted country, they are present at every victory and every defeat. All is watched by the angels, all is under control.[160]

To a lesser extent than in the First World War, the language of crusading was utilised to describe the character of the second conflict, perhaps because of the nervousness of appearing as belligerent as clerics had apparently done previously.[161] Yes, it was often stressed by the Church leadership that 'the cause for which we are fighting is undoubtedly the cause of right,'[162] but this war's suffering was dealt with much more in terms of its penitential and soul-making implications for the individual and the nation.[163] Nevertheless the term 'crusade' did on occasion emerge, this time, however, in less jingoistic and in more morally purposive tones. Claiming that the nation needed God's help to come through this ordeal, on the National Day of Prayer of 29 March 1942, the King described the war as a 'veritable crusade

160 *The Parish Magazine of St Alban's, Bordesley*, October 1941.
161 This did not stop those who had been previously assertive from reasserting their position: cf. Mews, 1983, p.412.
162 Archbishop Williams's Advent Pastoral Letter, 1940, p.4, St. Chad's Cathedral Archive.
163 Archbishop Williams's Lent Pastoral Letter, 1943, St. Chad's Cathedral Archive.

against the forces of darkness'.[164] In the assessment of some, this described the true character of this war and the spirit of the people entering it: Britain was perceived to be the custodian of those political values worthy of defence and creative of the climate in which the Christian religion flourishes. Thus, the British people were likened to the crusaders of old in the righteousness of their cause, and the realism of their devotion, rather than the militarism of their method. The vicar of Sparkbrook, Alban Tilt, commenting upon the invasion of 1944, hoped and prayed that the fighting forces 'are engaged upon a crusade to redeem the whole of European civilisation from Nazi slavery'.[165] Likening the sufferings of the civilian and the soldier to the sufferings of Christ he went on:

> Our Lord's victory [...] was won through pain and death: so today, wherever the fight for freedom is being waged, there is the cross of suffering to be borne by our gallant men. We at home are like the friends of Jesus who stood by the Cross, we have our vigil to keep. We must watch and pray. When at last victory breaks [we] need to become aware that this warfare is a part of the age-long battle between good and evil: that in the sufferings of the peoples and the sacrifices of our fighting men there is a Calvary, which must bring us to repentance, and enlist us as faithful soldiers and servants of Jesus Christ.[166]

Similarly, Cyril Alington, Dean of Durham, wrote:

> We believe we are fighting for some of those eternal values which are dear to God, and we cannot but hope that if, by His help, we are successful, one result of our victory will be to create an atmosphere in which the Christian message can be freely heard [...] like the Crusaders of old, we are clearing the way to the Holy Places [...] Few individuals, and no nation, are really worthy to bear the Cross. Like them, we are not quite clear what is our earthly goal: the United States of Europe may prove as short-lived a dream as the Crusading Kingdom of Jerusalem. Like them we have no certainty of sure or speedy victory: many a Crusader has died with his object unattained [...] we have deep down in our hearts a conviction, perhaps unreasoned but certainly not unreasonable, that our cause is one which God must bless: He must desire that there should be free

164 *The Birmingham Post*, 30 March 1942.
165 *The Fiery Cross*, the parish magazine of St. Agatha's, Sparkbrook, Vol. XIX, No. 9, September 1944.
166 *The Fiery Cross*, the parish magazine of St. Agatha's, Sparkbrook, Vol. XIX, No. 9, September 1944.

access to the 'Holy Places', whether they are envisaged as an earthly shrine or as the dwelling place of Freedom and Justice and Good Faith, and, like them, we are content to leave the issue in His hands.[167]

Equally, the nationalistic use of the crusading metaphor was occasionally in evidence in radio transmissions, as Siân Nicholas[168] notes of the broadcasts of Nathaniel Micklem. By contrast, the more frequently repeated claim of Birmingham's clerics was that this war was a fight for the very soul of the nation:

> War is a punishment of God for sin [...] we have our individual sins; we have our sins as a nation, for as a nation we have often set up false gods and worshipped them. We worship money and comfort and position [...] we allow injustice to the unemployed [...] insufficient wages [...] which make family life difficult [...] we allow an education which leaves boys and girls with only the vaguest notions of what God is or how they are to serve him [...] If we would claim to be fighting for Christian civilisation, we must be prepared to make sacrifices [...] Our reparation will be [...] repentance from our own individual sins [...] we must determine [...] to remove [...] injustice, falsehood and cruelty which we see in our society [...] the English people have a glorious history of kindness and charity [but] A nation which forgets its God soon begins to drift it knows not whither [...] May this war help us as a nation to come back to the knowledge and love of God, the only true foundation for any true and lasting peace.[169]

Thus, akin to the First World War, the Second was seized upon as an opportunity for spiritual advance, representative of the spiritual 'tug-of-war' between good and evil going on throughout history, victory in which was potentially transformative of the priorities and values of individuals and the structures of society.[170] In contrast to the Great War, however, the Churches came up with no similar nationally co-ordinated optimistic scheme, such as The National Mission of Repentance and Hope in England and The National Mission of Rededication in Scotland, in order to attempt to reap the harvest of its

---

167   Alington, 1940, pp.30 and 38.
168   Nicholas, 1996, p.156.
169   Archbishop Williams's Lent Pastoral Letter, 1940, pp.1 and 8.
170   Salter, 1942, p.51.

rhetoric.[171] Indeed, even the publication of *Towards the Conversion of England* in 1945 yielded little in the way of its title's suggested intent.[172] Instead, the Churches of the Second World War chose to focus their energies upon more diffuse means of spiritual support and evangelistic endeavour, through many publications and radio broadcasts, and such movements as the Sword of the Spirit and the Religion and Life weeks.[173] Perhaps because of this the clergy of the Second World War were protected from the demoralisation of unfulfilled revivalist expectations Stuart Mews ascribes to the clergy of the Great War.[174]

Dealing with Loss and Death

As well as adapting the pastoral task to particular wartime exigencies and developing a cosmic interpretation to rationalise events, clerics were called upon to function in their traditional roles, albeit in a more exacting way than in peacetime. For example, dealing with loss and bereavement was for the ordained minister grist to the mill. War, however, with new extremes of loss and a heavier incidence of bereavement, meant dealing with grief of a higher order and on a more frequent basis. Just as they had done as chaplains in the First World War, clerics were called upon in the Second 'to maintain the significance of death [after all, what did the] resurrection of the body mean to the soldiers who cleared and buried the rat-eaten pieces of flesh from the barbed wire'[175], or to the civil defence workers who pulled mutilated corpses from bombed out buildings? Somehow, clergy had to preserve the dignity of the body amidst the sacrilegious treatment meted out to it by the bombs and provide meaningful ritual

171 Explored in Thompson, 1983 and Brown, 1994.
172 Wilkinson, 1986, pp.222–223.
173 Wilkinson, 1986, pp.257–258.
174 Mews, 1973.
175 Wilkinson, 1978, p.174.

to mark a person's passing. It became routine for many of those caring in the aftermath to deal with death as the norm. It was left to clerics to cajole and remind others of the body's dignity. William Brooke recollects:

> I was at the vicarage when they came with news that the Moral Welfare Home [had been hit] Canon Tilt was the Chaplain, Canon Long was the chaplain on a voluntary basis, there was a house keeper and a warden [...] Canon Long was all right, his house keeper was killed by his side, the warden was missing and I think there was one girl missing, so we began to move things and gently go round and see if we could hear anything and then there was a noise; it turned out to be the girl [...] She came out alive, she was all right eventually but then we discovered the warden. One of the vivid memories is of her body on a lorry, it was covered in brick dust; it was like an effigy. It was just left there. And I remember saying to the services 'Is she dead or not? Either treat her as dead, as a corpse, or treat her as a living person.'[176]

Ministering in the aftermath of the blitz was a hectic and arduous round. It meant the routine of surveying one's community to see what damage had been done, who had been made homeless and who was in need. Clerics visited hospitals to see if there were any casualties. One Birmingham Roman Catholic cleric recalls a week in which he had a funeral each day, and another occasion when he had three bodies in the church at once. A lasting image for the same priest is of his church, St. Catherine, Horsefair, lined full length with coffins.[177] It is little wonder, with the taxing round of such a ministry, that the same priest spent his shelter hours dealing with such mundanities as filling in the parish baptism register.

The lot of breaking the bad news of the death of a loved one often fell to the clergy. John Jackson recalled:

> At that time where there were a tremendous number of casualties and obviously we did our very best first of all to give them spiritual counsel and comfort, which was very difficult under the circumstances. A normal bereavement is bad enough but when it is of somebody who as a result of war, particularly overseas where this information had been brought to them by the police that their loved one had died. There were occasions, sometimes, when even the police found it

---

176   Interview with Canon William E. Brooke, May 2000.
177   Conversation with Father John Welch, May 2000.

[difficult]; I remember one policeman found it very very difficult to convey this information to them, and we had a very good relationship with the police. I remember one policeman saying, 'Look I just can't do it, do you think you could do it, you're the best man to do it.' That's only an isolated incident but it just shows you the depth of feeling you had at that time for people who were under that tremendous stress of knowing that their loved ones had died.[178]

On occasion, the way of making sense of the death of a loved one lay in stressing its redemptive qualities to the deceased: thus, the sacrifice was not in vain. Much in the character of the 'magnificent' deaths of First World War combatants, a way of appeasing the pain was to imagine the nobility of the cause and the perfection of the deceased in it. One well circulated, and popularised example of this was the 'Letter of an Airman to his Mother', printed in *The Times* on 18 June 1940. Said to have been found amongst the personal belongings of an airman 'Missing, Believed Killed', this letter appeared in a parish magazines just after the Battle of Britain and at the height of the blitz. It idealises the dignity of wartime sacrifices of mothers as well as sons, on the home front as well as on the front line:

Dearest Mother, Though I feel no premonition at all, events are moving rapidly, and I have instructed that this letter be forwarded to you should I fail to return from one of the raids which we shall shortly be called upon to undertake. You must hope for a month, but at the end of that time you must accept the fact that I have handed over my task to the extremely capable hands of my comrades of the Royal Air Force [...] First, it will comfort you to know that my role in this war has been of the greatest importance [...] Though it will be difficult for you, you will disappoint me if you do not at least try to accept the facts dispassionately, for I shall have done my duty to the utmost of my ability. No man can do more, and no one calling himself a man could do less. I have always admired your amazing courage in the face of continual setbacks: in the way you have given me as good an education and background as anyone in the country; and always kept up appearances without ever losing faith in the future. My death would not mean that our struggle has been in vain. Far from it. It means that your sacrifice was as great as mine. Those who serve England must expect nothing from her; we debase ourselves if we regard our country as merely a place in which to eat and sleep. History resounds with illustrious names who have given all, yet their sacrifice has resulted in the British Empire, where there is a measure of peace, justice, freedom for all, and where a higher standard of civilization has evolved,

178 Interview with Prebendary John Jackson, March 2000.

and is still evolving, than anywhere else. But this is not only concerning our own land. Today we are faced with the greatest organized challenge to Christianity and civilisation that the world has ever seen, and I count myself lucky and honoured to be the right age and fully trained to throw my full weight into the scale. For this I have to thank you. Yet there is more work for you to do. The home front will have to stand united for years after the war is won. For all that can be said against it, I still maintain that this war is a very good thing; every individual is having the chance to give and dare all for his principles like the martyrs of old. However long the time may be, one thing can never be altered – I shall have lived and died an Englishman. Nothing else matters one jot nor can anything ever change it. You must not grieve for me, for if you really believe in religion and all that it entails that would be hypocrisy. I have no fear of death; only a queer elation [...] I would have it no other way. The universe is so vast and so ageless that the life of one man can only be justified by the measure of his sacrifice. We are sent to this world to acquire a personality and character to take with us that can never be taken from us. Those who just eat and sleep, prosper and procreate, are no better than the animals if all their lives they are at peace. I firmly and absolutely believe that evil things are sent into the world to try us; they are sent deliberately by our Creator to test our metal because He knows what is good for us. The Bible is full of cases where the easy way out has been discarded for moral principles. I count myself fortunate in that I have seen the whole country and known men of every calling. But with the final test of war I consider my character fully developed. Thus at my early age my earthly mission is fulfilled and I am prepared to die with just one regret, and one only – that I could not devote myself to making your declining years more happy by being with you; but you will live in peace and freedom and I shall have directly contributed to that, so here again my life will not have been in vain. Your loving Son.[179]

Similar sentiments expressive of the war's atoning effect inspired a poem of W.E. Harding, 'To the Fallen', published in the circular letter to those in the services from Erdington Congregational Church:

Pass friend, all's well! At least thy record's clear
Thou need'st not fear. Whatever be the cause
Of this betrayal, and these broken laws,
Thou are exempt from blame. There's nothing mean
In dying on the field. The great Unseen
Receive thee! Thou are through the gaping jaws;
Nor needest now the sound of our applause,
Beside still waters, and by pastures green.

179   *The Parish Magazine of St. Nicholas, Lower Tower Street*, December 1940.

There comes a shriving to the souls of men
Whose lives stand forfeit to the general sin.
Th' Accusing Angel put away his pen.
Christ, as we read, redeemed the souls in Hell
When He had paid this fee, entered in
With them to Paradise. Pass friend; all's well.[180]

Another parish magazine reprinted the words of the Bishop of Bradford in response to demands for a theodicy, entitled 'If You Have Lost a Son':

Why does God allow it? [...] Only because He cannot stop it without using force, and to use force would be to take away the freewill he has given us [...] We may well wonder at the depth and extent of the agony which men cause God to endure [...] He, too, saw a Son die. You know your own loss. There is a hole in your home and your heart. God help you. But do not talk of waste. For death is not the end. Life goes on [...] God wastes no spiritual possibilities in any of us [...]. The boy has higher flights to reach: a fuller life to live. He is more alive than when he was here [...] One can remember him in one's time of prayer, and have no doubt he remembers us [...] Hold on to a loving God to whom your son is dearer even than he is to you.[181]

Despite the grief attendant on bereavement, it was the bombings' carnage, sometimes blotted from recollection, oftentimes scarring the memory with abiding images, which most deeply affected the clergy. John Jackson recalls that the reality of war reared its head in the cruel randomness of the blitz:

I think one of the most tragic incidents was where we went out one night into Ravenhurst Street. [T]here was a house at the end of the road where [t]he[y] had to bring out three bodies. [It's] a memory that I shall always remember because it only reinforced my view of the stupidity of war.[182]

Bombing led to heavy casualties and mass funerals were common, even if accounts of such in Birmingham are not particularly well documented. However, the city of Coventry, which suffered large

---

180   Erdington Congregational Church, *Circular Letter 300*.
181   *The Fiery Cross*, the parish magazine of St. Agatha's Sparkbrook, Vol. XIX, No. 8, August 1944.
182   Interview with Prebendary John Jackson, March 2000.

numbers of fatalities in one infamous night, 14/15 November 1940, deemed it practical and fitting that many should be buried at the same time.[183] In this, the denominations of the Churches of Coventry worked ecumenically to mark the event.[184]

The clergy and lay Christians of Birmingham formed an important, albeit informal, part of the civil defence and caring operation during the blitz. Inspired by the example of the padres of the First World War, they helped sustain the population, and thereby civilian morale, by being present with the people as they endured the trials of home-front warfare. Christians worked in their localities to ease the stresses of the sheltering public, often acting as a calming and reassuring presence and sometimes providing food and drink. They helped deal with the physical and emotional debris on the morning after raids and they encouraged people to pay attention to the significance of death and mark the deaths of others with meaningful ritual. Clerics offered words of hope and pointed to the larger purposes unfolding behind events. The extent to which their voices were heard whilst Birmingham considered the shape of post-war society is the subject to which we now turn.

183   Chinn, 1996, p.101.
184   Longmate, 1976, pp.225–227.

4: The Churches' Vision of the Post-war World

The disaster of war may turn to our salvation, if it reawakens in us a living faith in the potential destiny of our people; if its stabs us awake and opens our eyes to the things that really matter.[1]

The way to victory lies in producing the conviction now among the masses that there are to be no more distressed areas, no more vast armies of unemployed, no more slums, no vast denial of genuine educational opportunity.[2]

These lines are being written [during] the gravest hours [...] – hours that are pregnant with incalculable possibilities [...] are we going to match the grave and critical times through which we are passing with a new and [...] *lasting* change of heart and mind, so that future men and women may say at such and such a period the British people began to [...] establish a new era of truth and justice on the earth – a step nearer to God's Kingdom? If we cannot or will not do this, we can at tremendous sacrifice win this war, but as certainly as last time we shall lose the peace [...] Surely, this is a possibility we dare not contemplate.[3]

Religion, Reconstruction and Morale

The political, polemical and ideological power struggle determining the shape that British society would take once the war had been won began well in advance of the hoped-for victory. As early as the Dunkirk evacuations and the fall of France, during May/June 1940, the

1   *The Christian News-Letter*, No. 35, 26 June 1940, published by J.H. Oldham for the Council on the Christian Faith and Common Life.
2   Harold Laski, writing the summer of 1940; quoted in Addison, 1994, p.184.
3   *The Messenger*, the magazine of Lozells Congregational Church, Wheeler St. Birmingham, June 1940: the editor's emphases.

theme of reconstruction began to be aired.[4] This was by no means a chance occurrence, for, as we have seen in the previous chapter, it had long been recognised by the powers that be that there is an inextricable link between sustaining the morale of the fighting forces and ultimate victory.[5] Promising a better world beyond war's ending, as an aspect of morale sustenance, had been an espoused practice during the First World War.[6] Unsurprisingly, therefore, it came to the fore as a method of influencing military morale in this second conflict,[7] especially under the auspices of the organised classes of the Army Bureau of Current Affairs.[8] Similarly, as it had become an accepted way of influencing those on the front line, now, in a total war context, it came to be recognized that civilian morale (upon which victory depended in this conflict perhaps more so than any other) needed to be galvanised by a similar process; that of creating a vision of things to come and distracting the public from the privations of the present. That is to say, making people believe that this war was worth fighting, encouraging them to think that a better world would result, and keeping them from dwelling on the mundanities and details of the war, would, it was believed, sustain their will to press on in spite of exigencies. It was clear to many that the discussion and debate of blueprints for such a new society gave substance to the oft-stated moral purpose of the war, thereby, it was held, increasing the determination of the people to win. William Beveridge, the architect of the substance of the proposals for post-war Britain, was one who recognised the power of moral ideals in shaping the ethos in which the conflict was fought. It was his stated belief that by establishing a moral purpose for the conflict the populace could be energised to greater dedication to the war effort. His broadcast words of 1942 reflect this, where he urged: 'A war of faith is

---

4   See, for example, the quote from Harold Laski above. See also Addison, 1985, p.9 for a discussion of the recognised political opportunity for change presented by the war. However, the link between civilian morale and proposals for post-war reform was not explicitly recognised until April 1942 according to McLaine (1979, p.173).

5   My thanks to Michael Snape for this insight.

6   See, for example, Gardner, 1917.

7   Addison, 1994, p.121.

8   Calder, 1969, p.251.

what the world is waiting for.'[9] Thus, by stressing the moral reasons for the fight, and the rewards attendant upon victory, the war was cast in the form of a spiritual battle. By characterising it in such terms, other quasi-religious concepts could also be utilised, and notions such as service, and self-sacrifice, could easily be drawn upon to frame wartime activities. Furthermore, by imagining the 'New Jerusalem' in this world, the rewards for the spiritual battle were made tangible and attainable.

Myriad voluntary groups and societies began to speculate about the future, even while victory seemed only a remote possibility.[10] Naturally, the Churches were ideally suited to the creation of such a 'faith' (*pace* Beveridge), their theology replete with readily applicable concepts and language that enabled the conflict to be so idealised. That the Churches used such motifs is already evident. Certainly, many churchmen saw the aims of the war as akin to their own, particularly those working in the Religions Division of the Ministry of Information.[11] Whatever the motivation for this, the utilisation of religious concepts, language and ideals came naturally because the Christian religion constituted a significant backdrop to the lives of the masses, supplying a strong thread in the discourse by which people lived. Whether the people had to deal with the austerity of war, the traumas of the blitz, or construct an ideal for post-war Britain, religious sentiment, terminology, concepts and ideals could be drawn on naturally because the people had a ready familiarity with them. Air-raid shelter spirituality, which was founded upon cultural conditions favourable to the use of Christian language and motif, had an eschatological dimension, which saw war's ending resulting in the creation of a new society.

Additionally, there were many cinematic projections of the 'brave new world' for which the British were told they were fighting and 'a strong claim can be made for the cinema's contribution to the radicalisation of the British electorate' by it.[12] Some of these films and

9   Addison, 1994, p.184.
10   Addison, 1994, p.162.
11   See Kirby, 1993, p.250.
12   Burton, 1995, p.74.

documentaries used religious motifs and semi-religious forms with which to mediate their message that the war presented a critical opportunity and a potential turning point. These films were often shown in public places such as schools, village halls, public shelters and in factories, and perhaps their message was made all the more powerful because of their religious texture. One such was directed by Humphrey Jennings, enlisting a narrative written by E.M. Forster, and telling the story of the early months of the baby Timothy, set against the conditions of the final months of the war. Moving between images of working-class life (with which Jennings was fascinated), high culture and Church choirs, the life of the baby is juxtaposed, presenting the apparent message of the equality of the people in their sacrifices for the next generation. The film portrays what in a literal sense is true, that the people have been fighting for this child, and for 'all the other babies'. The nation has fought for the promise of change, for freedom, and for 'the power to choose and the right to criticise'. Its concluding question relates to the promises made at the end of the First World War: must the same problems of unemployment and greed persist, or can the world finally be a different place? [13]

However, a number of Christians did not read the war as an opportunity for societal change; rather it was clear to them that events were for ripe for personal and national spiritual transformation. It was emphasised – interestingly across denominational bounds and ecclesiastical traditions – that it was a change of heart that was needed, not an alteration of society; a change in personal morality above a change in the social order. For many clerics the real problem, and the real enemy of this war, was materialism and lax personal morality. Therefore, it was towards personal moral reform, they argued, that resolve needed to be committed. As one Anglican cleric wrote, echoing the words of Winston Churchill:

> England has gone heathen and is not going to be reclaimed without sweat off [*sic*] blood and tears [...] The times are evil and call for heroic measures. Divorce, bad faith, dishonesty and uncleanness are the common habits of the people; and there is a tendency to imagine that happiness will be restored by a better political system and more elaborate social services. I warn you that all

13   *A Diary for Timothy* (1946), directed by Humphrey Jennings; Crown Film Unit.

these things will turn to the worsening of the conditions of England unless and until the people come to know God and to seek his righteousness first in all things.[14]

Yet, despite divergent tenor of comment the dominant voice supported societal 'reconstruction' with personal reform as a lesser part of this.

Furthermore, just as it has been commented that 'Hitler suffered a million deaths by typewriter'[15] from the considerable published polemic in favour of societal change emerging from this period, so too Christian intellectuals were similarly prolific. Indeed, the prophetic voice of the Church, though not silent prior to the war, was especially vociferous during it. Speaking and writing on a range of subjects, Churchmen and Christian intellectuals debated the moral principles and political ideals upon which post-war society should be re-organised. Upon many conference platforms up and down the land they debated, wrestled with and promulgated ideas for reconstruction. In numerous published volumes and series of studies, they called upon Christians to consider the moral and spiritual opportunities presented by the conflict. I refer here only to the some of the most significant of these on the national scene, instead focusing upon those individuals, movements and events most closely linked to the context of Birmingham. Birmingham's leading Christians saw that this was an opportune time not only for the nation and the city, but also for the status of Christianity as the nation's faith.

As well as exploring the particulars of the teaching and debate amongst Birmingham's clerics and congregations, some concluding remarks will be made about the issue of wartime reparations, the response to the use of the atom bomb and the way in which Birmingham officially marked the end of the war.

---

14 *The Fiery Cross*, the parish magazine of St. Agatha's, Sparkbrook, Vol. XVII, No. 11, November 1942. This echoes the sentiments of George Bell, Bishop of Chichester, in his *Christianity and World Order*, as noted by Machin, 1998, p.136.

15 Addison, 1994, p.184.

Some Contributions of National Influence

The question of the degree to which the Christian debate touched the lives of the majority, making a difference to their morale, must first be dealt with. It could be argued that Christian wranglings, in fact, made little impact and that 'a square meal and a good comedy programme on the radio [...] meant more to morale than a promise about post-war conditions.'[16] Notwithstanding the plausibility of this, evidence suggests that the Christian teaching on the subject of reconstruction was responded to favourably by those exposed to it. For instance, in response to a nationwide series of meetings instigated by William Temple at the height of the reconstruction debate,[17] a Mass-Observation survey found [of its cross-section of volunteers in November 1942] that not only was there a considerable degree of goodwill directed towards the Churches' and to clerics' pro-nouncements concerning post-war planning, but also that such utterances were not only expected but welcomed by 51% of its respondents.[18] Indeed, Mass-Observation's results reflected a greater faith in the Churches' declarations than those of the politicians. From this evidence it can be clearly seen that people did, at the very least, pay attention to what the Churches said in this area.

No discussion of the subject of post-war reconstruction would be complete without mention of William Temple, the dominant Church figure in relation to Christian social concern in the early part of the twentieth century. The influence of his ideas and personality on the tone, content and shape of the reconstruction debate is inestimable, and his contribution to it proved incalculable and lasting. It is not without significance that he came to be known as the 'People's Archbishop', because his support of societal reconstruction seemed to add promise to its realisation. The zenith of Temple's social thought was distilled and made accessible in his *Christianity and Social Order* published in

---

16   Addison, 1994, p.185.
17   At which, in Birmingham, large numbers attended to hear the archbishop speak. Calder, 1969, p.486.
18   Mass-Observation, FR 1525.

186

1942 selling some 140,000 copies at the time and being reprinted many times since. The major part of this piece of his published thinking concerned the manner and means of social change and how the foundations for such change may derive from Christian theology, especially rooted in the natural law. It is not until the final sections of the book that he outlined a number of specific policy statements of his own concerning childhood, the family, education, housing, incomes, industrial relations and leisure.[19] This book, coupled with Temple's involvement at the Malvern Conference a year earlier, proved to be of defining influence in the debate, and meant that when William Beveridge published his *Report on Social Insurance and Allied Services* ('The Beveridge Report') at the end of 1942, the Churches were in advance of this in their thinking about the shape of things to come.

Roman Catholics too were drawn into debating the rebuilding of post-war British society. Most notable amongst the formative influences among them were organisations such as the Sword of the Spirit. Founded in late 1940, partly in response to the need to demonstrate clear Roman Catholic support for the war effort,[20] this movement drew Catholics and non-Catholics together on the same platform, for a brief period at least. The Sword movement came under pressure from within Roman Catholic circles, in part because of the tentative nature of large-scale ecumenism at the time, but also because it appeared to pose a threat to more established Roman Catholic organisations of similar ilk, such as the Catholic Social Guild, chaired as it was by the wartime Archbishop of Birmingham, Thomas Williams.[21] Williams commented on the Sword movement in his Advent Pastoral Letter of 1941, arguing favourably that cooperation represented a positive witness to society in that it had the potential 'to restore and sustain a more Christian mode of life in our nation'. However, later in the same letter he demurred, saying that the Sword's cooperative methods dishonestly 'imply that we give up even one little bit of our beliefs and practices'.[22]

19 Temple, 1976 edition, p.96.
20 Mews, 1983, p.414.
21 For instance, see Williams's antagonism mentioned in Mews, 1983, p.421.
22 Archbishop Williams's Pastoral Letter, Advent 1941.

Writing of the Sword, a year into its existence, a leading Roman Catholic laywoman, Barbara Ward, commented upon the degree of confidence and hope engendered amongst intellectual Catholics by the work of the Sword:

> The British community is a free community because to a large extent it has preserved its Christian heritage and with it a great common stock of accepted belief. But that heritage in under fire [...] It must be the work of Christians in this generation to restore the basis of social agreement. The experience of the Sword of the Spirit Movement until now shows that, although the task is a difficult one, it can be accomplished, and that its challenge to Catholics is to play their part in leading the nations 'back from the broken cisterns of material and selfish interest to the living fountain of divine justice' [quoting the Pope's five peace points]. Catholics have resources of grace which are denied to others [...] It is because the evils of the world are in the last analysis spiritual evils that Catholics must be in the forefront of their solution [...] The Sword of the Spirit has tried – and hopes still – to be a creative response to the challenge of totalitarian war and social disintegration.[23]

Alongside the big platform meetings such as those provided by the Sword and its Protestant counterpart Religion and Life, the war seemed to generate an increase in the practice of small groups of Christians meeting to discuss and debate the nature of change. Parallel publications appeared, to support such cell groups, in the shape of the Sword of the Spirit's own tracts and the journal *The Christian News-Letter* (under the editorship of J.H. Oldham, architect of the Oxford Conference of 1937), alongside its associated books.[24] Likewise, a number of books in the Religious Book Club series emerged to debate the nature of the foundations of a new society and the shape of a reformed Church.[25]

One publication of the Religious Book Club was written by the leading Churchman, Leslie Weatherhead, a Methodist who, since 1936, had been minister at the Congregational City Temple, Holborn. In his book of 1940 *This is the Victory*, a follow-on from this *Thinking Aloud in Wartime*, Weatherhead addressed the practicalities of facing

23 Ward, 1941, p.192.
24 For example, Oldham, 1940.
25 For example, Allen, 1942.

up to the day-to-day events of the war. Towards the book's conclusion, he considered what the future might hold. In particular, he asked members of his young people's Friday Fellowship what they believed should be the changes wrought by the war. Recognising and supporting the suggested programmes of improvement in health, housing and education, as a socialist he, nevertheless, cautioned against the limits of political experiments:

> Jesus, one remembers, did not announce His Gospel in slogans like 'A living wage for every man.' But rather, 'Change your way of looking at life and believe the good news about God' [...] The Church's job is to change the would-be reformer, suggest and encourage the reforms, and condemn unsparingly all in our national and international life that is contrary to the spirit of Christ.[26]

British society was perceived by various Christian commentators to be ostensibly secular and in need of spiritual reform, whilst most regarded it still, and often at the same time, as a Christian country. The commentator's approach to and methods of change were fundamentally determined by their ecclesiology. To characterize, for Roman Catholic commentators loyalty to the Church meant the need for a degree of protectionism, for the Nonconformist it was easier to stand in tension with the state. The particulars of the Birmingham context mirrored the national dynamic and it is to the various contributions of local Churches and individuals that we now turn.

Some Local Contributions to the Vision

Significantly, just as Birmingham's Victorian civic identity had been driven and shaped by the city's Nonconformist forefathers and their 'civic gospel' – a process indivisible from the ministry of R.W. Dale and the city's Congregational base at Carrs Lane – the site for a major conference on the topic of the post-Second World War world, which

---

26   Weatherhead, 1940, pp.316 and 318.

drew together the city's intellectuals and dignitaries, was also, symbolically perhaps, located at that renowned church. As was the case at the city's Victorian zenith, municipal politics were seen to have pre-eminence over the national in matters of social reform.[27] Equally, it appears, change had to begin at home in the Birmingham of the post Second World War world. Now under the ministrations of Leslie Tizard, Carrs Lane Chapel was the venue for a series of lectures on Sunday evenings across the spring and summer of 1942, ahead of the national debate, for the Beveridge Report was not published until December of that year. These lectures, generically entitled *Christianity and Life*, were on a variety of subjects ranging from health and education through to the arts, science and the home. A civic, ecclesiastical or academic dignitary was invited to give an address to a public audience, at sessions appended to worship upon the same theme. The lectures drew together the city's elite and representatives from across denominational boundaries, and were later published, forming the focus of Birmingham's vision. Commented upon in *The Birmingham Post* on the day following each event, the conferences added significantly to the discourse concerning reconstruction at the time. It is possible to assert, from the evidence of the gatherings, that Christian principles and values still resonated in Birmingham, that the 'civic gospel' continued to be authoritative, and that the relationship between faith and politics in Birmingham life, established even before the Victorian era, continued to have vitality. Birmingham looked to its religious leaders for moral and spiritual leadership now as never before; clearly, Christianity remained the reference point. The confidence of the preface of the published addresses makes this clear. The stated purpose of the lectures was unambiguous, demonstrating that the Christian faith and the life of the city were intertwined in the minds of many. The editor proclaimed:

> 'Reconstruction' is in the air. If we are to rebuild society two things are necessary: 1. We must think afresh the principles on which a new order must be based. 2. We must discover a moral and spiritual dynamic which will overcome the obstacle of individual selfishness and which will inspire us to take common

27   See for example the quote from R.W. Dale in A. Briggs, 1990, p. 201.

action. Thousands of thinking men and women are convinced, as never before, that only the Christian religion can provide such principles and such dynamic.

The Lord Mayor of Birmingham, Norman Tiptaft, confident that the Church's voice would be heard, added in his foreword:

> The idea that the walls of the New Jerusalem will arise of themselves at the end of the war without adequate planning and hard work is utterly absurd. We shall no more win the peace than we shall win the war except by considered thinking and intense struggle.[28]

Clearly, for Tiptaft and Tizard, the discussion to be had about social change was most naturally carried out within the boundaries of Christian moral discourse. It was assumed that this discourse would be understood, and that that people would have a sufficient readiness with it to be able to utilise it. Tizard's opening sermons of the series provide further evidence of this belief: within them he adopts an unquestioning tone assuming that his prophetic monologues will be taken seriously and understood by all in his audience. In assuming this without question, he demonstrates the degree to which the Churches had a willing audience.

The guest speakers' (most of them non-clerics) addresses demonstrate the readiness and articulacy that Tizard assumes. The participants thereby understood one other because they spoke a common language. It is clear that, whatever the wider influence of these conferences, the wartime context in which they occurred was one in which religion was not peripheral, but automatically and naturally invoked as society sought to establish what should happen next.

In distinctly apocalyptic tones, Tizard spoke in his first sermon on the theme Christianity and Life, of 'Christianising' society, and of asserting the Lordship of Christ:

> Christianity is facing what may be its final trial of strength with the world. It must take up the challenge of Christianising public relationships. It dare not withdraw further. It dare not be any longer on the defensive. It must attack!

28 *Christianity and Life: a series of Sunday evening services and conferences for Birmingham men and women held at Carrs Lane Church during spring and summer, 1942*: Carrs Lane Church, 1942, preface and foreword.

[every part of life must be brought under] the control of Christian principles and the Spirit of Christ [...] asserting the Lordship of Christ over all human relationships, activities and culture.

Recalling the defining influence of Christianity upon the city's life Tizard advocated a return to the pervasive 'civic gospel' of old. Working with the notion that the authority of Christianity has been somewhat lost in the intervening years, and that the war was a sign of this loss, he saw this moment as critical:

When Carrs Lane made its tremendous impact upon the life of Birmingham, Dr. Dale was declaring, in the pulpit and out of it, that the authority of the living Christ extends to every province of human energy. To make that authority effective and supreme is the duty of the true Christian, who must live in the world and not apart from it, a force to leaven and purify [...] the Church in general has failed to make this assertion in a way which has commanded the attention and respect of the world, and the suffering and tragedy of the present time are an inevitable judgement of both the Church and the world [...] Here, surely, is the opportunity of the Christian Church – perhaps the last it will ever have – to stand before the bewildered minds of men as the custodian of values and to offer them the leadership they crave.[29]

For Tizard, what was envisaged is not only the physical reconstruction of society but also its complete moral reform and spiritual conversion:

The war has violently destroyed the past, which is perhaps a good thing. When we build again we must not strive to rebuild the old, but to plan afresh and build better [...] Let us put our trust in God and go forward into the darkness with courage.[30]

Tizard's sense of urgency, that the Church should take the initiative, did not lead him to excessive confidence in the Church, but in God's grand design. In rather Niebuhrian tones, echoing the prophet Isaiah's pronouncements concerning Cyrus, he stated that if the Church did not take this opportunity then God will use other means to bring about change: 'God will find some other instrument through which he can work out His purpose', even Stalin's Russia.[31]

29 *Christianity and Life*, 1942, pp. 4–6.
30 *Christianity and Life*, 1942, p.6.
31 *Christianity and Life*, 1942, p.10.

Tizard's predecessor at Carrs Lane, Leyton Richards, a renowned pacifist, moved early on in the war to the less conspicuous surroundings of the Birmingham Quaker College, Woodbrooke, to be its Warden. It was from this context he was called upon to give the Swarthmore Lectures of 1943. These annual lectures, begun in 1908 and named after the home of Margaret Fox, one of Quakerism's founders, were meant to be occasions when the intellectual and practical implications of the teaching of Society of Friends were outlined. Richards chose as the topical title for his contribution to Quaker thought 'Planning for Freedom'. Akin to other prominent Christian thinkers of the time, such as a number of the contributors to *The Christian News-Letter*,[32] Richards was concerned that the recent enthusiasm for a planned economy should not work to diminish the citizen's liberty and freedom of conscience: as a pacifist Richards no doubt knew the precariousness of such self-determination. In fearful tones, Richards reflected that 'in the interests of a planned economy, enforced by the imperial power of Rome, Jesus was nailed to a Cross.'[33] Despite such a demonic characterisation of state intervention he conceded, however, that

> Some measure of collectivism is inevitable, if personal liberty is not to suffer. No one, for instance, would propose that the roads should revert to private ownership [...] and that is [...] true of essential commodities such as gas, water, electricity, and so on. Here too is the justification for State railways.[34]

The irony for Richards was that it took 'total war' to galvanise people to effort rather than other moral challenges:

> If a people can mobilize against a foreign enemy, why not against poverty [...] If Mankind can organize for war, it can and must organize for peace [...] Planning of some sort, therefore there must be; and yet, in the name of liberty, it must somehow be reconciled with freedom of personality and the 'power to will' on

32   Cf. Reeves, 1999, p.60.
33   Richards, 1943, p.68.
34   Richards, 1943, p.56.

the part of every individual [that] no man is debarred from fulfilling the will of God [...] nor any penalty ensue upon the exercise of Christian loyalty.[35]

The people had spent their energy fighting the two great political ideologies of the mid-twentieth century, fascism and, less directly, communism, each proponents of state intervention. In tune with many Christian thinkers, Richards argued for a considered social planning that did not fall prey to such political extremism.[36]

Johannes Messner, the Austrian refugee priest in safe haven at the Birmingham Oratory, perceived a similar tension between state authority and free determination in political life. In an article for the *Dublin Review* of 1941 entitled 'Economic and Social Reconstruction' he explored the limits that a state may go to before infringing the treasured principle of liberty. He expressed it thus:

> Today the view is growing that liberty cannot be allowed to be unrestricted if it is not to become a destructive force in the cultural, economic and international life and in the life of the State. The great danger of the present day, however, is that in doing away with the misuse of liberty we may also do away with liberty itself, or, in other words, that we may do away with liberty in order to prevent its misuse. In the political sphere the Totalitarian states have followed this road, and in the economic sphere Socialism is about to go the same way. For Socialism aims at abolishing the system of free economy because liberty in economy has hitherto proved a failure. But put liberty in the right order and it will prove to be 'man's highest good' (Leo XIII); and it will also be proved that liberty within the framework of a natural economic order is the basis of the economic and social wellbeing of nations.[37]

Thus, though Birmingham's leading Christians, like their national counterparts, were almost universally in favour of societal change, some were as cautious as they were enthusiastic.[38] Perhaps, as well as reflecting their ecclesiology, this difference of opinion between clergy indicated that for some the 'Kingdom of God' represented a change of

---

35   Richards, 1943, p.67.
36   Machin, 1998, p.133.
37   Messner, 1941, p.161.
38   Though some on the right were opposed to policies outlined in Beveridge: cf. Pakenham, 1943, p.28.

heart rather than a determination for social reform, as the words of one Birmingham Methodist lay preacher demonstrated:

> Whilst the majority of people do not attend church and in most cases do not know why on earth they should this war is making many of them think […] we are frequently in contact with those who are beginning to think. Is it possible for us to lead such to seek Christ? […] He loved me and gave himself for me. When we can each affirm that with truth and sincerity and interpret it in our daily lives then and not till then shall we build Jerusalem in England's green and pleasant land.[39]

However, even those who were enthusiastic and hopeful of a new world order upon victory still displayed a nervousness of pragmatic proposals, being rather more confident in espousing the principles which might underlie such a new order. Few, if any, believed that British society could remain the same after the war, and in some small way the Christian community paved the way for the radical changes that came in the wake of victory.

Religious Education and the Spiritual Renewal of the People

> One wonders, Fred, what you fellows will really want when you get home at last […] of course, a good job, but what else? [...] I must not dilate upon schemes and present developments for fear of making you homesick […] You will have noticed, when you return, how youth has come to the fore. The state can't do enough for them […] It's all talk about education of a new type, for living, working, playing, and for fit bodies and fit minds and character. New sweeping reforms of the Education Bill have amazed us all. We can't hardly [sic] believe that the House will pass it, and yet, in our present mood it seems even harder not to pass it.[40]

---

39 Sermon preached on 20/2/43 by H.S. Cull, Methodist Lay Preacher (Birmingham Central Library).

40 Letter to a serviceman from Rev. E.H. Hardy of Coventry Road Methodist Church, 11 January 1944.

The most suitable memorials of our dead will be further provision for the religious needs of generations to come.[41]

The Education Act of 1944, especially its undertakings with regard to religious education and collective worship, startlingly exemplify the nation's self-belief in its Christian identity; embodying by its legislative promise a desire to continue to be faithful to it. Whether motivated by a sense of gratitude for the apparent favour of God upon the nation's cause, or in response to the call of the Churches for a national spiritual reconversion, the Act personified the will of the people that its Christian identity be strengthened and perpetuated.[42] According to Green, the 1944 Education Act was expressive of 'a measure of avowedly Christian stewardship: advanced by a Christian minister, passed by a Christian parliament, directed towards the goal of creating a truly Christian population [by means of] compulsory Christian education.'[43] The conditions of war, it seems, had created the political and religious climate for such an Act, whereas this goodwill hardly seemed possible even a few years prior to the conflict.[44] Of course, by making a regular religious diet in schools mandatory by statute, the Church and the state were not necessarily inventing new practices for schools to adopt. Hitherto, a religious curriculum and prayer of some sort were practices widely established in council schools as well as in Church schools. However, by legislating for a 'synthesis of denominationally uncontested, common, Christianity', and an act of collective worship the 1944 Act, the nation affirmed their previous status, and asserted their future priority in its post-war life.[45] Moreover, as E.R. Norman observes, the religious dimension of the Act was reflective not only of the government but of the people's wishes:

41 Barnes Papers EWB, 12/1/641, Diocesan Conference, Thursday 4 May 1944.

42 As observed also by John Wolffe in his God and Greater Britain: see Machin, 1998, p.135n. See also Norman, 1976, p.403 and his reference to Leeson, S., Christian Education (London, 1947), pp.193−194.

43 Green, 2000, p.149.

44 This was the observation of Canon Brown of Wakefield Diocese; see Green, 2000, p.149.

45 Green, 2000, p.161.

[T]here was a swell of public feeling [...] in favour of religious education in the state schools [...] a wide and deep desire was expressed, outside the Churches as well as within them, that Christianity be restored to its true and traditional place in English education.[46]

Thus, the results of a Birmingham essay competition organised by the Birmingham Reconstruction Committee show, to some extent, local people's support for the national moves, finding that over half the competitors who mentioned religious instruction in schools in their compositions were very enthusiastic about it.[47] Therefore, far from being the death knell of British Christianity, as Calder has asserted of the reform, the implicit popular support which compulsory religious education received is representative of the spontaneity of British religious attachments at the time, and the will of the people that any previous decline into irreligion be halted by a compulsory and quality religious education for all.[48] Moreover, the Act more or less embodied the desires of the Anglican archbishops,[49] whose proposals for the future of education were widely known as early as 1941, even amongst Birmingham's Anglican congregations.[50] Additionally, it is clear that R.A. Butler, chair of the Board of Education and architect of the reforms, managed to harness the popular climate of goodwill towards religion, as well as support of the leadership of the Protestant denominations, to his own vision for an anti-materialist, ethically Christian education.[51] Thus, the negotiations that took place between the Anglican archbishops, Nonconformist Church leaders, and the government about the place of religion in the future of the school curriculum managed to avoid a repeat of their 1902 debacle, resulting in the assurance of compulsory religious education and collective

46   Norman, 1976, p.402 quoting Spencer Leeson, *Christian Education* (London, 1947).
47   Davies, H., 'Reconstruction Essay Competition: Précis of Suggestions', Birmingham Reconstruction Committee, 1943. Source: Birmingham Central Library.
48   Calder, 1969, p.545; Green, 2000, p.152.
49   Grimley, 2004, pp.203–206.
50   *The Parish Magazine St Alban's, Bordesley*, July 1941. See also *The Times*, 13 February 1941.
51   Green, 2000, pp.155 and 161.

worship in all schools.[52] Consequently, this quasi-Lutheran unity between the purposes of the state and the Church created, in some quarters at least, a level of trust in the educational establishment which led some Christians to consider Church schools anachronistic.[53] For instance, the Birmingham Anglican diocesan synod voted on 11 June 1941 to abolish the dual system.[54] They, and others, decided that it was safe to relinquish the religious nurture of the young to local authority religious syllabi, though clearly Roman Catholic Christians were much more hesitant about doing so.[55] Arguably, the 1944 Education Act provides evidence that this society believed itself and its institutions to embody Christian values: not only this, but also that the British state was ordained to fulfil the purposes of God in this and other regards.

Some in Birmingham, however, were incredulous as to the newfound credence that Christianity seemed to have gained in national life. The vicar of St. James's, Ashted wrote of the proposals: 'this is all breathtaking to us who have been accustomed to Government departments being neutral on religious issues. At last it appears to be realised that unless our country has a Christian background the future is just not worth having.'[56] Moreover, for others in the Churches the religious dimensions of the Act were more about planning for a more secure religious future than having confidence in the existence of such an identity now. For the particularly Christian critic the Act was a way of making a nominally Christian nation a more thoroughgoing one. The nation was Christian, yes, many Christian commentators agreed, but not as convincingly as it should be. For example, the editor of *The Spiritual Issues of the War* opined:

> By common consent we are fighting to uphold the law of Christ against the law of paganism and brute force. Meanwhile, what is being done to strengthen the future of our national creed, and to ensure that the post-war England shall be,

52   Reeves, 1999, p.67.
53   Though, admittedly, there may have been alternative motivations in that the Churches could ill afford to pay the costs of upkeep on many of their schools. See Addison, 1985, pp.143 and 145.
54   *The Parish Magazine St Alban's, Bordesley*, July 1941.
55   Machin, 1998, p.134.
56   *The Parish Magazine of St James's Ashted*, January 1944.

more adequately than in the past, a Christian England? Because Christianity is a creed based upon a knowledge of historical facts, its future mainly depends, not upon an amiable state of mind, but upon an educational system in which the teaching of these facts is given foremost place.[57]

Likewise, the quality of the people's religion and its integrity was widely discussed, as was illustrated by an article in the journal *Theology*. Herein, John Drewett dealt with the character of popular English Christianity as problematic and as a challenge to 'real' Christianity. Drewett parodied the typical individual's faith in the following:

> His religion is one of works: he believes in giving the other fellow a helping hand; he is, or tries to be, a good neighbour. He is friendly to the Church and admires the work of many of the clergy, but he has little patience with doctrine or dogma [...] most Englishmen think themselves Christians because they give a cup of cold water to a stranger, they are in a sense spiritually inoculated. The more they do in the way of social service, A.R.P., etc., the more self-satisfied they become and further are they from that sense of need and dependence upon God which only comes as a result of conviction of sin. They are amongst those who think themselves better than others and are spiritually in the direct tradition of the Pharisees.[58]

For Drewett, the excess of wartime demands made upon citizens to greater effort served only to stultify this conceptualisation of Christianity as essentially an ethical religion rather than one demanding doctrinal conviction. War, according to Drewett, brought out the worst in the people's faith. The time had come, he argued, to recognise that it is impossible to tolerate such 'faith'; this is not real Christianity:

> No longer can we go on thinking that all Englishmen (or Anglicans) are Christians merely because there is a lot of good will amongst us. There is a real danger in times like these that the Church will try to 'cash in' on the rising emotional temper of the nation and think that by organising special services for the many community groups that have come into existence they are 'Christianizing' the nation [...] Too often we are satisfied to praise them for the services they are rendering and to suggest that, although they do not know it, they are Christians after all. [Likewise, in handing over responsibility for

---

57   *The Spiritual Issues of the War*, No. 44, 29 August 1940.
58   Drewett, 1942, pp.85 and 89.

religious instruction to the State we cannot] expect that the State will do the Church's job by converting the children to the Christian faith.[59]

However, Cyril Alington, Anglican Dean of Durham, demonstrated a contrasting optimism in relation to the character of popular Christianity. More attuned to the rhetoric of the clergy of the First World War, he preferred to endow this war with the qualities of a 'Crusade', arguing that:

> it is the Christian spirit latent in the nation which has taken us into this war[. It] has been called (in my opinion, justly) 'the greatest and most unselfish cause for which a nation has ever risked its all': it is a cause so great that, even if it failed, no patriot could regret so glorious an end.[60]

Writing of the need for education to further stimulate this latent Christianity and to make clear the aims of the fight, he put the case that:

> We are in fact a Christian country, ready to respond to Christian ideals [...] In no other way is it possible to explain the unanimity with which our country has responded to the call to sacrifice, and the dignity with which it is supporting the trial. [However], we are living on religious capital [...] It is indisputable that it is Christianity which has formed the British character [...] But what assurance have we that it will indefinitely endure? And what steps are we taking to secure its permanence? The obvious method is by ensuring that the rising generation is adequately instructed in the Christian faith [...] If it is indeed vital that the religion which their parents profess should be taught to children, it is the duty of the State to secure that the teaching is competently given, and given by those who are themselves convinced of its importance [we need] to set before the young a vision of God which will justify their instinct for worship [...] which will assure them that they are citizens not only of the United Kingdom of Great Britain and its Dominions but also of the United Kingdom of Heaven and Earth [...] If they are not, for what are they asked to fight? [...] We need to claim once more for religion a central place [...] As we consider what things we are fighting for, and why [England] knows what it is fighting for – like Cromwell's russet-coated captain, it 'knows what it is fighting for, and loves what it knows' [...] the cause of God.[61]

---

59   Drewett, 1942, p. 91.
60   Alington, 1940, pp.36–37.
61   Alington, 1940, pp.32–35.

200

In Birmingham, the Christian disposition of society was as often as not doubted, and, therefore, the importance of religious education to British wartime and post-war society affirmed. One vicar, writing to his parishioners at the height of the blitz, reminded his people of the definiteness of the cause, stirring them to deeper conviction in their faith:

> This country is committed to the service of a cause which might perhaps be described as 'keeping open the possibility of Christian civilisation' [*pace* Temple]. But this must depend upon *the continued vitality of the Christian Faith*, not military victory alone. But actual ignorance concerning what the Christian religion really was [*sic*] is extremely widespread. In recent years, astonishing change has taken place in the attitude of local authorities, who once thought that religious belief was so deeply rooted that there was no need for specific religious teaching in the schools, apart from a Bible lesson. That view hardly finds support today.[62]

Similarly, the Methodist local preacher H.S. Cull, in a sermon at King's Norton in September 1941, stated the pragmatic case for the evangelistic opportunity presented by the prospect of new legislation:

> You and I as part of our Christianity have got to care desperately that every child in our country has the chance of learning not just the facts of scripture but that he catches the true spirit of the Christian religion which is something far greater.[63]

There were clearly differences of opinion among the clergy as to the current character of the people's faith and how religious education in schools might improve upon it.[64] However, there was broad consensus about the fundamental need for, and the benefits of, religious instruction/education in the post-war world. As a Mass-Observation report established from a sample of London respondents, a greater

---

62   *The Parish Magazine St Alban's, Bordesley*, July 1941. My emphasis and bracketed comments.

63   Sermon preached by H.S. Cull, Lay Preacher, at Kings Norton, 3 September 1941.

64   For comments about the lack of religious knowledge amongst the populace see Green, 2000, p.152.

proportion of people were in favour of 'religious lessons' in schools than those against, some 51% in favour and 30% against.[65]

For the authors of *The Christian News-Letter*, denominational allegiance and partial bargaining over the 'religious' aspects of the curriculum had less import than plans to reconstruct an education system whose whole ethos socially engineered the new society. Christianity's domain was not limited to one aspect of the curriculum; it should embrace the whole curriculum and the whole of the growing child's experience. Writers such as J.H. Oldham held to such a holistic view of education and society. Moreover, successful religious nurture, he argued, depended upon a congruence of values across social life. The Sermon on the Mount had to be embodied in the social institutions and not simply taught about in schools.[66] What is more, the authors asserted that the religious knowledge propounded by schools could only be effective in delivering the desired Christian education of the nation if it took into account the child's broader experience, and if the Churches maintained some authority over what was taught.[67] The state, by its involvement in religious education, should not be implicated in a divorce between religious nurture, the Churches and the child. Arguably, thereby, the state's involvement in religious education, albeit it at the Churches' behest, led to a gradual erosion of the perceived necessity of Sunday-school attendance which existed prior to the Act.

The Closure of the Conflict

As the war ended, disillusionment about the envisioned 'New Jerusalem' which would come about as a result of the conflict very soon set in amongst some of the less patient members of Birmingham's Christian communities. For those whose view of the Kingdom was

65   Mass-Observation, FR 2017 (undated).
66   Reeves, 1999, pp.66–67.
67   Reeves, 1999, p.69.

more 'now' than 'not yet', the priority was the conversion of the soul rather than the alteration of society. One Methodist minister contrasted the anxiety and urgency of war with peacetime apathy:

> Since our last Anniversary dramatic events have taken place in the life of our nation. The war [...] has at long last come to an end. No longer do we get a sinking feeling in the pit of our stomach whenever we hear a plane overhead and it is with less anxiety that we open the door when the postman knocks. The war is ended [but] the fruits of peace elude us. Food is scarcer than at any time during the past six years. In spite of repeated assurances to the contrary the hideous monster 'unemployment' is raising his ugly head. Unofficial strikes and absenteeism are retarding industrial recovery. People who two years ago were talking enthusiastically about the 'New Britain' are now sceptical and not a few cynical [...] the best solution they can offer must remain inadequate because the root of the trouble is not in man's environment but in man himself; in his selfish desires, warped imagination and perverted will [...] Only new men can make a new world and a new Britain AND ONLY GOD CAN MAKE NEW MEN. We initiate and encourage recreational and cultural activities for young and old on this great estate but we regard it as our primary responsibility to introduce people to God and to create a fellowship which will effectively mediate His power. [68]

Though it was all too easy to be cynical about the reality of change, particularly with the slow pace of its advent, undoubtedly societal and ecclesiastical life could never quite be the same again. As early as January 1943, when the Christian Social Council hosted a conference on 'The Persecution and Massacre of the Jews', Birmingham's Christian communities began to be aware of the need to respond to the horrors of the Jewish persecution.[69] This led to the later founding of a local Council for Christians and Jews, and from this point on the realities of the sufferings of Jews would become increasingly apparent, demanding a practical as well as a theological response. In this developing awareness, films and newsreels played a significant part. Michael Parker, Vicar of King's Heath, was one of many who wrote to his parishioners in support of the task, sponsored by the Lord Mayor Birmingham, of providing clothes, needles and thread for those in

---

68 Sermon preached at Kingstanding Methodist Church, April 1946 by Dennis Robson (minister).

69 The Birmingham Christian Social Council: Annual Report and Accounts, 1943.

liberated Europe: 'many of you will have been shocked by the atrocities revealed by the films', he wrote. 'Here is a very simple opportunity to help.'[70]

The Second World War was concluded somewhat abruptly by the use of the atomic bomb. For many in the Churches its use was morally questionable if practically understandable. Typical of local reflections upon the manner of the war's closure was the pragmatic unease of William Brooke, by then Vicar of St. Jude's, central Birmingham. Brooke's statements reflected the official line taken on the issue by both the Archbishops of Canterbury and York, that the revulsion evoked by the use of the atomic bomb should be used to 'attack the general evil of war rather than the particular evil of nuclear weapons'.[71] In his parish magazine of September 1945, Brooke calmly measured the cost of using such a weapon, pointing forward to the necessary efforts towards peace that now needed to be made:

Everyone is thankful that the war is at last over; no one can rejoice at the way it ended. Many people have doubted whether the atomic bomb should have been used at all, or at any rate upon a thickly populated area. Possibly it hastened the end, and may, in the long run, have saved lives; but we can feel no pride that we have equalled the worst of our enemies in indiscriminate bombing. It is, however, of no use to be sentimental. There is no need to thrust all the blame on scientists, who have put their talents at the command of the Government; if that is a fault, it is one common to most of the population through the years of war. Nor is this invention so different in kind from many that have gone before and to which we have become accustomed. Rather, the end reveals the beginning. The atomic bomb shows clearly what has always been the character of war from the day the first caveman formed a club and intimidated his weaker neighbours. It is by its nature irrational and indiscriminate, and provides a rough and ready solution to a problem only by creating a dozen others. Mankind has to learn the childishness of an appeal to force to settle differences that should be settled by reason and consent. If the atomic bomb, by its very violence forces these lessons upon the attention of the nations, it will, apart from any more peaceful application, have been of lasting service. It is now the duty of all to look, and work, and pray for justice and peace, which are indivisible, and this duty falls especially upon Christian people, who are by their profession committed to belief in love and fellowship. It behoves us all to guard our thoughts and speech

70   *All Saints', King's Heath*, July 1945.
71   Kirby, 1993, p.252.

204

against hatred and bitterness, to witness boldly to the right [...] to bring about friendship with other people by any personal contacts [...] to influence public opinion so that the governments of Allied Nations may in all their actions [...] have the single aim of building up a world-wide community of nations.[72]

Bishop Barnes, preaching at Birmingham Parish Church in 1945, showed similar equanimity (despite his out-and-out pacifism) towards the nuclear technology. He imagined the benefits of nuclear power as transformative of daily life, rather optimistically assuming that 'We shall no longer need coal and firewood and oil [...] Personally, I rejoice to think that the Saltley gas-works may soon disappear.'[73] Gloomily – but accurately, however – he forecasted the effects of the likely holocaust if such a weapon were to be used upon cities like Birmingham. The advent of the atomic bomb, he argued, must, of necessity, lead to change in the international political climate. Pointing ahead to the delicate balance of nuclear deterrence which operated during much of the rest of the twentieth century, Barnes claimed that possession of nuclear weapons must one day lead to recognition of the futility of war:

> Nations in the future will not be able to threaten war. To make such a threat effective, they must possess a store of atomic bombs. Threats and counter-threats will end in the use of such weapons, however good be the resolutions against such use which men profess when they are being made [...] Nations, in fact, must say to themselves and to one another: we will not make war neither will we prepare for war. Need I say that in such a resolve they will follow the teaching of Jesus the Christ?[74]

Thus, the way in which the war ended dictated the moral and political agenda of the Churches for decades to come, as the Christian community sought to come to terms with the profound questions thrown up by the possession and use of such devices.

72   *St Jude's, Birmingham, A Monthly Letter*, September 1945.
73   Barnes Papers, EWB 12/1/661, 'The New Era – A sermon at Birmingham Parish Church on Sunday 11 November 1945'.
74   Barnes Papers, EWB 12/1/661, 'The New Era – A sermon at Birmingham Parish Church on Sunday 11 November 1945'.

During wartime, Bishop Barnes' pacifist energies had been channelled to, amongst other things, his monitoring of the tribunal procedures in relation to conscientious objectors, and to his personal support, via correspondence, of many of them in the process.[75] Now, as Birmingham sought his full involvement in a celebration of the conclusion of war in Europe, his natural outspokenness was freed from the restrictions placed on it by the wartime censor. Barnes's stubborn goodwill was directed towards a refusal to use the official liturgy, which had been given the imprimatur of the archbishops, objecting as he did to its designation as a service of 'Thanksgiving for Victory'.[76] Instead, Barnes, consulting widely and particularly by dint of the efforts of Archdeacon Michael Parker and Percy Harthill, the chair of the Anglican Pacifist Fellowship, submitted an alternative service for use at the City's celebrations entitled less exultantly a 'Service of Thanksgiving'.[77] Amongst the clear and obvious differences between the two forms were the latter's relative informality of language and its use of less formulaic prayers, its slightly penitential tone, and its inclusion of prayer for 'the wounded everywhere'.[78] Strikingly, the service begins with the matter-of-fact versicle 'The Cease Fire has sounded in Europe', to which the relieved response of the people is: 'Thank God'. The service proved popular with many. The Dean of Gloucester, for example, requested copies for use in his cathedral commenting that the form was: 'direct, sincere and human, and its language is "understanded of the people"', adding somewhat ironic-ally, 'but some of my dear colleagues – Tractarian, Anglo-Catholic, and impervious to a new idea – are so far, not co-operative in this matter. So I may not be able to use it on the day.'[79] The Lord Mayor of Birmingham was similarly appreciative of the service: describing it as 'outstanding in its simplicity and effectiveness' he noted, in particular, the effort Barnes had put into writing it.[80]

---

75   Barnes, 1979, pp.355–356.
76   Barnes Papers, EWB 8/30/5.
77   Barnes Papers, EWB 8/30/29.
78   Barnes Papers, EWB 8/30/29.
79   In a letter of 11 April 1945 (Barnes Papers, EWB 8/30/37).
80   Letter from the Lord Mayor dated 15 May 1945. Barnes Papers, EWB 8/30/43.

The people of Birmingham, along with those of many other European cities, had suffered much because of the war. At the height of the blitz one Mass-Observer reported what would seem to be the natural response that: 'In true Birmingham style bombed victims with whom I have come into contact, cursed and complained, vowing vengeance on the evil perpetrators.'[81] The clear demand of the Christian faith in response to the enemy who causes this suffering is one of love and forgiveness. How this command to continuous love would work out in reality was a matter of some wrestling by the Christian community at the end of the war. In a sermon preached in the University Church of St Mary the Virgin, Oxford on 19 November 1944, T.R. Milford reflected on the nature of forgiveness in the current conditions. Desiring an avoidance of the mistakes of the Versailles treaty, Milford argued that perpetuating the suffering of war by meting out punishment upon the defeated in actual fact leads to the moral disintegration of those meting it out. There is a difference between justice, judgement and punishment.[82] Forgiveness is the responsibility of those who suffer wrong, it is not for others to do it on their behalf: *we,* for example, cannot forgive the massacre of the Jews.[83] On an international level, forgiveness meant that the allies

> Must try to obtain security for themselves and a tolerable place in the world for Germany and Japan. They must rise above bitterness and revenge [because as a result of war] we become inevitably the instruments of judgement and also come under judgement [...] all alike have fallen below the requirements of justice [...] we have no right to arrogate to ourselves the right to punish.[84]

In Birmingham too, Church leaders sought to find a way of helping Christians grasp what forgiving one's enemies might mean in practice. Archbishop Williams characterised forgiveness pragmatically and bluntly. Forgiveness, he cautioned

> does not mean that we must feel any affection for our enemy [...] By his own evil behaviour our neighbour has made it necessary for us to [...] kill him; but

---

81   Letter dated 1 December 1940; TC23/8/D, Air Raids.
82   Milford, 1945, pp.124–125.
83   Milford, 1945, p.125.
84   Milford, 1945, p.126.

even while we hurt or kill him we remember that but for the God's grace we might be just as bad ourselves [we ought to] pray for the eternal rest and happiness of the man whom we have justifiably killed.[85]

Unfortunately, Bishop Barnes discouraged attempts to explore the meaning of forgiveness. Barnes had a tendency to equivocate with his colleagues in the Birmingham Christian Social Council, much to the frustration of Guy Rogers, the Rector of Birmingham. Though there was mutual respect between the bishop and the rector, on occasion the bishop's behaviour could embarrass this senior cleric, as Barnes often did not attend meetings, choosing instead to negotiate with the group through Rogers by correspondence. He would stall on joint decisions and object to the detail of joint statements. Typical of the bishop's behaviour was his dealings with the council concerning a study document written by its members with regard to the future of post-war Germany. To Barnes, the Christian imperative of forgiveness demanded that no territory should be taken from Germany:[86] should this happen, he argued, it would store up resentment, leading towards another war. In defence of the document, Rogers argued that it was not prescriptive in its answers, nor did it represent the collective views of the council. He went on:

> I fear after all the trouble that has been taken with this document if we are unable to agree to make some use of it we may precipitate a crisis amongst our members which would I feel be very regrettable and place me in a very difficult position.[87]

Despite this plea, Barnes continued to quibble, this time threatening his resignation if the council went ahead with the publication: 'The Birmingham Christian Social Council exists to consider social problems in Birmingham: it is not specifically qualified to give guidance as to the major issues of post-war European statesmanship.'[88] The council decided not to publish the document at their meeting later that month,

---

85   Archbishop Williams' Advent Pastoral, 1944.
86   Barnes Papers, EWB 9/1/32.
87   Barnes Papers, EWB 9/1/33.
88   Barnes Papers, EWB 9/1/34, 7 January 1945.

208

with the intention of finding some other use for it.[89] In correspondence with the bishop, Rogers asked him to reflect upon the episode:

> I fear our Free Church brethren begin to think our Anglican system tends to be despotic [...] I cannot find any trace in our action or in the proposed document of 'anti-Christian tolerance' [...] I wonder if you really think the Christian principle of forgiveness [...] is the founding principle of our Diocesan administration and Government [...] I hope it will help you to bear more patiently with this frank letter from an old friend and admirer who is not too happy with the way things are going at the moment – perhaps we all need to be more considerate.[90]

The handling of a number of other matters again suggests that Bishop Barnes was out of step with his clerical colleagues on the Christian Social Council. In correspondence between Rogers and Barnes in April 1945, Rogers requested permission to invite the Archbishop of York to speak on the issue of housing at a conference in the Town Hall. Barnes was incredulous at the timing of this, and replied:

> I should have thought that it was most undesirable that any such meeting should by any possibility clash with a general election [...] Within the next couple of months we ought to see the end of hostilities in Europe [...] With that knowledge a public meeting with regard to housing might valuably be arranged to take place when the new Parliament is determined.[91]

Incredibly, the bishop later refused to endorse the Council's provision of a Christian rationale for the recently formed United Nations Organisation, and later to give his approval to a statement, written by the leading city academic and pacifist, H.G. Wood, on the subject of the hydrogen bomb; on both occasions it was felt by him that the pacifism expressed therein was too moderate.[92]

By June 1941, the end of the heaviest 'blitz' period in Birmingham, around 8 churches had been destroyed and at least 135

89 Barnes Papers, EWB 9/1/36, 26 January 1945.
90 Barnes Papers, EWB 9/1/35, 15 January 1945.
91 Barnes Papers, EWB 9/1/37 and 38, 9 and 11 April 1945.
92 Barnes Papers, EWB 9/1/39, Letter of 9 March 1946; EWB 9/1/51, April 1950.

damaged.[93] Amongst those most severely damaged were Stoney Lane Congregational Church; Moseley Road Methodist Church; St. Anne's Church, Moseley; St. Bartholomew's, Masshouse Lane; St. John the Baptist, Deritend; All Saints' Roman Catholic Church, Small Heath and St. Thomas's Church, Bath Row.[94] By the middle of the war, a careful scheme had been put into place whereby compensation could be made to the Churches for buildings damaged by enemy action. Under the chairmanship of the Bishop of London, Geoffrey Fisher, the Churches Main Committee negotiated terms with the War Damage Commission. All of the principal British Christian denominations were represented, in an untypically ecumenical manner, by senior clerics including Benson Perkins (formerly of the Birmingham Central Hall) for the Methodist Church. By April 1944, the committee had worked out 'a statement of principles' whereby a fair decision could be made concerning requests for compensation.[95] These principles included the need to clearly define that the building in question was a 'church' and not simply a building used in connection with Church activities, for example a Church school. The committee then went on to prescribe the nature of the compensation; whether or not the church should be replaced like-for-like by a rebuilding; whether a church might better be replaced by the building of another in a different locality, or whether a simple monetary payment might be made. Astonishingly, it was not until the early 1960s that the Churches Main Committee's work was wound up, though it took until the latter part of the decade for final claims to be processed because evidence of subsequent dilapidation of buildings was often attributed to wartime buffeting.[96] By this time, 'the total of war damage payments made to churches in Britain had reached £40,500,000', twenty-one years after the first meeting of the committee.[97] The feeling of the Churches was that the Government had been generous in their compensation payments, having been in receipt of

93 Barnes, 1979, p.383.
94 There is no single definitive list of damaged and destroyed churches, and that here is not exhaustive. Sources: File on Architectural Losses, City Archive; Archbishop Williams's papers; Chinn, 1996.
95 Public Record Office, IR 34/682; letter dated 12 April 1944.
96 Public Record Office, IR 34/682, Note of Meeting, 2 February 1962.
97 *The Observer*, 18 March 1962.

war damage payments towards work on some 10,000 Anglican, 3,000 Methodist, and 1,000 Roman Catholic churches.[98]

Indicated by such things as the inclusion of a prayer for guidance for those with planning responsibilities in the rebuilding of Britain on the inside cover of the book *When We Build Again*, Christian ideals constituted a significant reference point for the population of Birmingham.[99] By constantly referring to the justifiable aims of the war and continually mentioning the hope for a different and better future the Churches may have played their part, not only in encouraging the populace to 'Keep Smiling Through', but in the subsequent Labour victory in the General Election of 1945.

98   *The Observer*, 18 March 1962.
99   Bournville Village Trust, 1941.

...on the character of popular religion during the Second World War, historians have created the false impression that these years were somehow in discontinuity with previous ones. Contrary to this, the nature of wartime British popular religion was similar in many respects to its character before the war. The reality was that Christianity's idiom, beliefs and practices were a ubiquitous backdrop to British social and cultural life into the wartime period. As David Hempton characterises the popular religion of earlier years, so in wartime:

> religion was not confined to the institutionally religious. Even non-churchgoers sent their children to Sunday School, dressed up on Sundays, used religion to get jobs and welfare relief, sang hymns as a means of cementing community solidarity, extolled 'practical Christian' virtues, relied heavily on Christian sexual ethics [...] derived comfort from religion in times of suffering and disaster.[1]

Furthermore, the Churches continued to play a relevant part in the communal life of the populace by the creation and maintenance of social networks, the provision of leisure opportunities, and by their worship and pastoral ministrations. Moreover, patterns of home-based religion, and religious instruction in schools, provided the wartime generation with Christian language, stories and morality at least as much as it had done previously. Thus, there are fundamental connections between pre-war and wartime popular religion: even so, the war years had their own popular religious integrity which inter-acted with the stated purposes of the conflict and notions of national and personal identity within it.

It is a tempting oversimplification to assume that because the war was so disruptive of normality, and because church congregations were so obviously depleted of their usual devotees, that these years mark a

1   Hempton, 1988, p.196.

nadir in religious observance.[2] However, this was clearly far from being the case: many continued to attend churches, despite the disruptions of the 'blackout' and altered time schedules. Furthermore, notwithstanding the thinning of the flock due to evacuation and conscription, and the sheer exhaustion of war work, core congregations persevered. In spite of adversity, this remnant remained determined that Church life would continue. Moreover, this remnant was complemented by huge numbers of people who attended churches to observe the national days of prayer. In addition, popular observance of radio's prayerful minute at nine o'clock each evening, and the evidence that recourse was made to prayer during air raids, demonstrates the vigour of wartime popular religiosity. Likewise, considerable numbers of people had the habit of listening to broadcast religious services, and other programmes with religious content enjoyed significant popularity. People saw visions and they were susceptible to a belief in miracles: they tended to have faith that the providential hand was working on their behalf, sometimes contrary to the evidence. Additionally, wartime citizens were avid cinemagoers, who happily sat through copious numbers of films that reflected cultural protocols replete with Christian imagery and motif. Such films utilised religious idiom precisely because such idiom was a constituent part of popular cultural life and resonated with the people. Consequently, films aimed at strengthening a sense of national identity were able to play upon this factor, and, therefore, popular religion was harnessed to the purposes of wartime propaganda.

By focusing upon Birmingham, a city at the heart of Britain's war machine, it has been possible to show that far from fitting in with previously accepted stories of religious decline and creeping secularisation, British popular religion was a continuing and vital seam of its socio-cultural life certainly up until 1945. What is more, there is every reason to believe that the apparent revival of fortunes experienced by Christianity after the war and into the 1950s came about because of the temporary strengthening of the populace's commitment to Christian protocols during the Second World War. Perhaps out of a sense of gratitude to God, or the Church, for their

2   Sutcliffe and Smith, 1974, p.256.

faithfulness to the people in the midst of wartime difficulty, the post-war revival of churchgoing, a situation which previously 'historians and sociologists have never come to terms with',[3] is explicable in light of the strength of wartime diffusive and discursive Christianity and the widespread wartime air-raid shelter spirituality.

Moreover, undoubtedly the Churches were far from marginal to neighbourhood life in Birmingham and other British cities during the Second World War. For instance, during the blitz many clergy and Church workers earned the respect of citizens because of the practical and spiritual support and consolation they offered to the sheltering public. Modelling their ministry upon that of the Great War padre, the pastoral practices of significant numbers of clergy and Church workers on the Home Front in the Second World War were effectively informed by the lessons learnt by chaplains in the Front Line in the last war. By dutiful personal sacrifice, often in the face of extreme danger, Church workers shared food and drink, kept up people's spirits and reassured them by their words and physical presence; they joined in with singing, they put out fires, they dug out the buried, and they comforted the bereaved, they were a valuable visible presence in a similar way to many padres in the First World War. Surprisingly unsung, the role of Church workers during the blitz deserves greater recognition than it has previously received in accounts of these years.

Furthermore, people's morale was strengthened by such practical interventions, and the moral and religious framework recurrently offered by clerics' wartime teaching influenced the people's resolve to 'Keep Smiling Through'. So obvious was the Churches' influence upon the morale of the local population that the government considered it in its official surveys of civilian morale. The voice and activities of clerics and Church communities mattered to the authorities, and propagandists manipulated its recognisable influence for the purposes of the war. Additionally, as war progressed, along with countless proposals from other sources, the Churches offered their vision of the form of post-war British society. Birmingham's Christian community was no less prolific in its debating of the principles and practicalities of social reform than the national Church. Indeed, it was

3   Brown, 2001, p.170. See also Green, 2000, p.164.

in the spirit of its history of civic religion that Birmingham drew together intellectuals, local politicians, and Church leaders from across the Protestant denominations to discuss the way ahead. Without a doubt, the wartime Churches of Birmingham made as great an ideological contribution to the city's public life as they did practically in the neighbourhood and parish setting.

Any variation in the stability of Church-attendance figures across the twentieth century, in the face of evidently persistent subscription to Christian protocols, begs the question: what does the loosening of bonds with the religious institutions of Christianity actually represent? As David Hempton puts it:

> The boundaries and categories constructed by historians to make sense of religion – official and popular, Christian and pagan, religious and irreligious, secular and sacred, rough and respectable, traditional and modern, imposed and indigenous – are insufficiently flexible to describe a much more complex reality. There must be enough scope to include life cycle changes, distinctions between male and female religiosity and the survival of religious frameworks and meanings in communities, ethics, even politics, long after formal religious adherence has declined.[4]

Jeffrey Cox argued that the Churches contributed to their own diminution by emphasising social service rather more than the commitment obtained by evangelism.[5] Dorothy Entwistle posits that

> the type of education provided by [the Churches'] mutual improvement classes [though] designed, not solely for educational purposes, but also to bind the adolescent male to the Church and Sunday school [...] in encouraging critical self-appraisal and self-confidence, paradoxically, also contributed to declining attendance.[6]

Thus, arguably, the Churches' endeavours to be relevant, and by its communal life to promulgate Christianity, has had a tendency to work against the numerical security of its institutions. Perhaps this paradoxical self-negation can equally be argued of the wartime Churches' enthusiastic support for statutory religious education in the

4   Hempton, 1988, p.202.
5   Cox, 1982.
6   Entwistle, 2001, p.37.

1944 Education Act. Because compulsory schooling delivered the basics of the Christian faith, why did the populace need any longer to send its children to Sunday school? Arguably, statutory religious education may have led to the further dilution of commitment to this traditional means of religious instruction. Equally, with the growth and recognised importance of religious broadcasting during the war, perhaps people's perception of the necessity for Church attendance altered; why attend Church when the staples of a spiritual diet can be found elsewhere? What is more, by providing first-rate oration and high-quality religious broadcasts, this diet could often be more varied and appealing than that which could be offered by most Churches. Why go to church when one can be in receipt of a better quality of religious music and teaching in the comforts of one's home? Therefore, by their deliberate efforts to make 'diffusive Christianity' even more pervasive in British cultural life, curiously the Churches may have precipitated further erosion of the obligation to Church attendance. If this is the case, any perceived alteration in patterns of churchgoing after the war needs to take into account the increasing number of alternative ways in which people could be religious, find meaning, and explore the spiritual without necessarily going to church.

Evidence of 'diffusive' and 'discursive Christianity' uncovered here demonstrates that Christianity remained a valid referent in the construction of individual identity and a source of meaning-making throughout wartime. Moreover, during wartime a sense of national identity was sometimes reinforced by use of religious idiom and narrative and delivered by the various means of popular culture. Similarly, just as social life was still being organised in part around Church-initiated social networks, and the Churches' rituals still successfully mapped key moments in community and family life, these were augmented in the Second World War by the civic religiosity of the national days of prayer. Certainly up until 1945 then, Christianity still captivated and informed British popular religious life.

Despite the evidence, however, there remains a continuing challenge to historians of religion who wish to treat such manifestations of popular religiosity and meaning-making outside of, or only loosely affiliated to, official Christian structures and protocols as authentic. Scepticism of the merits of such manifestations of popular religion pertained in wartime, and does so still amongst some historians and theologians. Thus, whilst the validity of the popular religious experience is in doubt the debate about the exact nature of secularisation is not yet done. It is my hope that this book contributes to the debate by helping to define the exact character as well as the authenticity of wartime religious life.

Appendix: Oral History Interviewees

Arthur Brownsword, born March 1925, Nechells. Father a hand-turner and screwer. Worshipped at Rocky Lane Methodist Church during wartime. Still a churchgoer at time of interview. Interviewed February 2000.

William E. Brooke, Anglican clergyman, born July 1913, Eastham, Worcestershire. Father a market gardener. Curate of St. Agatha's, Sparkbrook 1940–44, then Vicar of St. Jude's, central Birmingham. Interviewed May 2000.

Christopher Charles, born March 1929, Balsall Heath. Mother a shopkeeper. Began worshipping as an Anglican as a child. When interviewed did not attend church regularly. Interviewed March 2001.

Jean Cuthbert, born April 1928, Small Heath. Father a professional footballer. Non-churchgoer at the time of interview. Interviewed March 2002.

Martin Davies, born July 1933, city centre. A member of Birmingham's Jewish population. Interviewed October 1999.

Kitty Drummond, born September 1928, Brookfields, Hockley. Father a taxi-driver. Non-churchgoer at the time of interview. Interviewed March 2002.

Joan Evans, born July 1933, Hockley. Father a newsagent and packer. Non-churchgoer at the time of interview. Interviewed March 2002.

Laura Evans, born October 1910, Handsworth. Father a bricklayer's labourer. Attended an independent Evangelical Church at the time of interview. Interviewed May 1999.

Dennis Harris, born February 1932, Aston, Birmingham. Father a greengrocer/milkman. At the time of interview was a practising Methodist. Interviewed March 2001.

Winifred Harrison, born March 1909, Leeds. Father an export merchant. She was a Methodist Sunday-school Superintendent at Kings Heath, Birmingham. At the time of interview continued to be a churchgoer. Interviewed December 1999.

John W. Jackson, born October 1914, Moseley. Anglican curate of Bordesley, Holy Trinity 1940–41 and then of St. John's, Sparkhill 1941–44. Interviewed April 2000.

Betty Jones, born October 1935, Hockley Brook. Father a timber merchant. Mother did war work. An Anglican churchgoer at the time of interview. Interviewed March 2002.

Enfys Jones, born October 1917, North Wales. Father a coalminer. Family moved to South Wales to find work shortly after her birth. Schooled in the Rhondda, moved to Birmingham in the late 1930s to find work as a schoolteacher. At the time of interview continued to worship at a Welsh Nonconformist chapel in Birmingham. Interviewed September 1999.

Beryl Keith, born December 1920. Born and brought up in the central Birmingham district of Ashted. She was the daughter of a shopkeeper. An Anglican at the time of interview. Interviewed March 2001.

Penny Keel, born September 1930. Born and brought up in Hockley/Lozells area. Father an engraver, mother a cinema usherette. A non-churchgoer at the time of interview. Interviewed March 2002.

Betty Law, born May 1917, Ladywood, Birmingham. Father a lathe hand. A non-churchgoer at the time of interview. Interviewed January 2000.

Dorothy Leather, born November 1924, Nechells. Father was a gun finisher. Married to **Brian Leather**, born March 1925, Nechells, whose father was a polisher. Worshipped as Methodists at the time of interview. Interviewed February 2000.

Joan Oswald, born August 1928, Sparkbrook, Birmingham. Father an upholsterer. Married to **Norman Oswald**, born July 1926, Sparkbrook, Birmingham. Father worked for Co-operative Dairies. Joan worshipped as an Anglican at the time of interview; Norman was a non-churchgoer. Interviewed March 2002.

Martin Ryland, born September 1934 in Harborne, brought up at Bartley Green. Father a water engineer. Mother worked for the Admiralty prior to marriage. A non-churchgoer at the time of interview. Interviewed March 2002.

Iris Smith, born circa 1920 Edgbaston. Father a fitter and turner. Iris was baptised and worshipped at the Birmingham Oratory. At the time of interview she was a practising Roman Catholic. Interviewed August 2000.

Penny Stephens, born May 1921, Bearwood. Father a silversmith. An Anglican at the time of interview. Interviewed March 2000.

Ted Watson, born circa 1921, Birmingham. Father a university lecturer from Auckland, New Zealand, in wartime an R.A.F. navigator on night bombers, and later a P.O.W. An Anglican at the time of interview. Interviewed February 1999.

Ivy Westwood, born March 1909, Kidderminster, Worcestershire. Moved to Smethwick in her early childhood. An Anglican at the time of interview. Interviewed March 2000.

Peter Whitnall, born June 1907, Smethwick. Father worked at Guest, Keen and Nettlefold. An Anglican at the time of interview. Interviewed March 2000.

Questionnaire Respondents:

Monsignor James Crichton, born June 1907, Birmingham. Parish Priest of Shirley, 1941–47.

Father John Welch, born June 1915, Acocks Green. Parish priest of St. Catherine's, Birmingham 1940–49.

The Reverend Benjamin Clarke, born August 1908, Lancaster. Curate of Erdington 1937–40. Vicar of St. Matthias's, Birmingham 1940–46.

Bibliography

Archive Material

Archive of St. Chad's Cathedral, Birmingham

St. Chad's Cathedral Chronicle 1937–42, No. 21
Archdiocesan Directories
Archbishop Williams' Papers, including wartime correspondence
The Papers of Father Francis Drinkwater
Sermons of Father Bernard Salt
Mgr. John Power's Pastoral Notebook

Pamphlets and Tracts:

Air Raids: Five Spiritual Commandments for Protection against Air Raids
(prayer card)
Children into Ruffians: the new Nazi education. Watford: HMSO.
Newton, Douglas (undated). *The Catholic Church and the Crisis.*
The Sword of the Spirit, No. 14: *Nazism versus Christianity*
The Sword of the Spirit, No. 15: *Atlantic Charter*
Who Wants the New Order? (1941).

Birmingham Central Library

Carrs Lane Journal, 1939–45
Lozells Congregational Church: *The Messenger*
The Rocky Recorder (magazine of Rocky Lane Methodist Church, Nechells)
All Saints', Kings Heath parish magazine
The Fiery Cross (St. Agatha's, Sparkbrook parish magazine)
The Parish Magazine of St. Alban's, Bordesley
The Parish Magazine of St. James's, Ashted
The Parish Magazine of St. John the Evangelist, Sparkhill

St. Jude's, Birmingham, a Monthly Letter
The Parish Magazine of St. Luke's, Bristol Street
The Parish Magazine of St. Nicholas's, Lower Tower Street
The Birmingham Christian Social Council: Annual Report and Accounts.

Birmingham City Archive

Diocese of Birmingham Photographic Survey of Churches and Church Build-
    ings (1942–45)
Frank Lockwood Diaries
Papers of Roger Maxwell Jones R708–711, C708–711
Papers of Lily Catherine Moody
Papers of Sidney White C369–371
File on Blitz
File on Architectural Losses

Imperial War Museum

Barrowcliff, Miss J. 82/27/1
Cadenhead, W.G. 85/51/1
Clothier, H.R. 86/3/1
Dunkley, F.J. 80/27/1
Harper, J. 86/12/1
Lockwood, F.T. 96/52/1
Picken, Mrs J. 85/52/1
Platt, E. A. 78/59/1
Serraillier, I. 94/10/1
Smith, Miss E. 91/36/1
Stevens, F.J. 88/8/1
Willetts, Mrs R. 96/28/1
Miscellaneous 2730 85/2/1
Miscellaneous 2772 Misc 185(2772)

Mass-Observation

FR 23 Mass-Observation File Report on Religion (January 1940)

224

FR 312 Conscientious Objectors (July 1940)
FR 362 Spiritual Report (August 1940)
FR 363 Spiritual Report (August 1940)
FR 405 Report on Conscientious Objectors (16 September 1940)
FR 658 Easter Sunday (16 April 1941)
FR 692 Kings Norton By-Election (May 1941)
FR 769 Mass Astrology (1 August 1941)
FR 975 Superstition (November 1941)
FR 1200 Religion (April 1942)
FR 1263 Belief in the Supernatural (15 May 1942)
FR 1315 Death and the Supernatural (June 1943)
FR 1525 Religion and the Future (1 December 1942)
FR 1566 Religion and the People (January 1943)
FR 1572 Religion and the People (January 1943)
FR 1870 The Chaplain to the Forces
FR 1913 Pacifist in Wartime
FR 2017 Interim Report on Religious Instruction in Schools
FR 2112 Superstition (7 April 1944)
FR 2190E Spiritual Trends in Films (December 1944)
FR 2227 Post-Easter Peace Questionnaire (April 1945)
FR 2274 Religious Attitudes in a London Borough (August 1945)
FR 2284 Half-way Thinking: People's Beliefs, Religious and Moral (September 1945)
FR 8859/2 Ronald Selby Wright
TC Religion 3/B Superstition
TC/6/1/E Treatment of Conscientious Objectors in Birmingham (November 1940)
TC 23/8/D Air Raids in Birmingham (dated 1940)
TC47 Religion
TC 66/1/C Miscellaneous Printed Material
TC 66/1/F Town and District Surveys: Birmingham 1939-41

Mass-Observation Birmingham Diarists

DR 5061, 5064, 5110, 5114, 5123, 5132, 5149, 5174, 5175, 5176, 5228, 5307, 5406, 5419, 5420

Public Record Office

IR 34/682 The Churches and War Damage
IR 192/1217 Birmingham Random Sample: Change in Shelter Habits
IR 34/120 War Damage to Church Property (1941)
HO 192/1205 Birmingham Social and Economic Survey (12 January 1942)
HO 198/63 Bomb Census Report (Region 9)

The Birmingham Oratory Archive

The Birmingham Oratory Parish Magazine

Pamphlets and Tracts:

Put ye on the Armour of God

The Bodleian Library

The Christian News-Letter
The Spiritual Issues of the War

The Salvation Army, Birmingham

Birmingham Salvation Army Citadel Journal

The University of Birmingham: Special Collections

The Papers of Bishop Ernest Barnes

Published Local Primary Sources

Birmingham Parish Church: St. Martin's, Bull Ring. Blitz, April 10th, 1941. [Undated]. [Birmingham: St. Martin's Church].

Bournville Village Trust (1941). *When We Build Again*. London: George Allen & Unwin.

City of Birmingham Official Handbook 1937. (1937). Birmingham: City of Birmingham Information Bureau.

Cornish Brothers Ltd. (1939). *Cornish's Birmingham Year Book 1938–1939*. Birmingham: Cornish Brothers.

Davies, H. (1943). *Reconstruction Essay Competition: Précis of Suggestions*. Birmingham: Birmingham Reconstruction Committee.

Eyles, H. (ed.), (1931). *Birmingham and District: An Official Guide*. Birmingham: Chamber of Commerce.

Keogan, B. and Welch, J. (1945). *The Heart of England: An Anthology of Midlands Verse*. London: The Mitre Press.

Reed, Bryan H. (1950). *Eighty Thousand Adolescents: a study of the young people in the City of Birmingham by the staff and students of Westhill Training College for the Edward Cadbury Charitable Trust*. London: George Allen & Unwin.

Rev. T.J. Bevan 1919–1944: a tribute. [Undated]. [Publisher Unknown].

Richards, E.R. (1950). *Private View of a Public Man: The Life of Leyton Richards*. London: George Allen & Unwin.

Richards, L. (1937). *Christian Pacifism and the Present Crisis: Two Sermons Given at Carrs Lane Church October 17th, 24th 1937*.

Richards, L. (1943). *Planning for Freedom*. London: George Allen & Unwin.

Rogers, T.G. (1956). *A Rebel at Heart: The Autobiography of a Nonconforming Churchman*. London: Longmans, Green & Co.

Tizard, L. (1937). *Making Religion Real*. London: Camelot.

Tizard, L. (1941). *Facing Life with Confidence*. London: Independent Press.

"What Hath God Wrought." Short History of God's Dealing with the Undenominational Church of Wattville Road, Handsworth, Birmingham. 1871: 1876: 1925: 1961. [Undated]. [Place and publisher unknown].

Other Published Primary Sources

Newspapers and Religious Periodicals

Birmingham Post, 1938–45
Clergy Review, 1939–45
Dublin Review, 1939–45
Expository Times, 1938–42
The Month, 1939–45
Theology, 1939–45
The Times, 1938–45
The Universe, 1939–45

Books and Articles

'Absolution in Danger of Death'. *The Clergy Review*, Vol. XXIII, 3 March, 1943, pp.130–131.

Alington, Cyril (1940). *The Last Crusade*. London: Oxford University Press.

Allen, Geoffrey (1940). *The Call of God in Time of War*. London: SCM Press.

Allen, Geoffrey (1942). *Law with Liberty*. London: SCM Press.

Barber, D.H. (1946). *The Church Army in World War II*. London: SPCK.

Barry, F.R. (1937). *What has Christianity to say?* London: SCM Press.

Barth, Karl (1940). *A Letter to Great Britain from Switzerland*. London: Christian News-Letter Books.

Benson, Robert H. (1939). *A War-time Prayer Book*. London: Longmans Green & Co.

Bevan, Edwyn (1940). *Christians in a World War*. London: SCM Press.

Bevan, J.J. [Undated]. *God and This War: September 1939–*. London: Catholic Truth Society.

Britain Under Fire. [Undated]. London: Country Life Limited.

Brown, William A. (1942). *A Creed for Free Men: A Study of Loyalties*. London: SCM Press.

Cairns, D.S. (1919). *The Army and Religion: An Enquiry and its Bearing upon the Religious Life of the Nation*. London: Macmillan.

Carpenter, S.C. (1940). *Faith in Time of War*. London: Eyre and Spottis-woode.

Cassandra (1941). *The English at War*. London: Secker and Warburg.

Churchill, R.S. (ed.) (1947 edition). *Into Battle: Speeches by the Right Hon. W.S. Churchill.* London: Cassell.

Clitheroe, G.W. (1941). *Coventry Under Fire: An Impression of the Great Raids on Coventry in 1940 and 1941.* Gloucester: The British Publishing Company.

Cockin, F.A., Plaisted, E. and Gane, C. (*et al.*) (1941). *Three Men and a Parson: four discussions broadcast on February 26th–March 1st. Together with two addresses given on Sunday, March 2nd, and the addresses in the 'Lift Up Your Hearts' series, February 24th–March 1st, 1941.* London: Longmans Green & Co.

Cockin, F.A., Dodd, C.H., and Smith, R.L. (*et al.*) (1944). *Man's Dilemma and God's Answer: Broadcast Talks.* London: SCM Press.

Cunningham, B.K. (1926). 'The Clergy and Their Training'. In Marchant, J. *The Future of the Church of England.* London: Longmans, Green & Co.

Drewett, J. (1942). 'Diffused Christianity: asset or liability?' *Theology*, Vol. XLV, No. 266, August, pp.82–92.

Elliott, W. Thompson (1939). *Spiritual Issues of the War.* London: SCM.

Eppstein, John (1940). *Right Against Might.* Oxford: Catholic Social Guild.

Gardiner, L. (1917). *The Hope for Society: Essays on Social Reconstruction after the War, by Various Writers.* London: G. Bell & Sons.

Gibbard, S.M. (1941). 'The Church and Evacuation.' *Theology*, Vol. XLIII, 253, July, pp. 42–47.

Green, Harold G. (1944). *The Sign of the Cross: An Address given at St. Nicholas Church, Ipswich, May 14th, 1944.*

Green, Peter [Undated]. *Forty Short Prayers for War-time Based on Passages from the Holy Scriptures.* London: Hodder and Stoughton.

His Majesty's Stationery Office. (1942). *Front Line 1940–41: The Official Story of the Civil Defence of Britain.* London: HMSO.

Kirk, K.E. (1917). 'When the Priests Come Home'. In Macnutt, F.B. (ed.), *The Church in the Furnace: essays by seventeen temporary Church of England chaplains on active service in France and Flanders.* London: Macmillan & Co.

Lewis, C.S. (1940). *The Problem of Pain.* London: Geoffrey Bles.

Lloyd, Roger (1942). 'The Heresy of Fatalism'. *The Expository Times*, Vol. LIV, 7, April, pp. 229–231.

Lucas, W.W. (1940). *War and the Purposes of God: A Survey of Scripture Teaching.* London: Marshall, Morgan and Scott.

Matthews, W.R. (1946). *Saint Paul's Cathedral in Wartime 1939–1945.* London: Hutchinson & Co.

Macnutt, F.B. (ed.), (1917). *The Church in the Furnace: essays by seventeen contemporary Church of England chaplains on active service in France and Flanders.* London: Macmillan & Co.

Macpherson, Ian (1941). *The Cross in War-time.* London: Arthur Stockwell.

Malvern, 1941: The Life of the Church and the Order of Society. Being the Proceedings of the Archbishop of York's Conference. (1941). London: Longmans, Green & Co.

Martin, Hugh (1939). *The Christian as Soldier.* London: SCM Press.

Matthews, W.R. (1940). *The Moral Issues of the War.* London: Eyre & Spottiswoode.

Messner, J. (1941). 'Economic and Social Reconstruction'. *The Dublin Review,* No. 419, Oct., pp.161–165.

Milford, T.R. (1945). 'Can We Forgive?' *Theology,* Vol. XLVIII, June, 300, pp.121–127.

Moorman, John R.H. (1947). *B.K. Cunningham: A Memoir.* London: SCM Press.

Niebuhr, Reinhold (1940). *Why the Christian Church is not Pacifist.* London: SCM Press.

Oldham, J.H. (1940). *The Resurrection of Christendom.* London: The Sheldon Press.

Ourselves in Wartime: an illustrated survey of the home front in the Second World War, relating how an industrial mobilization unparalled in history was carried out, how resistance to air attack was organized, how a citizen army was formed, and how the nation saved for victory: and describing the endeavours, trials and triumphs of the people of Britain united in the fight for freedom. [Undated]. London: Odhams Press.

Pakenham, F. (1943). 'The Beveridge Report: some reflections'. *The Dublin Review,* No. 424, January, pp.28–33.

Priestley, J.B. (1968 edition). *English Journey: being the rambling but truthful account of what a man saw and heard and felt and thought during a journey through England during the autumn of the year 1933.* London: Heinemann.

Raven, Charles (1938). *War and the Christian.* London: SCM Press.

Raven, Charles (1940). *The Cross and the Crisis.* London: Fellowship of Reconciliation.

Richardson, Alan (1940). *The Message of the Bible in Wartime.* London: Christian Newsletter Books.

Rogers, C.F. (1941). *Astrology: In the Light of Science and Religion.* London: SCM.

Rogers, C.F. (1942). *Prediction in the Light of Science and Religion.* London: SCM Press.

Salter, F.A. (1942). *'Keep Smiling!': Sixteen Tonic Talks on Religion and Life.* London: Frederick Muller.

Selby Wright, Ronald (1942). *The Average Man: Broadcast Talks.* London: Longmans Green & Co.

Selby Wright, Ronald (1943). *Let's Ask the Padre: Some Broadcast Talks.* London: Oliver & Boyd.

Talbot, Neville (1917). *Thoughts on Religion at the Front.* London: Macmillan & Co.

Temple, William (1940). *Thoughts in War-time.* London: Macmillan & Co.

Temple, William (1943). *Social Witness and Evangelism.* London: Epworth Press.

Temple, William (1976 edition). *Christianity and Social Order.* London: Shepheard Walwyn/SPCK.

Vernon, Edward [Undated]. *The Lord's Prayer in Wartime: A Book for Those who Want to Pray.* London: James Clarke & Co.

Ward, B. (1941). 'The Sword of the Spirit: after one year'. *The Clergy Review*, Vol. XXI, No. 4, October, pp. 94–104.

Weatherhead, Leslie (1939). *Thinking Aloud in War-Time: An Attempt to See the Present Situation in the Light of the Christian Faith.* London: Hodder & Stoughton.

Weatherhead, Leslie (1940). *This is the Victory.* London: Hodder and Stoughton.

Woodward, C. Salisbury and Blackburne, Harry (1939). *Clergy in War-Time.* London: Hodder and Stoughton.

Secondary Sources

Addison, Paul (1985). *Now the War is Over.* London: Jonathan Cape.

Addison, Paul (1994). *The Road to 1945: British politics and the Second World War.* London: Pimlico.

Allen, M. (1989). *From Chapel to Church: 150 years of Methodism in Harborne.* Birmingham: [n.p.].

Akhtar, Miriam and Humphries, Steve (1999). *Far Out: The Dawning of New Age Britain.* Bristol: Sansom.

Bailey, Edward (1989). 'The Folk Religion of the English People'. In Badham, P. (ed). *Religion, State and Society in Modern Britain*. Lampeter: Edwin Mellor Press.

Ballard, P. (1985). *A City at War: Birmingham 1939–1945*. Birmingham: Museum and Art Gallery.

Baptist Union Directory, London: Baptist Union, 1980.

Barnes, John (1979). *Ahead of His Age: Bishop Barnes of Birmingham*. London: Collins.

Beaven, Brad and Griffiths, John (1998). *Mass-Observation and Civilian Morale: Working-Class Communities during the Blitz 1940–41*. Sussex: Mass-Observation Archive.

Black, H.J. (1957). *History of the Corporation of Birmingham*. Vols. 6 & 7. Birmingham: Birmingham Corporation.

Bourke, Joanna. (2005). *Fear: A Cultural History*. London: Virago.

Brewer, J.D. (1984). 'The British Union of Fascists and Anti-Semitism in Birmingham'. *Midlands History*, 9, pp.109–121.

Briggs, Asa (1952). *History of Birmingham*, Volume 2: *Borough and City 1865–1938*. London: Oxford University Press.

Briggs, Asa (1990). *Victorian Cities*. London: Penguin.

Briggs, S. (1975). *Keep Smiling Through: The Home Front 1939–1945*. London: Book Club Associates.

Brown, Callum (2001). *The Death of Christian Britain: Understanding Secularisation 1800–2000*. London: Routledge.

Brown, S.J. (1994). '"A Solemn Purification by Fire": Responses to the Great War in the Scottish Presbyterian Church'. *Journal of Ecclesiastical History*, 45, No. 1, pp.82–104.

Bullock, F.W.B. (1976). *A History of Training in the Church of England 1875–1974*. London: Home Words.

Burton, A. (1995). 'Projecting the New Jerusalem: The Workers' Film Association, 1938–1946'. In Kirkham, P. and Thoms, D. (eds.), *War Culture: Social Change and Changing Experience in World War Two Britain*. London: Lawrence and Wishart.

Butcher, H. (1999). *The Treacle Stick: Ladywood, Aston and Erdington 1917–1942*. Warwick: Quercus.

Calder, Angus (1969). *The People's War: Britain 1939–1945*. London: Pimlico.

Calder, Angus (1991). *The Myth of the Blitz*. London: Pimlico.

Campbell, Louise (1996). *Coventry Cathedral*. Oxford: Oxford University Press.

232

Cantwell, J. (1998). *The Second World War: A Guide to Documents in the Public Record Office.* Kew: Public Records Office.

Ceadel, Martin (1980). *Pacifism in Britain 1914–1945.* Oxford: Clarendon Press.

Ceadel, Martin (1983). 'Christian Pacifism in the Era of Two World Wars'. In Sheils, W.J. (ed.), *The Church and War.* Oxford: Blackwell.

Chandler, Andrew (1994). 'Munich and Morality: The Bishops of the Church of England and Appeasement'. *Twentieth-Century British History*, Vol. 5, No. 1, pp.77–99.

Chapman, Mark D. (1995). 'Theology, Nationalism and the First World War: Christian Ethics and the Constraints of Politics'. *Studies in Christian Ethics*, Vol. 8, No. 2, pp. 13–34.

Chapman, J. (1999). 'British Cinema and "The People's War"'. In Hayes, Nick and Hill, Jeff (eds.), *'Millions Like Us'?: British Culture in the Second World War.* Liverpool: Liverpool University Press.

Cherry, Gordon E. (1994). *Birmingham: A Study in Geography, History and Planning.* Chichester: John Wiley.

Chinn, C. (1996) *Brum Undaunted: Birmingham during the Blitz.* Birmingham: Birmingham Library Services.

Coleman, Peter G. (1991). 'Ageing and Life History: The Meaning of Reminiscence in Late Life'. In Dex, Shirley (ed.), *Life and Work History Analyses: Qualitative and Quantitative Developments.* London: Routledge.

Costello, J. (1985). *Love, Sex and War 1939–1945.* London: Collins.

Cox, Jeffrey (1982). *The English Churches in a Secular Society: Lambeth, 1870–1930.* Oxford: Oxford University Press.

Crerar, Duff (1995). *Padres in No Man's Land: Canadian Chaplains and the Great War.* Montreal: McGill-Queen's University Press.

Croal, Jonathan (1988). *Don't You Know There's a War On?* London: Hutchinson.

Currie, R., Gilbert, A. and Horsley, L. (1977). *Churches and Churchgoers: Patterns of Church Growth in the British Isles since 1700.* Oxford: OUP.

Donnelly, Mark (1999). *Britain in the Second World War.* London: Routledge.

Driver, A.H. (1948). *Carrs Lane 1748–1948.* Birmingham: Carrs Lane.

Ellis, John (1990). *The Sharp End: The Fighting Man in World War II.* London: Pimlico.

Entwistle, D. (2001). '"Hope, Colour and Comradeship": loyalty and opportunism in early twentieth-century church attendance among the working class in north-west England'. *Journal of Religious History*, XXV, February, pp.20–38.

Feiling, Keith (1946). *The Life of Neville Chamberlain*. London: Macmillan.

Finney, P. (ed.). (1997). *The Origins of the Second World War*. London: Arnold.

Freeman, Mark (1993). *Rewriting the Self: History, Memory, Narrative*. London: Routledge.

Fuller, J.G. (1990). *Troop Morale and Popular Culture in the British and Dominion Armies 1914–1918*. Oxford: Clarendon Press.

Fussell, Paul (1989). *Wartime: Understanding and Behaviour in the Second World War*. Oxford: Oxford University Press.

Gay, John D. (1971). *The Geography of Religion in England*. London: Duckworth.

Gilbert, Martin. (1995 edition). *Second World War*. London: Phoenix.

Gill, Conrad (1952). *History of Birmingham*, Volume One: *Manor and Borough to 1865*. London: Oxford University Press.

Gorer, Geoffrey (1955). *Exploring English Character*. London: Cresset Press.

Graham, Desmond (ed.), (1998). *Poetry of the Second World War*. London: Pimlico.

Green, S.J.D. (2000). 'The 1944 Education Act: A Church–State Perspective'. In Parry, J.P and Taylor, S. (eds.), *Parliament and the Church 1529–1960*. Edinburgh: EUP.

Greene, Graham (1974 edition). *The End of the Affair*. London: Heinemann.

Grimley, Matthew (2004). *Citizenship, Community and the Church of England: Liberal Anglican Theories of the State Between the Wars*. Oxford: Oxford University Press.

Guntrip, Harry (ed.), (1959). *Facing Life and Death: A Volume in Commemoration of the Late Rev. Leslie J. Tizard*. London: George Allen & Unwin.

Gusdorf, G. 'Conditions and Limits of Autobiography'. In Olney, J. (ed). (1980). *Autobiography: essays theoretical and critical*. Princeton, NJ: Princeton University Press.

Hall, Catherine (1977). 'Married Women in Birmingham in the 1920s and 1930s'. *Oral History*, Vol. 5, No. 2, pp.62–65.

Harrison, T. (1976). *Living through the Blitz*. London: Collins.

Hastings, Adrian (1991 edition). *A History of English Christianity: 1920–1990*. London: SCM.

Hastings, R.P. (1980). 'The Birmingham Labour Movement, 1918–1945'. *Midland History*, 5, pp.78–92.

234

Hayes, Nick and Hill, Jeff (eds.) (1999). *'Millions Like Us'? British Culture in the Second World War*. Liverpool: Liverpool University Press.

Hazelgrove, Jennifer (1999). 'Spiritualism after the Great War'. *Twentieth-Century British History,* Vol. 10, No. 4. pp.404–430.

Hazelgrove, Jennifer (2000). *Spiritualism and British Society between the Wars*. Manchester: Manchester University Press.

Hempton, David (1986). '"Popular Religion" 1800–1986'. In Thomas, Terence (ed.), *The British: Their Religious Beliefs and Practices 1800–1986*. London: Routledge.

Hennessy, Peter (1992). *Never Again: Britain 1945–1951*. London: Jonathan Cape.

Hodgson, Vere (1976 edition). *Few Eggs and No Oranges: A Diary Showing how Unimportant People in London and Birmingham Lived through the War Years 1940–1945*. London: Dennis Dobson.

Hoover, Arlie J. (1989). *God, Germany, and Britain in the Great War: A Study in Clerical Nationalism*. New York: Praeger.

Hoover, Arlie J. (1999). *God, Britain and Hitler in World War II: The View of the British Clergy, 1939–1945*. Westport, Connecticut: Praeger.

Hopkins, Eric (1990). 'Working Class Life in Birmingham Between the Wars, 1918–1939'. *Midland History*, 15, pp.129–149.

Iremonger, F.A. (1948). *William Temple Archbishop of Canterbury: His Life and Letters*. London: Oxford University Press.

Jenkins, Daniel (1975). *The British: Their Identity and Their Religion*. London: SCM Press.

Josephs, Zoë (1988). *Survivors: Jewish refugees in Birmingham 1933–1945*. West Midlands: Meridian Books.

Keegan, John (1997 edition). *The Second World War*. London: Pimlico.

Kent, John (1992). *William Temple: Church, State and Society in Britain, 1880–1950*. Cambridge: Cambridge University Press.

Kirby, Dianne (1993). 'The Church of England and the Cold War Nuclear Debate'. *Twentieth-Century British History*, Vol. 4, No. 3, pp. 250–283.

Kirkham, P. and Thoms, D. (eds.). (1995). *War Culture: Social Change and Changing Experience in World War Two*. London: Lawrence & Wishart.

Koppes, C.R. and Black, G.D. (2000 edition). *Hollywood Goes to War: Patriotism, Movies and the Second World War*. London: Tauris.

Laybourn, Keith (1990). *Britain on the Breadline: A Social and Political History of Britain 1918–1939*. Gloucestershire: Sutton.

Liddle, P., Bourne, J. and Whitehead, I. (eds.) (2000). *The Great World War*, Volume 1: *Lightning Strikes Twice*. London: Harper Collins.

Liddle, P., Bourne, J. and Whitehead, I. (eds.) (2001). *The Great World War 1914–45*, Volume 2: *The People's Experience*. London: Harper Collins.

Longmate, Norman (1971). *How We Lived Then: A History of Everyday Life during the Second World War*. London: Hutchinson & Co.

Longmate, Norman (1976). *Air Raid: The Bombing of Coventry, 1940*. London: Hutchinson.

Machin, G.I.T. (1992). 'British Church and the Cinema in the 1930s'. In Wood, D. (ed.), *The Church and the Arts*. Oxford: Blackwell.

Machin, G.I.T. (1998). *Churches and Social Issues in Twentieth-Century Britain*. Oxford: Clarendon Press.

Mackay, Robert (1999). *The Test of War*. London: UCL Press.

Marrin, Albert (1974). *The Last Crusade: The Church of England in the First World War*. Durham, NC: Duke University Press.

Marwick, Arthur (ed.), (1988). *Total War and Social Change*. London: Macmillan.

Mayall, David (1985). 'Palaces for Entertainment and Instruction: A Study of the Early Cinema in Birmingham, 1908–1918'. *Midland History*, Vol. X, pp.94–109.

McLaine, Ian (1979). *Ministry of Morale: Home Front Morale and the Ministry of Information in World War Two*. London: George Allen & Unwin.

McLeod, Hugh (1986). 'New Perspectives on Victorian Class Religion: The Oral Evidence'. *Oral History*, Vol. 14, No. 1, Spring, pp.31–47.

Mews, Stuart (1983). 'The Sword of the Spirit: a Catholic cultural crusade of 1940'. In Sheils, W.J. (ed.), *The Church and War*. Oxford: Blackwell.

Mews, Stuart (1994). 'Religious Life Between the Wars'. In Gilley, S. and Sheils W.J., *A History of Religion in Britain*. Oxford: Oxford University Press.

Nicholas, S. (1996). *The Echo of War: Home Front Propaganda and the Wartime BBC, 1939–45*. Manchester: Manchester University Press.

Noakes, J. (ed.), (1992). *The Civilian in War*. Exeter: Exeter University Press.

Norman, E.R. (1976). *Church and Society in England 1770–1970: A Historical Study*. Oxford: Clarendon Press.

O'Shaughnessy, M. (1995). '"What wouldn't I give to grow old in a place like that": A Canterbury Tale'. In Kirkham, P. and Thoms, D. (eds.), *War Culture: Social Change and Changing Experience in World War Two*. London: Lawrence & Wishart.

Payne, Ernest A. (1959). *The Baptist Union: A Short History*. London: The Carey Kingsgate Press.

Pedley, R. (ed.) (1951). *City of Birmingham Annual Abstract of Statistics, 1931–1949*. London: Central Statistical Office.

Phillips, A. (1995). *Orthodox Christianity and the English Tradition*. [n.p.]: English Orthodox Trust.

Power, W.S. (1970). *The Real Thing*. London: Cox & Wyman.

Reeves, Marjorie (1999). *Christian Thinking and Social Order: Conviction Politics from the 1930s to the Present Day*. London: Cassell.

Richards, J. (1983). 'The cinema and cinema-going in Birmingham in the 1930s'. In Walton, J.K. and Walvin, J., *Leisure in Britain: 1780–1939*. Manchester: Manchester University Press.

Richards, J. (1997). *Films and British National Identity: From Dickens to Dad's Army*. Manchester: Manchester University Press.

Robbins, Keith (1985). 'Britain, 1940 and "Christian Civilisation"'. In Beales, D. and Best, G. (eds.), *History, Society and the Churches: Essays in Honour of Owen Chadwick*. Cambridge: CUP.

Robbins, Keith (1995). 'Religion'. In Bear, I.C.B. and Foot, M.R.D. (eds.), *The Oxford Companion to the Second World War*. Oxford: OUP.

Robinson, Alan (1999). '"Lighten Our Darkness"? Army Chaplains of the British Empire during the World Wars'. *War in History*, Vol. 6, pp.479–485.

Rowntree, B. Seebohm and Lavers, G.R. (1951). *English Life and Leisure: A Social Study*. London: Longmans, Green & Co.

Samuels, Raphael and Thompson, Paul (1990). *The Myths We Live By*. London: Routledge.

Sheridan, Dorothy (1990). 'Ambivalent Memories: women and the 1939–45 war in Britain'. *Oral History*, Vol. 18, No. 1, Spring, pp.32–40.

Sheridan, Dorothy (2000). *Wartime Women: A Mass-Observation Anthology*. London: Phoenix Press.

Smith, A. (2003). 'Humphrey Jennings' *Heart of Britain* (1941): a reassessment'. *Historical Journal of Film, Radio and Television*, Vol. 23, No. 2, pp.133–151.

Smith, Harold L. (1996). *Britain in the Second World War: A Social History*. Manchester: Manchester University Press.

Snape, Michael F. (2002). 'British Catholicism and the British Army in the First World War'. *Recusant History*, October 2002, pp.314–358.

Snape, Michael F. and Parker, Stephen G. (2001). 'Keeping Faith and Coping: Belief, Popular Religiosity and the British People'. In Liddle, P., Bourne, J. and Whitehead, I. (eds.), *The Great World War*, Volume 2: *The People's Experience*. London: Harper Collins.

Sokoloff, Sally (1997). 'Soldiers or Civilians? The Impact of Army Service in World War Two on Birmingham Men'. *Oral History*, Autumn, pp.59–66.

Stevenson, John (1984). *British Society 1914–45*. The Penguin Social History of Britain. London: Penguin.

Suggate, Alan (1987). *William Temple and Christian Social Ethics Today*. Edinburgh: T & T Clark.

Summerfield, Penny (1998). *Reconstructing Women's Wartime Lives*. Manchester: Manchester University Press.

Sutcliffe, Anthony and Smith, Roger (1974). *A History of Birmingham*, Volume 3. London: Oxford University Press.

Thompson, David (1983). 'War, the Nation and the Kingdom of God: The Origins of the National Mission of Repentance and Hope, 1915–16'. In Sheils, W.J. (ed.), *The Church and War*. Oxford: Blackwell.

Thompson, Paul (1988 edition). *The Voice of the Past: Oral History*. Oxford: Oxford University Press.

Thoms, David (1989). *War, Industry and Society: The Midlands, 1939–1945*. London: Routledge.

Thorpe, Andrew (1994). *The Longman Companion to Britain in the Era of the Two World Wars 1914–45*. London: Longman.

Upton, Anthony (1992). *Burnt Roof: The Bombing of St. Laurence's Church, Foleshill, Coventry 29 October 1940*. Warwick: Privately Published.

Vidler, Alec R. (1974). 'Bishop Barnes: a centenary retrospect'. *The Modern Churchman*, Vol. XVIII, 3.

While, L.G. (undated). *Raiders over Rotton Park*. [Publisher's name and place not listed].

Wilkinson, Alan (1978). *The Church of England and the First World War*. London: SCM Press.

Wilkinson, Alan (1981). 'The Paradox of the Military Chaplain'. *Theology*, Vol. 84, No. 700, July, pp.249–257.

Wilkinson, Alan (1986). *Dissent or Conform: War, Peace and the English Churches*. London: SCM Press.

Wilkinson, Alan (1990). 'The Politics of the Anglican Modernists'. In Nichols, Aidan (ed.), *Chesterton and the Modernist Crisis*. London: Augustine Publishing Co.

Wilkinson, Alan (1997). 'Changing English Attitudes to Death in Two World Wars'. In Jupp, P. and Howarth, G. (eds.), *The Changing Face of Death*. London: Macmillan.

Williams, Sarah C. (1993). 'Urban Popular Religion and the Rites of Passage'. In McLeod, Hugh (ed.), *European Religion in the Age of the Great Cities: 1830–1930*. London: Routledge.

Williams, Sarah C. (1996). 'The Problem of Belief: the place of oral history in the study of popular religion'. *Oral History*, Autumn, pp. 27–34.

Williams, Sarah C. (1999). *Religious Belief and Popular Culture in Southwark c.1880–1939*. Oxford: Oxford University Press.

Wolfe, K. (1984). *The Churches and the British Broadcasting Corporation 1922–1956: The Politics of Broadcast Religion*. London: SCM Press.

Wolffe, John. (1994). *God and Greater Britain: Religion and National Life in Britain and Ireland 1843–1945*. London: Routledge.

Ziegler, P. (1998). *London at War: 1939–1945*. London: Arrow.

Unpublished Theses

Jones, Ian (2000). 'The "Mainstream" Churches in Birmingham, c. 1945–1998; The Local Church and Generational Change'. University of Birmingham: PhD thesis.

Mews, S. (1973). 'Religion and English Society in the First World War'. University of Cambridge: PhD thesis.

Sykes, R.P.M. (1999). 'Popular Religion in Dudley and the Gornals c.1914–1965'. University of Wolverhampton: PhD thesis.

Wasey, K. (2002). 'Character, Controversy and Community: Anglo-Catholic Churches and Working Classes in South East Birmingham 1865–1939'. University of Birmingham: M.Phil thesis.

Television

Canterbury Tales, series first broadcast in 1996 on Channel 4. Programme produced by Twenty–Twenty Television, London.

Films

A Canterbury Tale (1944). Written, produced and directed by Michael Powell and Emeric Pressburger.

A Diary for Timothy (1946). Directed by Humphrey Jennings; Crown Film Unit.

In Which We Serve (1942). Directed by Noel Coward and David Lean; Rank.

Listen to Britain (1942). Directed by Humphrey Jennings; Crown Film Unit.

Millions Like Us (1943). Directed by Frank Launder and Sidney Gilliat; Rank.

Mrs Miniver (1942). Directed by William Wyler; MGM.

Neighbours Under Fire (1941). Ministry of Information.

Religion and the People (1940). Directed by Andrew Buchanan; British Films.

The Heart of Britain (1940). Directed by Humphrey Jennings; Crown Film Unit.

Went the Day Well? (1943). Directed by Alberto Calvalcanti; Ealing Studios.

Index